CRIMINAL JUSTICE, WILDLIFE CONSERVATION AND ANIMAL RIGHTS IN THE ANTHROPOCENE

Edited by
Ragnhild A. Sollund and Martine S.B. Lie

First published in Great Britain in 2025 by

Bristol University Press
University of Bristol
1-9 Old Park Hill
Bristol
BS2 8BB
UK
t: +44 (0)117 374 6645
e: bup-info@bristol.ac.uk

Details of international sales and distribution partners are available at bristoluniversitypress.co.uk

© Bristol University Press 2025

British Library Cataloguing in Publication Data
A catalogue record for this book is available from the British Library

ISBN 978-1-5292-2335-4 hardcover
ISBN 978-1-5292-2336-1 paperback
ISBN 978-1-5292-2337-8 ePub
ISBN 978-1-5292-2338-5 ePdf

The right of Ragnhild A. Sollund and Martine S.B. Lie to be identified as editors of this work has been asserted by them in accordance with the Copyright, Designs and Patents Act 1988.

All rights reserved: no part of this publication may be reproduced, stored in a retrieval system, or transmitted in any form or by any means, electronic, mechanical, photocopying, recording, or otherwise without the prior permission of Bristol University Press.

Every reasonable effort has been made to obtain permission to reproduce copyrighted material. If, however, anyone knows of an oversight, please contact the publisher.

The statements and opinions contained within this publication are solely those of the editors and contributors and not of the University of Bristol or Bristol University Press. The University of Bristol and Bristol University Press disclaim responsibility for any injury to persons or property resulting from any material published in this publication.

Bristol University Press works to counter discrimination on grounds of gender, race, disability, age and sexuality.

Cover design: Nicky Borowiec
Front cover image: unsplash/ Ana Karla Parra, David Clode, Pierre Bamin and Richard Lee

Contents

List of Figures, Tables and Graphs		v
Notes on Contributors		vi
1	Introduction *Ragnhild A. Sollund and Martine S.B. Lie*	1
2	Legal Versus Illegal Hunts: A Species Justice Perspective on Wolf and Bear Theriocides in Norway *Martine S.B. Lie*	17
3	The Implementation of CITES in Norway: A Longitudinal Approach to the Assessment of Enforcement from a Species Justice Perspective *Ragnhild A. Sollund*	36
4	Online Illegal Trade in Reptiles in the Netherlands *Isabella Dominguez, Marjan Hindriks, Jordi Janssen and Daan van Uhm*	52
5	Countering Wildlife Crimes in Italy: The Case of Bird Poaching *Lorenzo Natali, Ciro Troiano, Sara Zoja and Anita Lavorgna*	70
6	Analysis of Social and Legal Factors Influencing the Effectiveness of Tackling the Illegal Killing of Wolves in Poland *Piotr J. Chmielewski and Agnieszka Serlikowska*	87
7	CITES in Spain: Blueprints and Challenges of Spanish Practice on CITES and Welfare of Trafficked Victims *Teresa Fajardo*	105
8	Paper Tigers and Local Perseverance: Wildlife Protection in Germany *Christoph H. Stefes*	125
9	The Norwegian Chain of Wildlife Treaty Effectiveness *David R. Goyes*	151
10	Rewilding in the UK: Harm or Justice? *Tanya Wyatt*	168

11	We Only See What We Know: Animal Conservation and Human Preservation *Mark T. Palermo*	185
12	Conclusion *Ragnhild A. Sollund and Martine S.B. Lie*	205

Index   215

List of Figures, Tables and Graphs

Figures

4.1	Organization of a network	62
5.1	*The Madonna del Cardellino* (Madonna of the goldfinch), oil on wood by the Italian Renaissance artist Raffaello Sanzio, 1506	75
5.2	A rescued goldfinch, which had been stuck to a branch and used as a decoy by poachers	76
8.1	Outlining the legal framework	130
8.2	Wildlife protection enforcement	135

Tables

3.1	Animal species that require tagging	48
6.1	Acceptance of motivations for killing wolves	99
6.2	Disagreement with motivations for killing wolves	99
8.1	Co-occurrence of general enforcement problems and disadvantages of decentralization	139
App A	List of Interviewees	147
App B	Panel Regression Models	149
10.1	Prohibited means and methods of killing, capturing and exploiting mammals	173

Graph

8.1	Degree of centralization and criminal violations of BNatSchG reported	142

Notes on Contributors

Piotr J. Chmielewski holds a Master's degree in environmental sciences. He is a PhD candidate at the Faculty of Artes Liberales at the University of Warsaw. His PhD thesis, in the field of environmental sociology, is titled 'The institutional context of the wolf (*Canis lupus*) conservation in Poland'. His research interests include human dimensions of wildlife and human–large carnivore coexistence. Additionally, he is a Chief Specialist in Green Deal Projects at the Polish National Centre for Research and Development.

Isabella Dominguez has a background in psychology, criminology, international relations and cyber security. She has researched the organization of criminal networks involved in the illegal tortoise and freshwater turtle trade.

Teresa Fajardo is Associate Professor at the University of Granada where she teaches Public International Law at the Faculty of Law, and International and European Environmental Law at the Science Faculty. Her research interests lie in the field of International and European environmental law, EU migration law and policy and Soft Law. She is a member of the Jean Monnet Chair on EU Environmental Law at the University of Barcelona. She has drawn up reports for the European Commission and the European Parliament on wildlife crime. Among her most recent publications are *To Criminalise or Not To Criminalise IUU Fishing: The EU's Choice* (Marine Policy, 2022), and *Biological Diversity and International Law: Challenges for the Post 2020 Scenario* (Springer, 2021).

David R. Goyes is a researcher at the University of Oslo. He holds a PhD in Criminology from the same university. He has contributed extensively to the study of global North–South relations, environmental conflicts and Indigenous issues. He is editor-in-chief of the *International Journal for Crime, Justice and Social Democracy* and member of several editorial boards. Goyes has a long publication record, with titles in English, Portuguese and Spanish. His first sole-authored book was *Southern Green Criminology* (Emerald, 2019). He has also contributed chapters to numerous edited volumes and articles to special issues of scientific journals.

NOTES ON CONTRIBUTORS

Marjan Hindriks is a Senior Legal Adviser on Circular Economy and Waste for Rijkswaterstaat, the executive agency of the Dutch Ministry of Infrastructure and Water Management. She has Master's degrees in International and European Law and in Criminal Investigation, both with a specialization in the environmental field. She enjoys using her skills and knowledge to try to improve our natural environment.

Jordi Janssen is an ecologist working for Monitor Conservation Research Society, and studies the legal and illegal wildlife trade with a particular interest in reptiles and amphibians. Over the last decade he has written several book chapters and over 30 publications on this trade. In addition, he is a PhD candidate at the Netherlands Institute for the Study of Crime and Law enforcement (NSCR) and Utrecht University in the Netherlands.

Anita Lavorgna is Associate Professor in the Department of Political and Social Sciences at the University of Bologna. After her PhD at the University of Trento, Lavorgna spent most of her academic career in the UK, where she was Associate Professor of Criminology at the University of Southampton until 2022. Her research pivots around cybercrimes, digital social harms and environmental crimes, and is mostly based on interdisciplinary approaches.

Martine S.B. Lie is a Doctoral Research Fellow in Criminology at the University of Oslo. In her PhD project she explores Norwegian large predator policies, including the implications of using the courts as an arena for the wolf conflict. The project is part of Criminal Justice, Wildlife Conservation and Animal Rights in the Anthropocene (CRIMEANTHROP) funded by the Research Council of Norway. Lie also has extensive experience from NGO work for the protection of animals. Among her publications are 'Humane Theriocides: Traces of Compassion for Animals in the Norwegian Legal Discourse on Illegal Bear and Wolf Killings' in *Revista Catalana de Dret Ambiental* 12(1), 2021, and '"Stepdogs" of Society: The Impact of Breed Bans in Norway' in *Critical Criminology* 25, 2017.

Lorenzo Natali is Associate Professor of Criminology at the School of Law, University of Milano-Bicocca, Italy. His research focuses on violent crime, symbolic and radical interactionism, green criminology and visual and sensory methodologies. He is the author of *A Visual Approach for Green Criminology: Exploring the Social Perception of Environmental Harm* (Palgrave, 2016), *Cosmologías violentas: Itinerarios criminológicos* (with Adolfo Ceretti; Marcial Pons, 2016) and *Green Criminology: Prospettive Emergenti sui Crimini Ambientali* (Giappichelli, 2015) and *Introdução à Criminologia Verde: Perspectivas Críticas, Descoloniais e do Sul* (with M. de Nardin Budó, D. Rodriguez Goyes, R. Sollund, and A. Brisman (eds); Tirant Brasil, 2022).

Mark T. Palermo is a psychiatrist and neurologist, chair of the Law, Art and Behavior Foundation. He is a social artist focusing on combating the medicalization of society using art as metaphor. In his research he attempts to circumvent academic sectarianism, drawing upon universal cultural foundations such as those found in literature, religion and philosophy. Recent publications include 'Scientism, Ethics and Evil: From Mens Rea to Cerebrum Reus' in *International Journal of Offender Therapy and Comparative Criminology*, 2022, 66(9), and 'From Social Deviance to Art: Vandalism, Illicit Dumping, and the Transformation of Matter and Form' in *Social Sciences*, 2020.

Agnieszka Serlikowska is an attorney at law and public servant with a PhD in Law. In 2020–22, she was associated with the Kazimierz Wielki University in Bydgoszcz. Her doctoral degree was awarded by the Faculty of Law and Administration of the University of Warsaw, for the thesis 'Fees and other charges imposed by competent authorities performing official food controls in European and national food and feed law' (Wolters Kluwer Poland, 2020). In her research and teaching, she focuses on the study of administrative responsibility.

Ragnhild A. Sollund is Professor of Criminology at the University of Oslo. She has published widely in the field of green criminology, particularly concerning wildlife crimes and harms, in addition to police racial profiling and migration. She is the author of: *The Crimes of Wildlife Trafficking: Issues of Justice, Legality and Morality* (Routledge, 2019) and *Green Harms and Crimes: Critical Criminology in a Changing World* (Palgrave, 2015). She has received the Energy Globe Award, Norway (2015) and the Lifetime Achievement Award from the DCCSJ of the American Society of Criminology (2021). From 2019 to 2023 she was in charge of the CRIMEANTHROP (Criminal Justice, Wildlife Conservation and Animal Rights in the Anthropocene) project, funded by the Research Council Norway. She was a partner to the EFFACE project funded by the European Union (2012–16).

Christoph H. Stefes, PhD, is Professor for Political Science at the University of Colorado Denver. In his research and teaching, he focuses on the study of political regimes, corruption, and environmental and energy policies. Among his most recent publications are 'Russia as a Norm Entrepreneur' in *Problems of Post-Communism* (with B. Jose; Taylor and Francis, 2022); 'Wildlife Protection in Germany: Sound Legislation and Deficient Implementation' in *Revista Catalana de Dret Ambiental* 12, 2021; 'Opposing Energy Transitions' in *Review of Policy Research* 37, 2020; and *Fighting Environmental Crime in Europe and Beyond* (with R. Sollund and A. R. Germani (eds); Palgrave Macmillan, 2017).

NOTES ON CONTRIBUTORS

Ciro Troiano is a criminologist, specializing in 'Criminal Anthropology and Investigative Methodologies'. He is trained in legal psychology and forensic psychopathology and is in charge of the LAV's Osservatorio Nazionale Zoomafia. Troiano is adjunct lecturer in 'Criminology of Crimes Against Animals', and has taught courses in 'Techniques for combating zoomafia' and 'Criminology of animal rights' at Police, Carabinieri and State Forestry Corps Academies. He edits the annual Zoomafia Report. Troiano is the author of numerous essays and articles. Among his latest texts: *Preso dal nervoso gli ho sparato: Vittime e offender nel maltrattamento di animali* (LAV, 2021); *La Guardia Zoofila – manuale a quiz* (Amazon, 2023).

Daan van Uhm is Associate Professor of Criminology, specializing in Green Criminology, at Utrecht University, the Netherlands. He has conducted research on various forms of environmental crime, including illegal mining in Latin America, wildlife trafficking in South East Asia, deforestation in Central Africa, and the criminalization of ecocide.

Tanya Wyatt is a former Professor of Criminology (Northumbria University in Newcastle, UK). Her specialism is crimes that affect the environment, including wildlife crime and trafficking and non-human animal abuse as well as the intersections with organized crime, corporate crime and corruption. Recent publications include *Wildlife Trafficking: A Deconstruction of the Crime, Victims and Offenders* (Palgrave Macmillan, 2022) and *Is CITES Protecting Wildlife? An assessment of implementation and compliance* (Earthscan, 2022).

Sara Zoja has been a psychologist and later a Jungian psychoanalyst based in Milan (Italy) since 2012. She got her Associate's and Master's degrees in clinical psychology from the university of Maine (USA) and the Vita-Salute San Raffaele university (Italy). She received her diploma in analytical psychology from the C. G. Jung Institute in Zurich. She trained in forensic psychopathology and clinical criminology (at San Raffaele university in Milan) and in child psychotherapy (at Il Ruolo Terapeutico school in Parma). She is a member of IAAP. Her research interests focus on dream therapy and on the relationship between animals and the unconscious.

1

Introduction

Ragnhild A. Sollund and Martine S.B. Lie

We live in the midst of a nature crisis in which we face not only global warming, but also the serious loss of other species.[1] The causes are anthropogenic, through which species are driven to extinction due to climate change, loss of habitat, hunting and wildlife trade. This represents a threat to ecosystems, to all living beings and therefore to the world as we know it. According to the last Living Planet index (WWF 2022), the world has suffered an average decline of 69 per cent in monitored species populations since 1970. This book addresses this crisis with results from research on the implementation and enforcement of two nature conservation conventions as a starting point, The Convention on International Trade in Endangered Species of Wild Fauna and Flora (CITES, 1975), and the Council of Europe's Convention on the Conservation of European Wildlife and Natural Habitats (the Bern Convention, 1979).

Species loss is usually regarded as a conservation issue, giving value to non-human animals[2] only at aggregated species level, rather than recognizing their individual intrinsic value (Sollund 2019), a perspective that is reflected in the two conventions. As a result of the focus on species conservation, the

---

[1] We are grateful to Nigel South for his valuable comments to an earlier version of the chapter.
[2] Animal is a speciesist word that categorizes all other than human animal species as the same and in contrast to the human animal. This is evidently wrong; contemplate, for example, the difference between a crab and an elephant and the similarities between a human and an orangutan. Scholars, therefore, often apply the term non-human animal to emphasize that humans also are animals, but this construct still implies an artificial divide. All such constructs are wordy, without really providing good solutions, which is why we in this chapter, with reservations and regret, simply retain the word 'animal' about all those animals on earth that are not human.

harms and loss of life resulting from anthropogenic acts such as hunting and wildlife trades that affect individual animals, their flocks and families, are usually overlooked. While a considerable amount of research on conservation is taking place within the natural sciences, and despite a growing body of work within the social sciences, there is still a lack of literature that combines conservation studies with a focus on animal rights and welfare, and animals' intrinsic value. This is an aim of this book, which is a fruit of the CRIMEANTHROP project; Criminal Justice, Wildlife Conservation and Animal Rights in the Anthropocene (2019–23).[3]

The CRIMEANTHROP project

This major research project, led by Ragnhild A. Sollund, ran for four years, from 2019 to 2023. It included case studies from the UK (by Tanya Wyatt), Spain (by Teresa Fajardo), Germany (by Christoph H. Stefes) and a larger study comprised of three case studies in Norway (by Ragnhild A. Sollund, David R. Goyes as a post-doctoral researcher, and PhD fellow Martine S.B. Lie). In this volume, the initial case studies have been added to by contributions from other scholars in order to cover human–wildlife relations more broadly and in other countries. The research project also benefited from two external advisers, Nigel South and Avi Brisman. The project was cross-disciplinary, including scholars within criminology, law and political science, but with an even broader theoretical approach, incorporating also literature from the natural sciences and humanities, as employed in *green criminology* (to be discussed later).

The project arose from a deep concern about the ways in which 'wildlife'[4] are used as commodities – regarded as resources for human exploitation – or as 'vermin', 'pests', and threats – animals whose extinction or near-extinction is sought by humans for economic reasons or to make our lives easier. Animals are traded as 'pets' in the international wildlife trade, they are eaten as exotic meat, experimented on, used in medicine, or are used as decorations, as when people traffic ivory in the form of artworks or souvenirs. Freeborn animals are hunted as trophies, as when Europeans travel to South Africa to shoot lions and legally (or illegally) import their trophies to their home

---

[3] CRIMEANTHROP – Department of Criminology and Sociology of Law, University of Oslo, Norway (www.uio.no). Funded by the Research Council Norway, project number 289285.

[4] Wildlife is another anthropocentric term that treats all freeborn animals as a 'mass' rather than as individuals. It should therefore be avoided, but will also be retained for simplicity, with the meaning above and still recognizing the individual, intrinsic value of each sentient freeborn animal, and animals whose defining features have not been altered by human control and dominion. 'Wildlife' sometimes also includes plants, but this is not the case here.

country, or when state licensed hunters pose with dead wolves in Norway during the annual culling.

This two-sided approach to wildlife, through which they, put simply, are either commodities or enemies, has a third aspect, namely that related to their aesthetic value; they should be preserved in order to provide future generations of *humans* with a state of nature rich in biodiversity. This third aspect, which, although it may benefit freeborn animals, also is anthropocentric, is part of the fundamental basis and logic of CITES and the Bern Convention. These two nature conservation conventions are central to the CRIMEANTHROP project, as well as to this book. They are part of the substantial body of International Environmental Law (see, for example, Rajamani 2021; Techera et al 2021), and are adopted by many states that are parties to the conventions: CITES, with 183 signatory states, plus the European Union, and the Bern Convention with 50 member states, including most European states and four African countries (see the next section). The EU has also ratified the Bern Convention (see the next section).

Even though the body of International Environmental Law has grown to considerable proportions, none of the environmental conventions truly protects animals from harm. There is no *international convention for animal rights*. A UN Convention on Animal Health and Protection[5] was drafted by NGOs in 2018 but, in this draft, it is still indirectly acknowledged that animals are used instrumentally for human purposes. The draft states in its preamble, among other points, that:

> Recalling the UN Mandate for a peaceful world, which is not limited to human beings but must be extended to all non-human individual animals, and; Recalling the UN World Charter for Nature stating that 'Every form of life is unique, warranting respect regardless of its worth to man, and, to accord other organisms such recognition, man must be guided by a moral code of action.'

The draft to the convention states further that among its basic guiding principles would be the internationally recognized five freedoms: (freedom from hunger, thirst and malnutrition; freedom from fear and distress; freedom from physical and thermal discomfort; freedom from pain, injury and disease; and freedom to express normal patterns of behaviour). These freedoms, were they to be respected, would be a huge step forward for animal rights, however, as we document in our research, these are freedoms animals who are subject to trade and nature 'management' do not enjoy.

---

[5] www.uncahp.org – About

CITES and the Bern Convention have played a crucial role in the protection of endangered species from trade and in the rewilding of European brown bears and wolves, however their implementation and enforcement in the member states can be variable and challenging, as is demonstrated in this book. Moreover, they do not incorporate to any meaningful degree, that freeborn animals are sentient beings with intrinsic value and interests (Regan 2004). A study into the successes and failures of the implementation and enforcement of these two conventions in the CRIMEANTHROP case study locations had to acknowledge this important and unregulated/overlooked aspect of wildlife conservation and protection. For example, when reptiles and parrots are legally abducted from their habitats to form part of the 'pet' trade chain, they suffer the harms of captivity for the rest of their lives even when they survive the journey, which is very often not the case, meaning these abductions also constitute a threat to their species (Sollund, this volume; Fajardo, this volume). Similarly, when endangered animals, such as large carnivores, are killed in licensed hunts or quota hunts, their species may survive but the harm that is done to each individual and their family groups (when they have one) is fatal and irreparable (Sollund, forthcoming; Lie, this volume).

Humans' protection of nature and the animals who belong there is frequently referred to as 'nature management' – a concept that is a euphemism for the act of killing animals recognized as endangered species. 'Conservation' is thus not wholehearted, and the efforts of conservation provided by conventions such as CITES and the Bern Convention are often unsuccessful in providing for viability and population growth, perhaps precisely because they become paperwork without 'teeth' (Trouwborst et al 2017; Goyes, this volume; Stefes, this volume). On the other hand, a sign of the success of the Bern Convention and the related Habitat Directive of the European Union is that wolves in Europe have increased considerably in numbers. Conversely, their increased numbers have led countries to try to lower their protection.[6] For example, Sweden decided in 2023 to cull 75 wolves of a population of 460,[7] which is a serious step in the wrong direction and undermines the conventions. In the current nature crisis, it would still harm conservation were nations to reject being party to such conventions. On the other hand, being a member state does not ensure that the goals of the conventions are actually met and that the conventions are meticulously enforced. They can, however, add to a country's image as taking

---

[6] https://eur-lex.europa.eu/legal-content/EN/TXT/PDF/?uri=CELEX:52022PC0543&from=EN

[7] 'Sweden risks EU ire with historic wolf hunt', POLITICO, www.politico.eu/article/sweden-hunt-conservation-animals-risks-eu-ire-with-historic-wolf-hunt/

responsibility for nature (Sollund and Runhovde 2020) and, more seriously, create an *image* of protecting endangered species while the opposite is the case. In this way, killing endangered animals can be legitimated through a country's affiliation to a convention.

Research that was the starting point for the development of CRIMEANTHROP (for example, Sollund 2016, 2017, 2019), thus pointed to CITES and the Bern Convention being implemented and enforced in a paradoxical manner in Norway, rather than providing animals of endangered species genuine protection. For example, animals who are protected under CITES were killed in the hands of authorities, and critically endangered wolves were lawfully shot in geographical zones where they are supposed to enjoy special protection. It therefore became urgent to explore whether such paradoxical implementation and enforcement were mirrored in other countries, and to investigate what may be success and failure factors for the functioning of these conventions in more European countries. As mentioned, CRIMEANTHROP includes several disciplines and theoretical perspectives. The project's basis is, nevertheless, within the interdisciplinary field of green criminology.

Green criminology

The era of the Anthropocene prolongs the logic of anthropocentrism that to date has favoured the human species above all others, leading to ecological disaster – ecocide (Higgins et al 2013), speciecide (Sollund forthcoming), and widespread animal harm at the individual level. We have taken it upon ourselves to 'manage' nature and other animals, by which we threaten the existence of all beings on planet Earth (Palermo, this volume). Green criminology is a field of criminology that is particularly well tailored to incorporate animals and nature, with its perspectives on victimology and field of study.

Green criminology studies harms towards nature, humans and other animals. The victims of these ecological harms may be ecosystems, the atmosphere, animals and humans of both current and future generations. As many ecological harms are legal in name, such as destruction of habitats and abduction of wild animals in the legal wildlife trade, both legal and illegal harms are investigated in green criminology, building on the field's critical criminological inheritance (see, for example, Sollund 2015; Lie this volume). The state may even be seen as an enabler or accomplice in harmful practices, by for example, poor regulation and control, or subsidizing harmful industries (for example, Brisman and South 2019; Stretesky et al 2013).

As mentioned, much research on humans' 'management' of nature and animals employs an anthropocentric perspective, focusing on how policies affect humans and human interests, either on a short-term basis or for later generations. In contrast to this, green criminological enquiries may employ a human-oriented *environmental*, ecosystem-based *ecological*, or animal-centred *species justice* perspective when investigating ecological harms (White 2013, 2018; Brisman and South 2019; see also, Sollund this volume; Lie this volume).

Environmental justice focuses on enhancing the right to, and ability to access, a healthy environment for all humans across the globe – environmental rights (see, for example, White 2013). In that respect, environmental justice maintains the human focus, but in an inclusive way, acknowledging the right of all humans to live in a safe environment, both now and for future generations. Ecological justice acknowledges the intrinsic value of ecosystems and extends rights to them, including a right not to be altered and destroyed (see, for example, White 2013). Here, humans are seen as only one of many components of ecosystems, and the goal is to protect and enhance 'ecological wellbeing' for the ecosystems for their own sake. Those advocating for species justice extend their victimological scope to include animals, both as species and individuals (see, for example, White 2013). Animals' intrinsic value is acknowledged, including their right not to suffer abuse. Species justice, therefore, seeks to protect animals from abuse, degradation and other harms, whether it is direct or indirect, physical or psychological, one-on-one or institutionalized. Together, the three green justice perspectives constitute ecojustice (White 2013).

Empathy with the more-than-human may also be a starting point of many green criminological enquiries, such as for CRIMEANTHROP and this book. It is accepted that emotions such as empathy are crucial for our thinking and, consequently, also for our actions (Sollund 2017). Gruen (2015) defines empathy as:

> A type of caring perception focused on attending to another's experience of wellbeing. An experiential process involving a blend of emotion and cognition in which we recognize we are in relationships with others and are called upon to be responsive and responsible in these relationships by attending to another's needs, interests, desires, vulnerabilities, hopes and sensitivities. (p 1)

Although most of the contributions herein do not explore the emotional sides of the implementation and enforcement of CITES and the Bern Convention directly, emotions still set the stage to the degree that the case studies point to weaknesses in the treaties' implementation and enforcement.

The focus on enhancing justice and empathy with animals and nature makes green criminology a normative research field, invested to improve the living conditions for nature, non-human and human animals. Legislation may suppress nature and non-human animals' intrinsic value and rights, but can also be a central instrument to enhance their status and protection. Critical analysis of any legal framework, its scope, implementation, enforcement and 'blind spots' is, therefore, central to studies within the field. The analysis offered in this book, of the implementation and enforcement of CITES and the Bern Convention in several European countries, fits well within this framework but is unique in its extent.

CITES

CITES is a trade regulation. The meaning and implications of this fact cannot be underestimated, since it therefore encourages, facilitates and legitimates the trade in wildlife, whether in animals or plants. It was implemented in 1975 and most of the world's nations are parties to the convention. It was thus established at a time when the subject of animal rights had not yet reached public debate to any significant extent, yet the problems of factory farming and systemic animal abuse were on the rise. The convention works through an appendix system which means that species are listed on three appendices according to the degree of threat that is reported for the species. Appendix I includes species threatened with extinction. Trade in individuals of these species is permitted only in exceptional circumstances. Appendix II includes species not necessarily threatened with extinction, but in which trade must be controlled in order to avoid utilization incompatible with their survival. Appendix III contains species that are protected in at least one country, which has asked other CITES parties for assistance in controlling the trade.[8] CITES arose due to a concern that animals, such as elephants, were actually being traded to extinction, and a regulation of the trade was seen as the necessary response to ensure that the source countries of wildlife trade could continue to benefit from their resources at that point and in the future. Decisions about which species shall be listed and where, are made at meetings of the Conferences of the Parties (COPs) that take place every second to third year. For example, in the CoP in Panama in 2022, many shark species were listed. In 2016, the African Grey parrots were up listed to Appendix I as endangered after 'unsustainable' exploitation for the 'pet' trade.

Each party to CITES is obliged to submit an annual trade report to the CITES secretariat. It should contain a summary of information about the number and type of permits and certificates granted, the states with which such trade occurred, the quantities and types of individuals subjected to trade, whether animals and plants, and the names of species as included in Appendices I, II and III. If states fail to submit an annual report for three consecutive years without providing adequate justification, this could lead

---

[8] 'How CITES works', https://cites.org/eng/disc/how.php

to the Standing Committee recommending to all parties to suspend trade with the party concerned.[9] This does not mean that all parties to CITES actually submit the required reports; in fact, many fail to do so (Wyatt 2021). This means that even what is traded under the umbrella of CITES fails to be adequately reported and registered.

Currently (May 2023) the convention has listed roughly 6,610 species of animals and 34,310 species of plants. A problem with CITES is, however, that many species that are never listed are driven to extinction, including from trade (Janssen and Leupen 2017; Dominguez et al this volume). Another problem is that many countries fail to submit the annual reports that are expected, meaning that much of the trade in listed species also goes under the radar of CITES (Wyatt 2021).

In addition, CITES has been criticized for legitimating and prolonging the trade and practices that involve animal abuse, despite decorative amendments to the convention meant to reduce the evident harms of the trade for the animal victims involved (Goyes and Sollund 2016; Sollund, forthcoming, see Fajardo, this volume).

The Bern Convention

The Bern Convention was introduced by the Council of Europe in 1979. Its stated aim is 'to ensure conservation of wild flora and fauna species and their natural habitats', especially endangered and vulnerable species, including migratory species (Council of Europe 1979, Article 1). The convention acknowledges wild fauna and flora's values from an anthropocentric perspective, such as their economic, cultural and aesthetic importance, but also their intrinsic value (preamble), and promotes cooperation between states to ensure the conservation of species and habitats. Included in the convention are four appendices, covering 'Strictly protected flora species', 'Strictly protected fauna species', 'Protected fauna species' and 'Prohibited means and methods of killing, capture and other forms of exploitation'.

The convention includes both commitments and prohibitions. For example, the parties are required to promote national conservation policies (Article 3,1), and to promote education and spread information about the need for conservation of wild animals and their habitats (Article 3,3). Protection of the habitats and species listed in Appendices I–III of specially protected flora and fauna is highlighted as especially important. Article 6a states that 'all forms of deliberate capture and keeping and deliberate killing' of animals listed in Appendix II of 'strictly protected fauna species' is forbidden. Regarding species listed as 'protected', exploitation shall be 'regulated to keep

---

[9] 'Annual report', https://cites.org/eng/imp/reporting_requirements/annual_report

the populations out of danger' (Article 7,2). Article 8 prohibits 'the use of all indiscriminate means of capture and killing and the use of all means capable of causing local disappearance of, or serious disturbance to, populations of a species', and lists concrete unacceptable killing methods in Appendix IV. The parties may make exceptions to the convention's provisions if that is the only satisfactory solution to solve certain specified and substantial challenges (Article 9,1), but such exceptions must not be 'detrimental to the survival of the population concerned' (Article 9,2).

Anyone may file complaints regarding a nation's compliance with the convention, which are first handled by a secretariat, who may decide to forward the complaint to the convention's governing body, the Standing Committee (Jen 1999; Epstein 2014). The committee will then discuss the case at their annual meeting and might open a so-called 'case file' on the matter, and agree to either close the case or make public recommendations to the party in question (Jen 1999; Fleurke and Trouwborst 2014). The convention has a diplomatic character, however, which means that, in practice, the Standing Committee rarely opens case files or issues such reprimands to signatory parties (Epstein 2013). The convention also includes an article on arbitration, which has never been employed in practice (Jen 1999; Epstein 2013, 2014).[10]

The Bern Convention is implemented in the European Union through the Birds and Habitats Directives, which protect wild birds and over a thousand specified other species in the EU, as well as habitats. The Bern Convention and EU directives are closely connected and formulated similarly, albeit with some differences with regards to the species protected, protection of areas, and a more vigorous enforcement apparatus in the directives, including the European Court of Justice (Epstein 2014; Fleurke and Trouwborst 2014). The Bern Convention, on the other hand, places a stronger emphasis on transboundary cooperation than the directives (Fleurke and Trouwborst 2014).

Their different scopes and strengths enable the three treaties and their governing bodies to supplement each other (Epstein 2014), but can also lead to differences in practice. For example, unlike the Bern Convention, the Habitats Directive Art 2 has a stated objective of ensuring 'favourable conservation status' for the species and habitats it covers (Epstein 2013, 2014; Fleurke and Trouwborst 2014). Following this, as well as the Habitats Directive's more robust enforcement apparatus, Sweden has a considerably larger wolf population than neighbouring Norway, who is not in the EU

---

[10] See, however, this recent development: 'Applying International Environmental Law Conventions in Occupied Territory: The Azerbaijan v. Armenia Case under the Bern Convention', www.ejiltalk.org

and therefore only bound by the Bern Convention (see also, Fleurke and Trouwborst 2014). As Epstein (2013: 551) states, 'the legal situation for an animal changes significantly when it crosses political borders'.

The EU is an influential member of the Bern Convention, by supporting the convention and its activities financially and since the EU states constitute the majority of the Standing Committee (Epstein 2014). The convention has become synergistically interwoven with the Habitats Directive (Epstein 2014). Not only is the Bern Convention the precursor of the Habitats Directive, which is clear from the directive's form and formulations, but the Habitats Directive and its operation are also influential to the Bern Convention and its application. For example, the Bern Convention has, on some occasions, urged signatory states to pursue a 'favourable conservation status', clearly impacted by the Habitats Directive (Epstein 2014).

Presentation of the contributions

The anthology presents case studies from the countries investigated in CRIMEANTHROP, as well as other European states – the Netherlands, Italy and Poland – enabling us to cover major parts of the continent.

More specifically, implications of CITES and the Bern Convention for animals in various European states are presented and discussed. The contributions explore various aspects of this, from the enforcement of the conventions by local bureaucrats to their implementation in national legislation and violations of such legislation, to national efforts to combat extinction and even repopulate extinct animals. The methodologies and theoretical perspectives employed are also diverse, including approaches such as network, comparative and legal analysis, philosophical and political theory.

The studied countries' efforts to adhere to the conventions vary. For example, while the Norwegian government wilfully maintains the large predator populations on a level registered as endangered, even critically, some countries move beyond restricting hunting and trade of endangered animals to comply with the minimum demands of international commitments, and actively engage in restoring populations. This happens in Spain and the United Kingdom where they are taking steps to rewild lynx (see Wyatt, this volume).

In Chapter 2, 'Legal versus illegal hunts: a species justice perspective on wolf and bear theriocides in Norway', Martine S.B. Lie investigates Norway's mentioned policies towards large predators, which are meant to implement the Bern Convention. These policies are an excellent example of 'nature management' predominantly based on killing endangered animals. Wolves, brown bears and wolverines are shot in licensed hunts in Norway, while lynx are victims of regular quota hunts. Lie undertakes a comparison of the legal wolf and bear hunts and illegal hunts, based on analysis of verdicts, hunting guidelines and regulations. The analysis uncovers similarities in actors and methods between the legal and the illegal killings. Lie goes on to investigate whether there are differences in the amount of harm the hunts cause to the individual animal victims, asking if the legal hunts can be justified by focusing more on species justice than the illegal hunts.

In Chapter 3, 'The implementation of CITES in Norway, a longitudinal approach to the assessment of enforcement from a species justice perspective', Ragnhild A. Sollund builds on research carried out over more than a decade. At different stages the author has interviewed enforcement agents and analysed case file material concerning CITES crimes. The chapter concentrates on the development of priorities and changes concerning law enforcement and animal harm related to wildlife trade that appear from these data. One important step in the wrong direction was to introduce a partial lifting of the ban against the keeping of exotic reptiles in Norway. This has meant that reptiles are now traded mainly on the internet and illegal reptiles may easily be laundered into the legal trade. On the other hand, there have been revisions in the CITES regulations in Norway which have the potential for increased control of the trade in live wildlife, such as tagging/labelling. The author finds, however, that there is still a lack of transparency in relation to CITES crimes, which makes it impossible for researchers to get an overview of the problem in Norway for lack of registration and available statistics.

In Chapter 4, 'Online illegal trade in reptiles in the Netherlands', Isabella Dominguez, Marjan Hindriks, Jordi Janssen and Daan van Uhm explore another aspect of CITES crimes, namely online sales of protected reptiles in the Netherlands. In addition to analysing expert interviews and police files, the authors present an innovative network analysis of how the trade is organized. The growth of the internet plays an increasing role in the illegal wildlife trade, including the trade in reptiles in the Netherlands. Protected reptile species are sold on various digital platforms and live animals become victims of this lively online underworld. Reptiles are often laundered online which results in illegal and legal activities intertwining. The digital era has enabled traders, buyers, but also criminal actors, to communicate easily with each other, which complicates law enforcement of CITES in the Netherlands. Digital platforms, such as social media, are flexible and can accommodate forums where traders advertise animals to targeted groups, and arrange sales and payments. What may look like one advertisement for a small number of animals can in reality be big business.

In Chapter 5, 'Countering wildlife crimes in Italy: the case of bird poaching', Lorenzo Natali, Ciro Troiano, Sara Zoja and Anita Lavorgna study wildlife crimes in Italy. Italy is one of the European countries with the richest biodiversity, but its precious heritage is at risk, with wildlife crimes, and particularly the abductions and killing of animals in its various manifestations, being one of the main threats to the survival of rare or endangered species. This review chapter focuses on bird abductions/killings as a case study, presenting trends, phenomenology and characteristics, and describing the related wildlife markets in Italy and their impact on wildlife conservation. The authors also offer a brief overview of the relevant national legislation and its implementation, suggesting how the system currently in place is not always adequate to confront a diffuse and socially embedded phenomenon whose social and environmental harms are too often not yet fully recognized. The chapter also presents Italy's legislative efforts to combat wildlife crimes and ensure conservation, identifying central challenges and shortcomings that halt the enforcement of CITES and the Bern Convention and related national legislation.

In Chapter 6, 'Analysis of social and legal factors influencing the effectiveness of tackling the illegal killing of wolves in Poland', Piotr J. Chmielewski and Agnieszka Serlikowska investigate the legal framework for wolf protection in Poland. They look into what factors influence the jurisprudence of this country's courts in cases concerning the illegal killing of wolves, and the Polish people's tolerance to wolves. They perform a literature review, analyse legislation and court decisions and find that the Polish legal framework is complicated when it comes to criminal regulations related to wolf protection and that the Polish criminal justice system has an anthropocentric (mainly economical) approach to illegal wolf killing.

In Chapter 7, 'CITES in Spain: blueprints and challenges of Spanish practice on CITES and welfare of trafficked victims', Teresa Fajardo explores the implementation of CITES in Spain, focusing on the introduction of the Spanish Action Plan against illegal trafficking and international trafficking of wildlife species (TIFIES). The chapter is based on analysis of a wide range of data, including judicial decisions, crime statistics and expert interviews with judges and NGOs, among others. She finds that the TIFIES plan is a positive contribution to combat illegal wildlife trafficking and species extinction, in that it calls for increased specialization of all authorities involved in CITES enforcement. However, she identifies that the low budgetary priority given to enforcement of environmental regulation is also an issue in Spain. When it comes to the policy and practice related to the handling of trafficking victims, Fajardo finds that Spain goes beyond the requirements set by CITES and makes more efforts both to rehome and to repatriate the animal victims of trade.

In Chapter 8, 'Paper tigers and local perseverance: wildlife protection in Germany', Christoph H. Stefes also explores the implementation of CITES, The Bern Convention and other wildlife treaties in practice, but with a focus on Germany and the enforcement of the conventions and its challenges. Germany is an active participant in international meetings, where its delegations regularly advocate for expanding the protection of endangered species. It could, therefore, be expected that Germany would be an exemplary protector of endangered wildlife at home. Stefes analyses how Germany's federal structure of enforcement impacts on its efficiency, and compares the results of centralized, cooperative and decentralized enforcement based on both interviews with enforcers and quantitative analysis of reported offences. He finds that although Germany has faithfully incorporated international treaties and European law into federal legislation, law enforcement is wanting and sentencing is routinely too lenient to have a deterring effect. Germany's wildlife protection legislation is thereby rendered into a paper tiger.

In Chapter 9, 'The Norwegian chain of wildlife treaty effectiveness', David R. Goyes explores the grounds for the weaknesses in implementation and enforcement of CITES and the Bern Convention in Norway by asking how the country fares vis-à-vis the chain of wildlife treaty effectiveness. The text of a treaty alone has little effect on the practices that harm wildlife. Rather, for a treaty to be effective in preserving nature, he finds that many links in a chain have to work smoothly and strongly. States have to: (1) be willing to ratify the treaty; (2) change their domestic legislation to adopt the goals of the treaty; and (3) allocate resources to implement the measures through which the goals will be achieved. Stakeholders must: (1) know, directly or indirectly, of the treaty and their goals; (2) embrace the treaty contents by incorporating them into their worldviews; and (3) act following the treaty mandates. Goyes finds that the stakeholders have not incorporated the conventions into their worldviews and their work, and contends that this might explain and substantiate allegations of Norway's mistreatment of wildlife.

In Chapter 10, 'Rewilding in the UK: harm or justice?', Tanya Wyatt looks into the interest in rewilding of lynx in the UK. She considers how rewilding fits with the framework of CITES and the Bern Convention, and analyses the public debate following the rewilding initiative. The exploration is twofold – first, the chapter examines the narratives of opposition and support for return of the lynx, focusing on the animal and environmental harms and benefits that are predicted. Second, the chapter analyses how the Bern Convention and CITES, as they are transposed in UK legislation, can account for rewilding. Considering both the supportive and the opposing arguments, Wyatt discusses the rewilding of lynx from a species justice perspective, focusing on the potential harms and benefits it might bring for animals and the environment.

In Chapter 11, 'We only see what we know: animal conservation and human preservation', Mark T. Palermo reflects upon the current anthropocentric relationship between humans, other animals and nature, including the potential and challenges of international wildlife treaties in ensuring animal and nature protection. He takes his point of departure in pre-religious and shamanistic cultures, where the relationship with the natural world was strong, reality based and pragmatic. In an age of trans-humanist urges and struggles for non-human animal conservation and representation, however, the relationship with nature has become a matter of policy. Moral impossibilities relevant to the commodification of life are pervasive and acceptable when it comes to non-humans. Notwithstanding animistic revivals, urbanization and a recreational, consumeristic and medicalized relationship with the natural world further distance us from nature from an ontological perspective. The author's objective is to strengthen the all-encompassing nature of green criminology as it relates to animal conservation with a cross-disciplinary theoretical engagement approach, and to outline important shortcomings of current animal conservation.

In Chapter 12, editors Sollund and Lie summarize the case studies, describing the main findings and overall conclusions concerning the status of species conservation in Europe and consideration of the individual rights and welfare of freeborn animals and species justice.

Many of the contributions point to weaknesses and challenges in the implementation and enforcement of CITES and the Bern Convention. There is hope that the nature diversity agreement reached in Montreal (UNEP COP 15, 2022) will reduce the pace of extinction, however, there is also a danger that this agreement will become yet another document with little practical impact for endangered wildlife. As we show in this volume, freeborn animals are victims of human greed and consumption, reaffirming that human interests are given primacy and that too little respect and concern are paid to the protection of wildlife in Europe.

References

Brisman, A. and South, N. (2019) 'Green criminology and environmental crimes and harms', *Sociology Compass*, 13(1), pp 1–12.

CITES (no date) 'How CITES works', https://cites.org/eng/disc/how.php

Council of Europe (1979) *Convention on the Conservation of European Wildlife and Natural Habitats*, ETS No. 104. Available at: www.coe.int/en/web/conventions/full-list (accessed 29 December 2020).

Epstein, Y. (2013) 'Population-based species management across legal boundaries: the Bern Convention, Habitats Directive, and the gray wolf in Scandinavia', *Georgetown International Environmental Law Review*, 25(4), pp 549–88.

Epstein, Y. (2014) 'The Habitats Directive and Bern Convention: synergy and dysfunction in public international and EU law', *Georgetown International Environmental Law Review*, 26(2), pp 139–73.

Fleurke, F. and Trouwborst, A. (2014) 'European Regional Approaches to the Transboundary Conservation of Biodiversity: The Bern Convention and the EU Birds and Habitats Directives', in M. Kotze and T. Marauhn (eds) *Transboundary Governance of Biodiversity*. Martinus Nijhoff Publishers, pp 128–62.

Goyes, D. and Sollund, R. (2016) 'Contesting and contextualising CITES: wildlife trafficking in Colombia and Brazil', *International Journal for Crime, Justice and Social Democracy*, 5(4), p 87.

Gruen, L. (2015) *Entangled Empathy: An Alternative Ethic for our Relationships with Animals*. Lantern Books.

Higgins, P., Short, D. and South, N. (2013) 'Protecting the planet: a proposal for a law of ecocide', *Crime, Law and Social Change*, 59(3), pp 251–66.

Janssen, J. and Leupen, B. T. (2019) 'Traded under the radar: poor documentation of trade in nationally-protected non-CITES species can cause fraudulent trade to go undetected', *Biodiversity and Conservation*, 28(11), pp 2797–804.

Jen, S. (1999) 'The Convention on the Conservation of European Wildlife and Natural Habitats (Bern, 1979): procedures of application in practice', *Journal of International Wildlife Law & Policy*, 2(2), pp 224–38.

Rajamani, L. (2021) 'Table of Legislation', in L. Rajamani and J. Peel (eds) *The Oxford Handbook of International Environmental Law*. Oxford University Press, pp xxix–lxxxiii.

Regan, T. (2004) *The Case for Animal Rights*. University of California Press.

Sollund, R. (2015) 'Introduction: Critical Green Criminology – An Agenda for Change', in R. Sollund (ed) *Green Harms and Crimes: Critical Criminology in a Changing World*. Palgrave Macmillan, pp 1–26.

Sollund, R. (2016) 'The Animal Other: Legal and Illegal Theriocide', in M. Hall, J. Maher, A. Nurse, G. Potter, N. South and T. Wyatt (eds) *Greening Criminology in the 21st Century: Contemporary Debates and Future Directions in the Study of Environmental Harm*. Routledge (Green Criminology Series), pp 79–99.

Sollund, R. (2017) 'Doing green, critical criminology with an auto-ethnographic, feminist approach', *Critical Criminology*, 25(2), pp 245–60.

Sollund, R. (2019) *The Crimes of Wildlife Trafficking: Issues of Justice, Legality and Morality*, Routledge.

Sollund, R. (forthcoming) 'Species restorative justice: a call to end anthropogenic wildlife destruction' (in review).

Sollund, R. and Runhovde, S. (2020) 'Responses to wildlife crime in postcolonial times. Who fares best?', *The British Journal of Criminology*, 60(4), pp 1014–33.

Stretesky, P., Long, M. and Lynch, M. (2013) *The Treadmill of Crime: Political Economy and Green Criminology*, Routledge.

Techera, E., Lindley, J., Scott, K. N. and Telesetsky A. (eds) (2021) *Routledge Handbook of International Environmental Law*, 2nd edn, Routledge.

Trouwborst, A., Fleurke, F. M. and Linnell, J. D. (2017) 'Norway's wolf policy and the Bern Convention on European wildlife: avoiding the "manifestly absurd"', *Journal of International Wildlife Law & Policy*, 20(2), pp 155–67.

UNEP COP 15 (2022) *UN Biodiversity Conference (COP 15)*, www.unep.org

White, R. (2013) *Environmental Harm: An Eco-Justice Perspective*, Policy Press.

White, R. (2018) 'Green victimology and non-human victims', *International Review of Victimology*, 24(2), pp 239–55.

WWF (2022) '69% average decline in wildlife populations since 1970, says new WWF report', press release 13 October, www.worldwildlife.org

Wyatt, T. (2021) *Is CITES Protecting Wildlife? Assessing Implementation and Compliance*, Routledge.

2

Legal Versus Illegal Hunts: A Species Justice Perspective on Wolf and Bear Theriocides in Norway

Martine S.B. Lie

Introduction

Norwegian grey wolves and brown bears are endangered and critically endangered, respectively, in Norway (Artsdatabanken 2021). Although they are protected by the Convention on the Conservation of European Wildlife and Natural Habitats (the Bern Convention), which Norway ratified in 1986, they are victims of both legal and illegal theriocides (killings of animals by humans; see Beirne 2014; Sollund 2017a), through practices including illegal hunts, state-mandated hunts, and killings in defence of humans or their animals.[1] This chapter is based on comparative analysis of verdicts from Norwegian court cases on illegal wolf and bear theriocides or attempted theriocides, and legislation and guidelines for legal large predator hunts.[2] I identify several similarities between the legal and illegal hunts, and this finding raises the question of whether the legal hunts are more justified than

---
[1] The use of the word 'animal', as distinct from 'human', is misleading and conceals the fact that *Homo sapiens* are also animals. Regrettably, they will still be used in this chapter for the sake of simplicity.
[2] This study is produced as part of the project Criminal Justice, Wildlife Conservation and Animal Rights in the Anthropocene (CRIMEANTHROP), at the Department of Criminology and Sociology of Law, University of Oslo. It is funded by the granting Committee for the Humanities and Social Sciences (FRIPRO) of the Research Council Norway, project number 289285. I am grateful to Professors Nigel South and Avi Brisman for their valuable comments to an earlier version of the chapter.

the illegal hunts from an animal welfare-based species justice perspective –
that is, whether they cause the victims less suffering.

I begin by presenting the species justice perspective and related research
on large predator hunts in Nordic countries. From here, I describe the
sample of verdicts that I examined and my methods for analysis, before
introducing Norwegian wolf and bear policies based on so-called 'lethal
control'. Following this, I discuss the (attempted) illegal theriocides as they
are described in the verdicts, before comparing them with legal hunts. Finally,
I consider the justifiability of 'lethal control' of endangered predators as a
policy strategy.

Theoretical perspective

This inquiry into the distinction between legal and illegal large predator
hunts and its justifiability fits well within green criminology's interest in
legal definitions of ecological harm (see, for example, Brisman and South
2019). Because Norwegian brown bears are endangered and Norwegian
wolves are critically endangered, the hunts affect them both as individuals
and as species, threatening biodiversity and, thereby, also affecting humans'
interests in maintaining wildlife across the planet. This chapter adopts a
species justice perspective as its point of departure, seeing the hunted animals
as victims (Brisman and South 2019: 6) and focusing on the hunts' effect on
them *as individuals*.

Human dimensions of large predator management and illegal hunting in
the Nordic countries are well studied. Skogen and Krange (for example,
2020; Skogen et al 2013), Pohja-Mykrä (2016, 2017) and von Essen (for
example, von Essen and Allen 2020; von Essen et al 2015; see also Skogen
et al 2022), among others, have analysed the conflict over large predator
policies, illegal hunts and the reluctance to report such crimes. The human–
predator conflict is found to be interconnected with other, deeper conflicts,
such as those between rural and urban interests (see, for example, Skogen
et al 2013), and illegal hunts are seen as an expression of certain hunters'
resistance to the large predator management (Pohja-Mykrä 2016, 2017;
von Essen et al 2015; Skogen and Krange 2020). Epstein (2013, 2016), and
Trouwborst et al (2017) have examined the Nordic countries' compliance
with the Bern Convention and the related Habitats Directive (which is
not in force in Norway because Norway is not a member of the European
Union) regarding wolf conservation. Larsson (2019, 2020) has analysed the
investigation of illegal wolf hunts by Norwegian police,[3] while Sollund and

---

[3] Including cases O2 (Larsson 2019), D2 and D4 (Larsson 2020) analysed here (see 'Illegal theriocides' for a description of the cases).

Goyes (2021) have discussed the cultural background of licensed wolf hunts in Norway. Additionally, Sollund (2020a) has analysed gendered aspects of wildlife crimes, including illegal large predator hunts.

Sollund (2017a, 2017b, 2020b) has also examined Norwegian large predator hunts from a non-anthropocentric perspective, criticizing both legal and illegal hunts for breaching the intrinsic rights of animals and ecosystems. She points out how what is essentially the same act of killing an endangered animal may be both legal and illegal (Sollund 2017b), inspiring my systematic comparison of legal and illegal hunts. Sollund (2016, 2017a, 2017b) has also analysed verdicts from illegal theriocides, and five of the cases in her analyses overlap with the cases analysed here.[4] Most of the cases she has analysed, however, predate the Nature Diversity Act of 2009 (the NDA), which was meant to coordinate and strengthen the protection of nature in Norway (Økokrim 2009); six of the eight cases analysed in this chapter were adjudicated under this Act. Sollund's rights-based perspective also differs from the welfare-based species justice perspective I employ here, as explained next.

White (2012: 27) describes 'species justice' as focused on 'non-human animals and their intrinsic right not to suffer abuse, whether this be one-on-one harm, institutionalized harm or harm arising from human actions that affect climates and environments on a global scale'. From a strict animal rights-based species justice perspective, individual animals hold an intrinsic right to life (see, for example, Regan 1983; Sollund 2017a, 2020b). As both legal and illegal hunts clearly breach this, any analysis of how they are conducted and are differentiated is unnecessary to reach such a conclusion. A broader understanding of species justice is therefore employed here – one that involves concern for individual animals' welfare and avoidance of (some) harm to them, but not necessarily avoidance of death (see also Lie 2021). A utilitarian animal welfare approach to animal protection, originating from Singer (1991), is therefore the starting point. This approach is expanded by what Donovan (1996) calls 'a feminist caring ethic', employing sympathy and imagination to understand individual animal harm, not just abstract equations of harm (see also Adams and Gruen 2014). More concretely, I explore whether the data show signs of more concern for harm avoidance and the individual hunting victims' welfare in legal theriocides than with the illegal theriocides. Can legal hunts be justified by upholding more of a commitment to species justice than illegal hunts?

---

[4] These are cases O1, D2, D3 (Sollund 2016), O2 and A2 (Sollund 2017a) (see 'Illegal theriocides' for a description of the cases).

Methodology

The chapter is based on qualitative analysis of verdicts regarding illegal theriocides of wolves and bears in Norway, as well as an analysis of guidelines and legislation regulating legal hunts. Using NVivo, I uncovered three categories of illegal theriocides and coded these, as well as similarities between the theriocides or attempted theriocides and legal hunts.

The legislation analysed to understand the basis for legal hunts are the NDA, the Predator Regulation (2005), and the Wildlife Act (1981). In addition, I analysed four booklets for hunters about wolf, bear, lynx and wolverine hunting, published by the Norwegian Association of Hunters and Anglers and The Norwegian Institute for Nature Research (Odden et al 2013a, 2013b, 2017; Swenson et al 2013), as well as a guide for carrying out culling orders from the Norwegian Environment Agency (2019). The sample of verdicts dates from 2009 to 2023 and consists of eight verdicts from district courts, six from Eidsivating Appeal Court, and one from the Supreme Court. The verdicts cover eight cases in total, two of these (a wolf theriocide and an unsuccessful illegal wolf hunt) handled in the same verdicts. Three verdicts were gathered directly from district courts, the rest from Lovdata.[5] I found no verdicts issued after 2009 regarding theriocides of lynx or wolverines in Lovdata, which is curiously contrary to Sollund's (2016, 2017a) sample of mostly older verdicts.

In all of the cases, the accused individuals were found guilty of illegally killing wolves or bears, attempting to do so, or contributing to such a crime, except one individual, whose involvement in an organized hunt was not proven beyond a reasonable doubt. In four of the cases, the accused individuals were convicted of violating the Penal Code §152/240 (old/new version), which provides that reducing 'a natural population of protected organisms that are threatened by extinction nationally or internationally' (Lovdata's translation) is punishable by up to six years imprisonment. As this section of the code is intended for the most serious environmental crimes, most of the cases were seemingly not perceived as that serious by the judges. In two of the cases, the actual offences were committed before the NDA came into force in 2009. They were, therefore, prosecuted and decided under the Wildlife Act, but the judges also make reference to and interpret the NDA in the verdicts, as it was enacted before the verdicts were issued. The rest of the accused were convicted for breaching Section 15 of the NDA. Eleven of the accused were also found guilty of breaching weapons and dogs legislation, while one was found guilty of breaching animal welfare legislation for chasing four wolves with his car, in addition to breaching

---

[5] Lovdata is a database with all recent verdicts from Norwegian appeal courts, the Supreme Court, and some verdicts from district courts.

the Wildlife Act by shooting a bear. I do not comment on the wolf chase because theriocide does not appear to be the motive for it.

Norwegian large predator management through 'lethal control'

Norwegian large predators were subjects of eradication policies until the 1970s (Sollund and Goyes 2021). Now, predator policies are marked by a tension between the traditional anthropocentric interest of prioritizing hunting and farming, and commitments to the Bern Convention (Sollund and Goyes 2021). Wolves and bears are listed on the Bern Convention's Appendix II of 'strictly protected fauna species' and can be killed only in exceptional circumstances – if it is the only 'satisfactory solution' and if it is not detrimental to the populations' survival (Bern Convention Art 9.1; see Sollund and Lie's Introduction to this volume). Norwegian legislation and policies implementing the Bern Convention, however, provide them only with *conditional* protection depending on their numbers, location and, to some extent, behaviour, reproduction and genetics (see also Goyes, this volume). Despite this, Norway has never been critiqued by the convention bodies for this policy,[6] which is not that surprising, considering the convention's diplomatic character and practice.

Annual licensed hunts for wolves and bears have been granted as a means to secure farming and hunting interests (see, for example, Innst. 330 S). The hunting quotas are determined based on region-specific population goals of 13 brown bear litters and just four to six wolf litters[7] (The Predator Regulation §3). The quotas are normally set by politically appointed regional predator boards, and appeals may be made to the Ministry of Climate and Environment (The Predator Regulation §§4, 7, 18). The Norwegian Environment Agency can also authorise hunts, even if the population goals are not met (The Predator Regulation §13). In addition, specific individuals can be killed to prevent more concrete risks of attack on livestock (*skadefelling*) (Norwegian Environment Agency 2019).

Rovdata monitors large predators in Norway and registered approximately 175 brown bears in 2022, and 89–92 wolves (including cross-border habitants) in the winter season 2022–23.[8] The number of brown bear litters (9.5 in 2022) is consequently well below the population goal, but licensed

---

[6] At the time of writing (June 2023) a complaint on the quotas for licensed wolf hunts in the 2022–23 hunting season is however on stand-by, scheduled for follow-up fall 2024.

[7] This figure includes cross-border wolves residing in both Norway and Sweden, which are counted as 0.5 of a litter.

[8] 'Bjørn – Bestandsstatus', https://rovdata.no/Brunbj%C3%B8rn/Bestandsstatus.aspx (accessed 8 June 2023); 'Ulv – Bestandsstatus', https://rovdata.no/Ulv/Bestandsstatus.aspx (accessed 8 June 2023).

hunts are still approved every year. The wolf population goal was reached but wolves are still critically endangered (Artsdatabanken 2021). Crucially, this means that Norwegian authorities wish to maintain the population at a level where they still remain critically endangered.

In practice, wolves are welcome only in the so-called 'wolf zone' in eastern and inland Norway, covering 5 per cent of the land surface, while farming is prioritized outside the zone (Innst. 330 S; Trouwborst et al 2017: 157). Yet, licensed hunts may also target wolves inside the wolf zone (Innst. 330 S: 9) – a policy that is controversial and has been the subject of litigation, but was approved by the Supreme Court in 2023.[9]

The hunts are carried out by registered hunting teams that shoot the victims with hunting rifles, with help from dogs used for tracking (Swenson et al 2013; Odden et al 2017). Individual hunters may also hunt large predators, for example by using bait and killing them when they come to eat (Swenson et al 2013; Odden et al 2017). Because hunting wolves and bears presents challenges for hunters, the hunts are usually well planned (Swenson et al 2013; Odden et al 2017). A wolf hunt held in January 2020 is illustrative of this. The hunters planned the hunt for two and a half months while they awaited the outcome of an appeal to the Ministry; 180 people subsequently participated and killed four wolves within the first 24 hours (Bugge and Myrvang 2020).

To participate in the wolf and bear hunts, one must hold a hunting licence, register to hunt each species, and must have passed a shooting test specific for large predator hunts (Swenson et al 2013; Odden et al 2017). Municipalities also appoint and compensate hunting teams who are called on to kill specific individuals considered extra prone to attack (The Predator Regulation 2005: §9a). In some instances, The Norwegian Nature Inspectorate (SNO), a division of the Environment Agency, conducts the hunts. They sometimes hunt by helicopter (see Sollund 2020b), which can cause the victims much stress and is generally prohibited under the Bern Convention's Appendix IV.[10] In addition to these planned hunts, wolves and bears can be killed legally if required to stop 'an immediate and serious threat' to humans or to thwart an 'ongoing or imminent attack'[11] on livestock or dogs, and where killing them 'is seen as required'[12] to prevent the attack (Nature Diversity Act §17 [author's translations]). In four of the cases, the accused individuals asserted this right to shoot in defence.

---

[9] HR-2023-936-A.

[10] Exceptions can be made on the same grounds as for killing species listed in Appendix II (explained earlier).

[11] The original formulation was altered in 2020 from requiring a *direct* attack to 'an ongoing or imminent attack' (Lovvedtak 121).

[12] This formulation was added in 2020 to be in line with the Bern Convention (Lovvedtak 121).

Illegal theriocides

Illegal wolf and bear hunts are a significant problem in Norway and pose a considerable threat to both species' survival, especially for wolves (Liberg et al 2012; Innst. 330 S). Sollund (2016) notes that some of these theriocides follow some form of contact between the predator victims and farm animals. Larsson (2020) differentiates between instances where wolves are shot if the possibility presents itself during hunts of other animals and systematic, organized hunts. Planned hunts, theriocides following what is claimed to be predator attacks about to happen, and shots fired at predators during other hunts are all found among the verdicts analysed here.

Organized illegal hunts

Two cases, where several hunters communicated and operated as 'hunting teams', appear more planned and intentional than the other cases. In the cases, involving two hunts for a wolf and a bear, the accused appear to be part of a network of hunters, who notify each other of wolf and bear sightings, and who stand ready to convene quickly if hunting possibilities arise. In the bear hunt (O1),[13] five men traced and chased a male bear, some of them with hunting dogs, before one of the accused shot him. The courts were unsure, however, whether all five were planning on killing him, or just chase him to train their dogs.

The wolf hunt (O2)[14] was planned to the extent that the prosecutor charged the hunters with a violation of the former Penal Code's Section 60a for offences committed by an organized group. The Appeal Court rejected the use of the Penal Code 60a, but its use by the prosecution, accepted by the District Court, still illustrates the extent to which planning and cooperation are involved in illegal large predator hunts. The case also allowed the police to wiretap the suspects' telephones, making phone transcripts available as evidence in court (Larsson 2020). The verdicts, therefore, include detailed descriptions of the event. For example, after having observed a wolf family of three over time, an instigator 'gathered crew for the hunt, some to follow tracks in the terrain and others to sit in stand' (LE-2015-83191, p 15 [author's translation]). The hunters also ploughed logging roads to keep the wolves inside a designated area. The hunt was instigated when the female wolf was in heat in order to keep the wolves from breeding. Three shots were fired at the wolves, but they failed to hit them. The instigator, therefore,

---

[13] Described in verdicts TSOST-2009-103124 and LE-2010-12617.
[14] Described in verdicts TSOST-2014-168573, LE-2015-83191, HR-2016-1857-A and LE-2016-182913.

'organised a form of follow-up the day after' (LE-2015–83191, p 15 [author's translation]). The case was ultimately decided by the Supreme Court, with five hunters convicted and one acquitted. The instigator was simultaneously convicted for shooting a wolf on his own during a fox hunt – a theriocide I describe later.

Although there are no such cases in the verdicts, predators are also killed deliberately and illegally by means other than with rifles. This may involve especially harmful killing methods, such as poisoning (Larsson 2020). Such theriocides obviously cause the victims great pain and clearly breach the Animal Welfare Act §12 and Wildlife Act §§19 and 20 regarding killing methods. Poisoning may also harm animals other than those targeted if, for example, they happen to eat bait that has been adulterated. Moreover, illegal traps and poisoned bait are often hard to trace back to a particular suspect (Larsson 2020: 130), which may explain why there are no such cases among the verdicts.

Theriocides in defence

Five cases involved theriocides (or attempts) where the convicted individuals argued that they were defending themselves or their animals. The judges, however, found that none of the cases fulfilled the criteria necessary to render legal these theriocides.

An accused who supposedly shot a bear in self-defence (D1)[15] claims to have first tried to scare off the bear by screaming and throwing some wood at him (which is not supported by evidence or witness statements). When this did not work, the accused asserted that he fired a warning shot from a distance of around 7–10 metres, which resulted in the bear trying to escape. Because he thought that he had accidentally hit the bear with the warning shot, he followed him and fired another shot from 30–40 metres distance, but the bear survived and ran away. An autopsy conducted when the bear was killed eight months later largely disproves that he was hit by the first shot, but it found 22 encapsulated pellets within a 35-cm radius on his genitalia and hind part from the second shot. The court chastised the accused for using ammunition not suitable for bears. Before the shots, the bear had scared horses on the accused's property.

In another case (D2),[16] the convicted individual was alerted about the wolf by a tenant and could see from his window that a wolf was heading towards his sheep. The individual then ran out and shot the wolf immediately, instead of trying to scare him off. According to the defendant, he shot the wolf from a distance of 84 metres, and the wolf fell dead immediately,

---

[15] Described in verdicts THEDM-2012-51106 and LE-2012-108373.
[16] Described in verdict TOVRO-2012-30478.

In yet another case, the defendant killed a bear to protect sheep (D3).[17] According to the defendant, the bear was 210 metres from the defendant and 140 metres from the sheep enclosure when he was shot the first time. The defendant, his dog and his acquaintance hunted him down (by foot, car and ATV) over a longer distance. The defendant did not try to scare the bear away, but first shot at the bear on an open road. The bear was wounded and tried to escape. The accused and his neighbour followed him and the accused shot him once more on the road. The bear then tried to escape by swimming across a lake. The two men followed him and the accused fired two more shots, leading the bear to turn and swim back towards the dog chasing him. The accused then shot the bear in the head and killed him in the lake.

In the fourth case (D4),[18] the accused was alerted by phone about a wolf's presence near his house. After unsuccessfully calling for his dog, who was running loose, he brought his rifle outside on the grounds that he was worried about the dog. He shouted to scare the wolf, who then walked away but reappeared shortly thereafter on the back side of the house, where the accused shot him head-on from 34 metres' distance, claiming he did this to protect his dog, even though (s)he was not to be seen at that point. The shot hit the wolf in the heart and he died quickly.

In the last of these cases (D5),[19] a reindeer owner shot a mother bear and two cubs. The defendant understood from his reindeers' GPS monitoring that there were predators present. Alongside other reindeer owners, as well as a representative from SNO, he monitored the bears for five days. The men tried to move the bears by chasing them on snowmobiles over 17.6 kilometres. One of the cubs was transported on the back of the snowmobile, as (s)he could not keep up with the others. The bears however returned the next morning. The defendant then lit up a cairn to alert the bears to the group's presence. During the five days, the bears killed at least 14 reindeer calves. The men found calf corpses, and saw the bears chasing reindeer and eating from the corpses, as well as reindeer mothers looking for their calves. On the second day, the defendant called the Environment Agency, applying for permission to kill the bears as *skadefelling*. They denied his application verbally, and later in writing, as I will elaborate upon below. On the fifth day, the bears were once again eating reindeer calves and the defendant decided to kill them under the right to defence, stating in court that he thought another attempt to chase the bears away would do them more harm than good, and that they would return anyway. At this point,

---

[17] Described in verdict TNOST-2010-57617.
[18] Described in verdicts TSOST-2016-183971 and LE-2017-6392.
[19] Described in verdict TTRO-2022-176914.

there were only two cubs.[20] He followed the bears down a mountain side on snowmobile and continued by foot, guided by one of the colleagues sitting on stand. After 45–60 minutes, he saw the mother bear raising her head and shot her and the two cubs with his rifle from a distance of about 30 metres, then notifying the police and the SNO representative of the killings. When he fired the deadly shots, the bears were calm. The majority of the court, therefore, denied the defendant's claim of shooting in defence, as an attack was not imminent.[21]

Alleged accidental illegal theriocides

A wolf theriocide and an attempt occurred during legal hunts. In the first case (A1),[22] the hunter stated that he mistakenly thought the season for licensed wolf hunts had started when he shot a wolf from a 50 metres distance during an elk hunt. The wolf survived the shot, but traces of blood followed him for 'several kilometres'. In the other case (A2),[23] the hunter, who also instigated the organized wolf hunt described earlier, claimed to have thought he shot a fox instead of a wolf during an overnight foxhunt. He fired the shot from a distance of 70 metres and waited around six hours to check on the wolf, who was heavily wounded but alive. The wolf suffered all this time before the offender killed him.

Comparison of the legal and illegal theriocides

Legal wolf and bear hunts and the illegal theriocides described in the verdicts resemble each other in terms of actors and methods. Arguably, both types of theriocides also cause the animal victims suffering, although reproductively 'valuable individuals' are usually protected from legal hunts.

Actors and means

All the defendants are male hunters. This is a finding shared by Sollund (2016, 2017a), who has called the hunting experience a 'prerequisite to the crime' (2017a: 91), and who considers illegal hunting as a 'crime of hegemonic

---

[20] The verdict does not state what happened to the third cub but says that one of them climbed a tree after the snowmobile chase and this was the last time (s)he was seen.

[21] One of the lay judges claimed that the defendant should be acquitted since it was clear that the bears would attack the reindeer again shortly after their rest. He also emphasized the defendant and the others' attempt at moving the bears and the bears' repeated killings of the reindeer.

[22] Described in verdicts TSGUD-2019-69611 and LE-2019-148163.

[23] Described in verdicts TSOST-2014-168573, LE-2015-83191 and HR-2016-1857-A.

masculinity' (2020a). Approximately 96 per cent of those who hunted large predators legally in Norway in the 2015–16 hunting season were also men (Rundtom and Steinset 2016). Eight of the defendants had registered for, or participated in, licensed wolf and bear hunts, according to the verdicts. At least three were also appointed members of their municipality's predator hunting team, which means they killed predators illegally while being trusted representatives of official predator policies.

The convicted also conducted their crimes in similar ways and with similar means to those in legal hunts. The two organized illegal hunts were carried out in much the same way as licensed predator hunts – planned and by a collaborative group of hunters with rifles and hunting dogs, who tracked and shot the victims. This was also pointed out by the prosecutor regarding the bear hunt. The District Court, however, disagreed that the hunt was 'organized the same way that an ordinary hunting team would have done it' because it appeared less organized in the beginning (TSOST-2009-103124: 16). The two so-called 'accidental' cases even happened during legal hunts of other wildlife, which also occurred with rifles. Even the alleged 'defensive' theriocides were conducted by hunters with their regular hunting rifles and would have been legal, had the criteria been met. In D5 the bear theriocides would have been legal had the Environment Agency accepted the defendant's application for *skadefelling*. As mentioned earlier, the accused in D1, however, used ammunition unsuitable for killing a bear, and was therefore convicted for breaching the NDA §15 by causing the victim unnecessary suffering.

Protection of reproductively 'valuable individuals'

A difference between the legal and illegal theriocides may be the genetic and reproductive 'value' of the victims, as explained regarding case O2:

> When a hunting permit is given for a protected wolf, a very thorough assessment is usually made in advance of the significance of taking out this specific individual for the possibility of achieving the management goals. ... A concrete and individual assessment is thus made of the significance of the culling for the management of the wolf population. When individuals or groups pursue their own population regulation (impulsively or systematically), the culling of individuals is not scientifically assessed or determined, but controlled by which individuals one can get within shooting range of or in other ways is able to kill. We are then speaking of 'targets of opportunity', and not scientifically assessed cullings where the consequences have been carefully evaluated. ... The consequences of the culling can for the strain/population be very different. (District Court verdict, TSOST-2014-168573, p 17 [author's translation])

The Environment Agency's rejection of the defendant's application for *skadefelling* in D5, even though the bears were killing reindeer and alternative solutions were tried, similarly demonstrates how female bears enjoy more protection than male bears, because of their reproductive value:

> The threshold for killing female bears with cubs is generally very high. Additionally, the bear population is below the management goal for region 6. In the fringe areas of the Scandinavian bear population there are relatively few female bears, and the few that exist are crucial for the population to develop in the right direction in relation to the goal for the region. (Rejection quoted in TTRO-2022-176914, p 6 [author's translation]).

Norwegian predators are monitored closely through DNA analysis and sometimes heavy collars with radio transmitters, which are placed under stressful conditions (Tønnesen 2013; Sollund 2016: 4–5; Rovdata n.d.). 'Genetically valuable individuals' – wolves from the Russian-Finnish population – enjoy special protection from legal hunts because they represent new genes of value to the massively inbred southern Scandinavian wolf population (Ministry of Climate and Environment 2014: 60). These 'immigrants', so to speak, are monitored closely and sometimes even moved closer to possible mates in extensive and expensive operations to counteract the risk that the considerable inbreeding poses to the species' survival (see, for example, Vollan et al 2021).

In case O2, the hunters also monitored the victims, and strategically started the hunt when discovering that the female was in heat, to keep the couple from reproducing more wolves. Contrary to the District Court's statement above, this implies that victims of organized illegal hunts may not be solely 'targets of opportunity', but indeed strategically chosen in order to optimize the effects of the hunt – diminish the predator population as much as possible.

Although the protection of 'immigrant' wolves is not based on consideration for individual animals, it might still indirectly have a positive effect on the wolves' welfare. The inbreeding rate is equivalent to siblings mating, and the health consequences inflict suffering on them also as individuals (see, for example, Räikkönen et al 2013). Efforts to reduce inbreeding can, therefore, also improve individual wolves' life quality. Nevertheless, the protection of 'immigrant' wolves is arguably a remedy to treat a symptom – inbreeding – rather than to treat the cause – the scarcity of wolves. Similarly, the higher threshold for shooting female bears, as demonstrated in D5, is also a remedy to adhere to the Bern Convention while willingly keeping the population at a scarce, vulnerable level. Moreover, the protection of these 'valuable individuals' is not bullet proof, literally speaking, as the wolf killed in D4 was 'genetically valuable'. The frequency of 'immigrating' wolves is also found to be insufficient for securing survival of the southern Scandinavian wolf population (see, for example, Laikre et al 2016). Nevertheless, Norwegian authorities mandate wolf hunts.

The animals' suffering

With equal killing methods, the legal and illegal theriocides also have similar potential for suffering for the victims, as the District Court remarked in O1: 'Nor can the court see that the killing method for the bear indicates that there are especially aggravating circumstances. It was euthanized with one shot, and fell dead. Even skadefelling and licensed hunts cannot be expected to be carried out in a gentler way for the bear'[24] (TSOST-2009-103124, p 16 [author's translation]).

The court does not, however, acknowledge the loss of life as suffering in itself. The additional harm caused when killing a whole family by shooting the mother in front of her young in D5 is not emphasized by the court. Evaluations of animal welfare and rights in the verdicts are largely limited to evaluation of whether the killings were 'humane' or not, meaning whether the victims died quickly or not (see Lie 2021). As previously described, some of the victims were hurt and not killed immediately. The bear in D1 was wounded but lived for another eight months with the wound and embedded pellets, partly due to unsuitable ammunition. The victims in cases A1 and A2 were also wounded but did not die right away.

Legal hunts may also cause the victims suffering. Wolves and bears are actually more prone to being wounded by missed shots than other so-called 'game animals', according to Stokke and colleagues (2012). The predators' relatively small size (underneath the fur in bears' case) makes them challenging targets, and their rarity may lead hunters to pull the trigger despite not being sure of accuracy, because they see the moment as a unique opportunity (Stokke et al 2012). Awareness that bears might attack the hunter may also lead to premature shots (Stokke et al 2012), as might have been the case with the first shot in D1. Stokke and colleagues (2012) also see a risk of unsuitable ammunition meant for other animals being used in legal large predator hunts, as in D1. In addition, they find that 'aversion to predators can lower the threshold for humane hunting so that there is greater acceptance for hurting shots failing to kill within the hunting team' (Stokke et al 2012: 4).

As mentioned earlier, cruel methods, such as poisoning, are also employed to kill predators illegally, and cause them considerable pain and suffering.

---

[24] The word 'euthanize' (*avlive*), diminishes the brutality of the killing – as though it had been conducted out of compassion for the animal (Lie 2021). As mentioned earlier, *skadefelling* refers to the culling of specific individuals to prevent more concrete risks of attack.

Some forms of legal hunts, however, also cause the victims suffering beyond being shot and killed, such as when hunters use helicopters. Wolverines and lynx may also be lured into traps, where they can be encaged for hours before being shot (Odden et al 2013a, 2013b), and the Environment Agency kills wolverine families in front of each other's eyes in the den during the breeding season, causing the animals huge stress and suffering (Sollund 2020b: 359).

It is worth mentioning that predators also cause pain and death to other animals, as demonstrated in D5. It is in their nature and a necessity for them to hunt. This analysis, however, focuses on *theriocides*, the *human caused* suffering and death resulting from legal and illegal hunts.

The 'species justifiability' of legal hunts

Norwegian large predator management has been and continues to be highly debated and politicized. It is a typical issue for negotiations between political parties in power, and parties that wish to gain power often have to weigh in on the issue. This contested basis for their protection means that the large predator populations' survival is vulnerable to, and heavily influenced by, political change, although the Bern Convention implies that measures are to be taken to ensure their survival. In practice, such measures are currently essentially limited to the protection of reproductively 'valuable individuals'.

The continual changes in predator policies and political guidelines indicate that the matter of which particular predator theriocides are legal and which are not is a political construct and not based on substantial differences between the theriocides. Moreover, the illegal hunts are *mala prohibita* – illegal simply because they are defined as such at the time of the hunt, not based on a normative understanding shared by the human public that such hunts are fundamentally 'wrong' and that lawful hunts are inherently legitimate (Larsson 2020). To the contrary, the acts are essentially the same except for their definition in law – one that is controversial. Furthermore, legal hunts may, in fact, facilitate illegal hunts by providing those eager to reduce the predator populations with the necessary training and equipment to kill them (Sollund 2016, 2017b; Lie, under review).

From a species justice perspective, the legalistic definition that makes some wolf and bear theriocides legal and others not appears ambiguous and paradoxical, as these animals are culled legally in much the same way and by some of the same people as in the illegal killings: some of the killers are indeed even trusted members of officially appointed hunting teams. As Sollund (2017b: 5) writes, 'the crime of killing a wolf may be perceived as a serious crime, while at the same time being an act that is permitted and encouraged by the authorities'. Moreover, the scarcity of wolves and bears is, indeed, a result of deliberate politics mandating legal hunts that maintain their endangered statuses.

Pohja-Mykrä (2016) and von Essen and colleagues (2015) argue that licensed predator hunts reduce conflicts over large predator management and restore hunters' sense of codetermination and feelings of being respected. The Norwegian Parliament also sees the hunts as a measure to reduce the conflict over large predators' presence in Norway (Innst. 330 S, pp 3, 9). Such arguments imply that some animals are offered as 'scapegoats' (Sollund 2017b: 7) – killed because of hunters' anger and pride – ignoring the animal victims' interests. Whether one is endangered or not, or shot legally or illegally, is obviously insignificant for the individual victim.

Conclusion

As this chapter has discussed, critically endangered Norwegian wolves and bears are victims of a variety of theriocides, some of which are legal but disputed and problematic from a species justice perspective. No substantive qualitative differences can be found between the legal and illegal theriocides, other than their statutory status, which is vulnerable to the political climate. Individual animals considered as reproductively 'valuable' are, however, largely protected from legal hunts. Otherwise, the illegal theriocides are found to be similar to legal hunts with regards to actors, methods and animal harm, and both threaten the species' survival. This reflects Norwegian large predator conservation's ambiguous and paradoxical nature.

The legal hunts uphold humans' interests in keeping the wolf and bear populations low, while letting some of them live in order to fulfil the minimum requirements of the Bern Convention. Both legal and illegal wolf and bear hunts cause individual animal suffering and threaten the species' survival. Thus, legal hunts cannot be defended as being substantially more 'species just' than illegal hunts, not even from a welfarist perspective. Legal *and* illegal hunts both hold significant potential for harm in that respect.

References

Adams, C. J. and Gruen, L. (2014) 'Introduction', in C. J. Adams and L. Gruen (eds) *Ecofeminism: Feminist Intersections with Other Animals and the Earth*, New York: Bloomsbury, pp 1–7.

Artsdatabanken (2021) *Norsk rødliste for arter 2021 [Norwegian redlist for species 2021]*. Available: https://artsdatabanken.no/lister/rodlisteforarter/2021 (accessed 1 September 2022).

Beirne, P. (2014) 'Theriocide: naming animal killing', *International Journal for Crime, Justice and Social Democracy*, 3(2): 49–66.

Bern Convention (1979) *Convention on the Conservation of European Wildlife and Natural Habitats*, ETS No. 104, Council of Europe. Available: www.coe.int/en/web/bern-convention (accessed 29 December 2020).

Brisman, A. and South, N. (2019) 'Green criminology and environmental crimes and harms', *Sociology Compass*, 13(1): 1–12.

Bugge, S. and Myrvang, S. E. (2020) '180 jegere deltok: Skjøt fire ulver på få timer [180 hunters participated: Shot four wolves in a few hours]', *VG*, [online] 2 January. Available: www.vg.no/i/jd1ndq (accessed 29 December 2020).

Donovan, J. (1996) 'Attention to suffering: a feminist caring ethic for the treatment of animals', *Journal of Social Philosophy*, 27(1): 81–102.

Epstein, Y. (2013) 'Population-based species management across legal boundaries: The Bern Convention, Habitats Directive, and the gray wolf in Scandinavia', *Georgetown International Environmental Law Review*, 25(4): 549–88.

Epstein, Y. (2016) 'Favourable conservation status for species: examining the Habitats Directive's key concept through a case study of the Swedish wolf', *Journal of Environmental Law*, 28(2): 221–44.

Innst. 330 S (2015–16) *Innstilling fra energi- og miljøkomiteen om Ulv i norsk natur. Bestandsmål for ulv og ulvesone [Recommendation from The Standing Committee on Energy and the Environment about wolves in Norwegian nature. Population goals for wolves and wolf zone]*. Available: www.stortinget.no/no/Saker-og-publikasjoner/Publikasjoner/Innstillinger/Stortinget/2015-2016/inns-201516-330/?lvl=0 (accessed 15 March 2021).

Laikre, L., Olsson, F., Jansson, E., Hössjer, O. and Ryman, N. (2016) 'Metapopulation effective size and conservation genetic goals for the Fennoscandian wolf (*Canis lupus*) population', *Heredity*, 117(4): 279–89.

Larsson, P. (2019) 'On the Hunt: Aspects of the Use of Communication Control in Norway', in N. Fyfe, H. O. Gundhus and K. V. Rønn (eds) *Moral Issues in Intelligence-led Policing*. London: Routledge, pp 104–20.

Larsson, P. (2020) 'Etterforskning av illegal ulvejakt [Investigation of illegal wolf hunts]', *Nordisk Tidsskrift for Kriminalvidenskab*, 107(2): 122–40.

Liberg, O., Chapron, G., Wabakken P., Pedersen, H. C., Thompson Hobbs, N. and Sand, H. (2012) 'Shoot, shovel and shut up: cryptic poaching slows restoration of a large carnivore in Europe', *Proceedings of the Royal Society B: Biological Sciences*, 279(1730): 910–15.

Lie, M. S. B. (2021) '"Humane theriocides": traces of compassion for animals in the Norwegian legal discourse on illegal bear and wolf killings', *Revista Catalana de Dret Ambiental*, 12(1): 1–28.

Lie, M. S. B. (under review) 'Illegal bear and wolf killings as situational action fuelled by legal hunts'.

Lovvedtak 121 (2019–20) *Vedtak til lov om endringer i naturmangfoldloven (nødverge til forsvar for bufe mv)* [Resolution to the Amendment Act to the Nature Diversity Act]. Available: www.stortinget.no/no/Saker-og-publikasjoner/Vedtak/Beslutninger/Lovvedtak/2019-2020/vedtak-201920-121/?all=true (accessed 20 April 2023).

Ministry of Climate and Environment (2014) 'Faggrunnlag for bestandsmål for ulv og ulvesonen [Scientific basis for the population goals for wolves and the wolf zone]'. Available: www.regjeringen.no/no/aktuelt/Faggrunnlag-for-bestandsmal-for-ulv-og-ulvesonen/id2351064/ (accessed 20 April 2023).

Nature Diversity Act (2009) Lov om forvaltning av naturens mangfold, LOV-2009-06-19-100.

Norwegian Environment Agency (2019) *Veileder for gjennomføring av fellingsoppdrag [Guide for executing culling assignments]*. M—1440. Available: www.miljodirektoratet.no/globalassets/publikasjoner/m1440/m1440.pdf (accessed 29 December 2020).

Odden, J., Andersen, R., May, R., Bruset, B., Mattison, J., Solberg, H. O., et al (2013a) *Jakt på jerv i Norge [Hunting of wolverines in Norway]*, Trondheim: Norwegian Association of Hunters and Anglers, and Norwegian Institute for Nature Research.

Odden, J., Linnell, J., Solberg, H. O., Lurås, E., Lundby, R. and Parmann, S. (2013b) *Jakt på gaupe i Norge [Hunting of lynx in Norway]*, Trondheim: Norwegian Association of Hunters and Anglers, and Norwegian Institute for Nature Research.

Odden, J., Flagstad, Ø., Lundby, R., Lurås, E. and Parmann, S. (2017) *Jakt på ulv i Norge [Hunting of wolves in Norway]*, Trondheim: Norwegian Association of Hunters and Anglers, and Norwegian Institute for Nature Research.

Økokrim (2009) 'Nye lover og forskrifter 2009: Ny naturmangfoldlov [New laws and regulations 2009: New Nature Diversity Act]', *Miljøkrim*, 12(2): 38–9.

Pohja-Mykrä, M. (2016) 'Felony or act of justice? Illegal killing of large carnivores as defiance of authorities', *Journal of Rural Studies*, 44: 46–54.

Pohja-Mykrä, M. (2017) 'Community power over conservation regimes: techniques for neutralizing the illegal killing of large carnivores in Finland', *Crime, Law and Social Change*, 4(67): 439–60.

Räikkönen, J., Vucetich, J. A., Vucetich, L. M., Peterson, R. O. and Nelson, M. P. (2013) 'What the inbred Scandinavian wolf population tells us about the nature of conservation', *PLoS One*, 8(6): e67218.

Regan, T. (1983) *The Case for Animal Rights*, Berkeley: University of California Press.

Rovdata (n.d.) *Om overvåkingsprogrammet [About the monitoring program]*. Available: https://rovdata.no/Nasjonaltoverv%C3%A5kingsprogram/Omoverv%C3%A5kingsprogrammet.aspx (accessed 6 August 2021).

Rundtom, T. O. and Steinset, T. A. (2016) 'Hvem er jeger? [Who is a hunter?]', *Samfunnsspeilet*, 3: 3–8.

Singer, P. (1991) *Animal Liberation* (2nd edn), London: Thorsons.

Skogen, K. and Krange, O. (2020) 'The political dimensions of illegal wolf hunting: anti-elitism, lack of trust in institutions and acceptance of illegal wolf killing among Norwegian hunters', *Sociologica Ruralis*, 60(3): 551–73.

Skogen, K., Krange, O. and Figari, H. (2013) *Ulvekonflikter: En sosiologisk studie [Wolf conflicts: A sociological survey]*, Oslo: Akademika.

Skogen, K., von Essen, E., Krange, O. (2022) 'Hunters who will not report illegal wolf killing: self-policing or resistance with political overtones?', *Ambio*, 51: 743–53.

Sollund, R. (2016) 'With or Without a License to Kill: Human-Predator Conflicts and Theriocide in Norway', in A. Brisman, N. South and R. White (eds) *Environmental Crime and Social Conflict: Contemporary and Emerging Issues*, Farnham: Ashgate, pp 95–124.

Sollund, R. (2017a) 'The Animal Other: Legal and Illegal Theriocide', in M. Hall, J. Maher, A. Nurse, G. Potter, N. South and T. Wyatt (eds) *Greening Criminology in the 21st Century: Contemporary Debates and Future Directions in the Study of Environmental Harm*, London: Routledge, pp 79–99.

Sollund, R. (2017b) 'Perceptions and law enforcement of illegal and legal wolf killing in Norway: organized crime or folk crime?', *Palgrave Communications*, 3(1): 1–9.

Sollund, R. (2020a) 'Wildlife crime: a crime of hegemonic masculinity?', *Social Sciences*, 9(6): 93.

Sollund, R. (2020b) 'Wildlife management, species injustice and ecocide in the Anthropocene', *Critical Criminology*, 28(3): 351–69.

Sollund, R. and Goyes, D. R. (2021) 'State-organized crime and the killing of wolves in Norway', *Trends in Organized Crime*, 24: 467–84.

Stokke, S., Arnemo, J. M., Söderberg, A. and Kraabøl, M. (2012) *Skadeskyting av rovvilt. Begrepsforståelse, kunnskapsstatus og kvantifisering [Shoot and wounding of predators. Conceptual understanding, knowledge status and quantification]*. NINA-rapport 838. Norwegian Institute for Nature Research (Norsk institutt for naturforskning). Available: https://brage.nina.no/nina-xmlui/handle/11250/2643010 (accessed 29 December 2020).

Swenson, J., Stokke, S., Solberg, H. O., Lundby, R. and Parmann, S. (2013) *Jakt på bjørn i Norge [Hunting of bears in Norway]*, Trondheim: Norwegian Association of Hunters and Anglers, and Norwegian Institute for Nature Research.

The Predator Regulation (2005) Forskrift om forvaltning av rovvilt, *FOR-2005-03-18-242*.

Tønnesen, M. (2013) 'Hvem er villest i landet her? Et ulveliv [Who is the wildest in this country? A wolf life]', in R. A. Sollund, G. Larsen and M. Tønnesen (eds) *Hvem er villest i landet her? Råskap mot dyr og natur i antropocen, menneskets tidsalder*, Oslo: Scandinavian Academic Press, pp 79–99.

Trouwborst, A., Fleurke, F. M. and Linnell, J. D. C. (2017) 'Norway's wolf policy and the Bern Convention on European Wildlife: avoiding the "manifestly absurd"', *Journal of International Wildlife Law & Policy*, 20(2): 155–67.

Vollan, M., Slåen, G. O. and Løberg, A. K. (2021) 'Flytta kjendisulven for andre gang [Moved the celebrity wolf for the second time]', *NRK*, 3 January. Available: www.nrk.no/innlandet/her-flyttes-den-genetisk-vikt ige-ulven-fra-beiteomradet-1.15310784 (accessed 6 January 2021).

von Essen, E., Allen, M. (2020) '"Not the wolf itself": distinguishing hunters' criticisms of wolves from procedures for making wolf management decisions', *Ethics, Policy & Environment*, 23(1): 97–113.

von Essen, E., Hansen, H., Källström, H., Peterson, M. N. and Peterson, T. (2015) 'The radicalisation of rural resistance: how hunting counterpublics in the Nordic countries contribute to illegal hunting', *Journal of Rural Studies*, 39: 199–209.

White, R. (2012) 'The Foundations of Eco-global Criminology', in R. Ellefsen, R. Sollund and G. Larsen (eds) *Eco-Global Crimes: Contemporary Problems and Future Challenges*, London: Routledge, pp 15–33.

3

The Implementation of CITES in Norway: A Longitudinal Approach to the Assessment of Enforcement from a Species Justice Perspective

Ragnhild A. Sollund

Introduction

In 2010, I began research on wildlife[1] trafficking (WLT) and its law enforcement. The focus herein is on the trafficking in live animals and products of their bodies – species that are listed in the appendices of CITES, and how this convention has been implemented and enforced in Norway.[2] In 2020, I did follow-up research with new data collection under the umbrella

---

[1] 'Wildlife' is an anthropocentric term, which includes both plants and animals, and through which freeborn animals are perceived and valued as a 'mass' rather than as individuals with individual traits and needs. It is merely one example of anthropocentric language that serves to create an artificial dichotomy between the human animal and non-human animals, through which, for example a crab and an elephant are categorized as 'animals' despite their striking biological differences, and the similar features that exist between humans and elephants in that they are both mammals. Such language serves to perpetuate speciesism and animal abuse. With this reservation and for simplicity I still use the terms 'wildlife' and 'animal' herein, the first referring to freeborn non-human animals and those who have been locally bred for so few generations that they can still be regarded as 'wild' and undomesticated.

[2] I am grateful to Nigel South for comments to previous versions of this chapter.

of the CRIMEANTHROP[3] [Criminal Justice, Wildlife Conservation and Animal Rights in the Anthropocene] project. In this chapter I concentrate on the illegal trade, although I acknowledge that the *legal* trade may be equally harmful to the animal victims who are abducted (Sollund 2011) or killed in their habitats and deprived of the life to which they were entitled (Sollund 2019).

CITES *regulates* wildlife trade and there are currently 183 parties – nation states, as well as the EU as one partner – to the convention. It is urgent to underline that the mandate of CITES is not to put an end to wildlife trade. It is a trade convention that regulates which species are allowed in trade, and which are not. CITES does not protect animals from trade *before* their species is threatened with extinction. CITES also has little concern for the welfare of *individual* animals who are victims of trade (Múla Arribas 2015; Goyes and Sollund 2016; Sollund 2019; Wyatt et al 2022), and partial protection is awarded only to species that are listed on the CITES appendices. Currently 6,610 species of animals and 34,310 species of plants have some protection in CITES. Because most species are not subject to any trade regulation, species may become extinct without ever being listed or even discovered (for example, Frank and Wilcove 2019). In regards to its ability to protect species from extinction, this is a weakness. But CITES is also criticized for other reasons, for example in regards to its capacity to create a reliable overview of the trade in species it is supposed to protect, and in terms of animal welfare (Reeve 2014; Goyes and Sollund 2016; Sollund 2019; Wyatt 2021).

CITES is an anthropocentric trade convention objectifying animals (Goyes and Sollund 2016; Sollund 2019), which is out of touch with what is known about the cognitive abilities and social needs of animals (Pepperberg 2009). It is a general problem concerning the implementation of CITES that many parties simply fail to fulfil their obligations, such as submitting the required annual and biannual trade reports to the secretariat (Wyatt 2021), leaving the trade largely in the shadows. CITES can thereby create an illusion that wildlife trade is subject to controls and enforcement efforts that are actually lacking. Since the goal of CITES is not to protect wildlife from harm, perhaps it is too much to ask of this convention to ensure that animals who are subject to trade should not suffer harm due to the trade. However, in recent years there has been more focus on the harm animals are subjected to through trade, also within the convention, exemplified for example through changes made in this regard in the Norwegian CITES regulation,

---

[3] Funded by the Norwegian research Council as project No. 289285. The project studies the implementation and enforcement of CITES and the Bern Convention in Norway, the UK, Spain and Germany and runs for four years.

that mirrors the decisions made at the COP (Conferences of the Parties) and meetings of CITES.[4]

Species are grouped in the appendices according to how threatened they are. Appendix I includes species threatened with extinction. Trade in these species is permitted only in 'exceptional' circumstances, such as for science experiments. There are, nonetheless, also exemptions for animals who are part of a travelling collection or exhibition, such as a circus,[5] which clearly underline the anthropocentrism of the convention. This allows the trafficking of endangered wildlife for them to be exploited in circuses and zoos.

Appendix II includes species not yet threatened with extinction, but in which trade is controlled to avoid exploitation incompatible with species survival. Appendix III species are protected in at least one country, which has asked other CITES parties for assistance in controlling the trade. Parties to the convention must implement the convention through national legislation and through the establishment of a management authority. In Norway, currently, CITES is implemented through the Nature Diversity Act (2009) under the management authority of the Norwegian Environment Agency (henceforth NEA). The level of protection accorded to a species impacts not only on the level of punishment for the offender (Sollund 2019), but also on the fate of the victim, which are issues to which I return later.

In this chapter I focus particularly on changes that took place in the enforcement of CITES in Norway through the period of my research. The first set of changes concerns the reptile trade. Up to 15 August 2017, all keeping and trade in exotic reptiles were banned in Norway, with only a very few exceptions.[6] The ban was lifted and a list of 19 permitted species was introduced. This leads to questions about whether such change is a positive development, and how it has impacted on the enforcement of CITES in Norway, as well as on animal welfare? The second changes relate to the ways in which CITES regulations have been revised several times during the last decade. One change of potential importance concerns the killing of confiscated animals (see Sollund 2019). My aim is to assess empirically parts of the development concerning the enforcement of CITES in Norway over a decade, with a special focus on the above issues.

---

[4] See, for example: 'CITES Secretary-General's welcoming remarks at the 28th Meeting of the CITES Animals Committee – Tel Aviv', https://cites.org/eng/node/18383
[5] 'How CITES works', https://cites.org/eng/disc/how.php. See also Resolutions, https://cites.org/eng/res/index.php
[6] For example, people who were allergic to dogs and cats could apply for permission to keep a tortoise.

Methodology

The research methodology, approved by the Norwegian Centre for Research Data,[7] is primarily qualitative but broad-based in also drawing upon police and customs statistics concerning CITES-related crimes, where these existed. The lack of statistical data on CITES crimes, which is due to a lack of registration code for CITES in the police system,[8] led me to request permission to accumulate all police case files that could potentially concern wildlife trafficking from all Norwegian police districts. The police case files and verdicts have been subject to a content analysis (see, for example, Sollund 2019). In addition, I acquired access to seizure reports[9] from customs, both during the first part of the research (2010–13) and covering 2017–20. I have interviewed customs inspectors, police officers, district veterinarians and advisers at the Norwegian Environment Agency, both between 2010 and 2013, and in 2020; 34 in total. I also interviewed five persons who kept reptiles illegally, some of whom had trafficked reptiles to Norway from abroad during the ban. I have coded the interview data thematically and subjected them to analysis. Since one important change concerns the lifting of the reptile ban, I describe features of the international reptile trade below.

The transnational reptile trade

Reptiles are heavily traded for the 'pet'[10] industry, although many reptiles are unfit for this purpose; for example, many, such as anoles and chameleons, should not be handled (Hedley et al 2019; see also Sollund 2019). The trade in live reptiles persists on a global scale. Europe, particularly the European Union, is an important destination for many (van Uhm 2016; Altherr and Lameter 2020; see also Dominguez et al this volume; Stefes, this volume). Endemic species from Cuba, Mexico and Australia that are not CITES listed, or which may be endangered, are trafficked from these countries and sold on websites such as terraristik.com (Altherr et al 2019). Between 2004 and 2014, 20,788,747 live reptiles were imported to EU member countries. These imports include animals who are CITES listed and species that are not but which nonetheless should have protection in their source countries.

---

[7] https://search.nsd.no/en/series/ed271b1c-2595-47e4-8c97-3fcc00f02368
[8] Statistics Norway and the police publish crime statistics based on data from the police's penal case file system STRASAK, and the codes of different sorts of crime. When there are no codes for CITES crimes, these 'disappear'.
[9] For an overview of seizure reports see Sollund (2019) and Sollund (forthcoming).
[10] The word 'pet' is another anthropocentric term indicating that animals exist to be kept instrumentally for humans' social needs or even for other reasons such as to add status and pastime to the owner.

Regardless of this, they are sold openly in the EU (Auliya et al 2016; Altherr and Lameter 2020).

An article by Marshall et al (2020) likewise documents that much of the online trade in reptiles is unsustainable and endangers many species' survival. According to the study, 35 per cent of the reptile species are traded online. Three-quarters of this trade is in species that are not covered by CITES. These include numerous endangered or range-restricted species, especially from hotspots within Asia. Approximately 90 per cent of traded reptile species and half of traded individuals are abducted from the wild. Exploitation can even occur immediately after a species has just been discovered and scientifically described, leaving new endemic species especially vulnerable to traders seeking to profit from scarcity and novelty (Marshall et al 2020: 1).

The abusive exploitation of reptiles takes place not only at species level. One must not underestimate all the individual animal abuse entailed by this part of the global wildlife trade. After birds, reptiles are the most heavily trafficked taxa. According to Auliya et al (2016) there have been 10,247 reptile species registered around in the world, of which only 8 per cent of the trade is regulated through CITES and European rules. As noted also by Marshall et al (2020),[11] this means many species are threatened because there is no monitoring of the number of animals subjected to trade or of their overall populations. A minimum of 36 per cent of reptile species were traded, many coming from wild populations. A minimum of 79 per cent of traded reptile species are not subject to CITES trade regulation, including newly discovered species (Marshall et al 2020: 6). Auliya et al (2016) base their article on case studies from a whole range of countries, including Australia, New Zealand, Indonesia, Japan and countries in Central America, Europe and the EU, and West Africa.

At least 13,000 species (including more than 10,000 vertebrate species, and more fish than other species) are traded and kept as 'pets' (Warwick et al 2018). The diversity of species who are traded as 'pets' is on the rise (Scheffers et al 2019). For most traded species, especially reptiles, there is a lack of knowledge about their biology and hence their needs, preventing a reliable basis for husbandry guidance (Warwick et al 2018).

The greatest importer of live reptiles to the EU in 2004–14 was Germany with roughly 6 million animals, next comes the UK with almost 3 million; the Czech republic with almost 2 million and Italy with almost 1.8 million reptiles (Auliya et al 2016). Many of these animals have been abducted and deprived of a life in natural environments, thereafter they are trafficked in

---

[11] Marshall et al examined how species present on the most species-rich website (834 species) discovered in our 2019 snapshot changed between 2004 and 2018 (excluding 2002, 2003 and 2019 because few archived pages were available) (Marshall et al 2020: 3).

containers and suitcases across the world. If they survive the journey, they end up in a glass box to entertain collectors and other aficionados. Rare reptiles may be sold for several thousand euros in the EU (Altherr et al 2019). Although Europe is a large market, the US is even more significant, taking 56.1 per cent of the total market for import of live reptiles against the EU's 18.2 per cent (Auliya et al 2016).

The most exporting reptile countries are in Mesoamerica, closely followed by sub-Saharan Africa. South America was the third largest exporting region, followed by South and South East Asia, and West and Central Asia (Robinson et al 2015). The trade does not come without costs. An assessment of 10,000 reptile species by the International Union for Conservation of Nature (IUCN) published in 2022 showed that 21 per cent of all reptile species are at risk of extinction.[12]

Changes in the implementation of CITES and wildlife trade regulation in Norway

The lifting of the reptile ban in Norway meant that reptiles moved from being clandestinely sold to being subject to openly commercialized sale on the internet, particularly on the website *Finn.no*. For example, on 26 April 2023, there were 851 hits on reptiles on the website. Although many of the advertisements were for equipment, they also included snakes, such as python regius, and lizards, such as geckos and bearded dragons. The same day there were 326 hits for parrots. The birds on sale included Amazon parrots and African grey parrots, the latter is listed as endangered on Appendix I of CITES, after being severely exploited in trade from various Central African countries. While they have been trafficked in millions to Europe and the US for the 'pet' trade, locally they are also used for medicinal and supernatural purposes, such as using heads as luck charms and as protection from witchcraft (Assou et al 2021).

In contrast to the reptile trade, the parrot trade was never forbidden in Norway. However, in a regulation of the Animal Welfare Act of 1977, just after Norway joined CITES, the trade in exotic species was regulated and implied that CITES-listed exotic birds must be accompanied by a CITES export and import permit, the latter extended by the NEA contingent on the export permit.

A potentially important change in the Norwegian CITES regulation is that which was made in April 2021, concerning species listed in CITES Appendix I. This says, under §29, that before a confiscated 'live specimen'

---

[12] 'World's reptiles comprehensively assessed', www.iucn.org

listed on Appendix I is euthanized,[13] the NEA shall consider the possibility for rehoming the 'specimen', or return the animal to the state of export. Previously, they were killed more or less as routine (Sollund 2019).

Another change concerns exceptions to the rules about an import permit to Norway, if the individual animal listed on Appendix II (B) has previously been imported to the European Union or an EEA[14] state, and where the individual is accompanied by an export permit. In cases concerning parrots who may be long lived, they may have been in the country before a requirement of tagging in the revised CITES regulation came into force. Owners of such individuals must produce an owner certificate by applying to the NEA. The deadline was set to 1 July 2021. For the NEA to grant this certificate, the individual must have been in the possession of the owner before 1 July 2018.

Lack of transparency of CITES enforcement in Norway

There are both advantages and disadvantages related to the changes in the implementation of CITES in Norway. Before discussing these, it is essential to provide some background about previous practice in the enforcement of CITES. I have documented elsewhere that in the past CITES had a low priority among Norwegian enforcement agencies (Sollund 2013). This persists today and is particularly salient with regard to the lack of transparency and public statistics concerning CITES crimes and penal reactions. At my request, customs officials have subsequently entered different cases manually and managed to establish what reaction was directed at various offenders (Sollund 2019; Sollund forthcoming), but there are still no public statistics that can tell us about the prevalence of such cases and how they are punished generally. In order to produce such statistics, the police would need a specific code for CITES crimes, preferably several; for example, for live animals, for animal products, live plants and plant products. From coding, it could be possible to make statistics like other statistics produced by Statistics Norway[15] concerning crimes, offenders and penalties in Norway.

Since neither the police nor customs have statistics of CITES crimes and ensuing penalties, I contacted the NEA, the CITES management authority in Norway. I wrote to them in October 2021, requesting statistics of CITES

---

[13] The word to euthanize implies that the killing of an animal is 'humane', it is a euphemism for the brutality of this act of taking a life. I find it more accurate to describe this act as killing, since the killing is not done out of mercy for the animals, in the way that one may take the life of an old dog, but as an enforcement measure.

[14] Signatories to the European Economic Area agreement.

[15] 'Norway crime rate & statistics 1990–2022', www.macrotrends.net

crimes (animals) and penal reactions, and was told that they would have to 'dig them out' and this could take some time. After several repeated requests over nearly two years, I received Excel overviews of CITES seizures between 2010 and 2020, however an overview of penal reactions does not exist. This lack of transparency is a serious weakness of the implementation of CITES. Further, an important requirement for people to abstain from crimes is that they are aware that the act they are about to commit is actually a crime. The potential of creating public awareness about these crimes is lost when the type and extent of these crimes are not made publicly known, something to which a statistical overview could contribute. Although general information relating to CITES and CITES regulations can be found both on the websites of NEA and the Food Safety Authority (FSA), it is questionable whether potential offenders ever really acquaint themselves with such rules before they commit a CITES crime, although that would depend on the degree of their deliberations prior to committing the offence.

Much wildlife trafficking is not premeditated; people buy and traffic wildlife and wildlife products as tourists, on a whim, and on the internet (Lavorgna 2014; Sollund 2019; Wyatt et al 2022). It is therefore crucial that barriers against committing crimes are produced, such as awareness of the risk of potential punishment, of the severity and certainty about punishment if caught, of the risk of being caught, and not the least of the harms that are unavoidable in these crimes for the animal victims. Information about CITES, therefore, needs to extend beyond the specific websites of these enforcement agencies. This can be achieved through media campaigns and publicly available data about the punishment for these crimes to produce deterrence (Sollund 2019).

The lifting of the reptile ban: consequences for law enforcement and animal welfare

As noted, the lifting of the ban did not imply that trade in all exotic reptiles was legalized in Norway, rather a positive list was introduced. Of the 19 allowed species, 15 are listed either as vulnerable on the IUCN or on Appendix II of CITES, which means they require a CITES export and import permit. It is a condition by the FSA that they shall not be caught in the wild and I will return to this issue and the difficulties this may provide in terms of enforcement. First, I wish to address problems related to introducing positive lists. The positive lists of reptiles that may be subject to trade and possession, introduced by various governments, may have other criteria than the degree of threat to the species, although all countries that are parties to CITES must also pay attention to CITES rules. For example, the docility of a species, whether individuals pertaining to the different species may be handled, or whether they are 'stationary' (not in need of a lot of space to run). A study of the criteria of such lists internationally, nationally, and regionally in Europe, the United States and Canada found that they were inconsistent or non-specific (Toland et al 2020).

The change of the CITES regulation implying that CITES Appendix I species can no longer be killed as a matter of policy practice, means that the Norwegian CITES authorities will now at least aim to save the lives of Appendix I[16] (A) species. It is too early to assess the wider implications of this change. However, it may only have an impact on the chances for survival of CITES Appendix I species seized by Norwegian authorities. Appendix II and III species will still likely be killed, as will non-listed species. This exemplifies a (hierarchical) speciesism in which only the rarest species are accorded protection and disregards the individual, intrinsic value of each animal and her/his interest in life. Nevertheless, had this change been implemented earlier, potentially many parrots who have been killed as a consequence of being seized (Sollund 2019), could have been saved. For example in 2019, three African grey parrot babies were killed at Oslo airport (Sollund 2021), but could have lived had the regulation been changed earlier, as they are CITES Appendix I species.

Animal welfare issues were among the concerns for the Norwegian FSA when they wanted to lift the reptile ban, and in their recommendations for which species should be on the positive list. One important issue was the welfare of the approximately 100,000 reptiles that were estimated to be kept illegally in the country (Sunde 2010). In the years prior to 2017 when the ban was lifted, stakeholder organizations such as *Reptilforum*, as well as the FSA, argued that it would improve animal welfare if the species on the positive list were legalized. While reptile aficionados argued that it had not been difficult to find veterinary care for their reptiles even during the ban (Sollund 2019), the FSA meant that veterinarians would reject such patients, and that owners would not bring them to veterinary care because they were illegal and their owners would fear being reported. Another issue was veterinarians' lack of qualifications in treating reptiles. Certainly, there must have been cases where veterinarians lacked needed skills and where reptile owners would hesitate before bringing their reptiles to the vet because of the ban. The extent to which these issues really were a problem was, nonetheless, not empirically assessed.

An issue that has been documented, is that many people who were evidently incapable of caring for reptiles kept such species during the ban (Sollund 2019; Sollund forthcoming). Extensive case file material that included 366 cases involving the trafficking and keeping of illegal reptiles – a crime that was most often one of many crimes of which the offenders were

---

[16] [of the Norwegian regulation], list A (equivalent to CITES Appendix I species).

guilty – showed that these offenders often were poor carers. For example, reptiles were often 'second hand'; they lived in unsatisfactory conditions, for example, in bare glass boxes (or terrariums without any form of enriched environment), in closets or even under a glass cover in a table. Their owners were in most of the cases involved in drug crimes, violence and more, testifying to their inability to care for themselves as well as for other animals in their possession. The large majority of these animals were likely kept for extrinsic reasons; for example, posing with a large snake could add to social status among their peers (Sollund 2019; see Maher and Pierpoint 2011, for the case of status dogs).

To assess the welfare of a reptile requires both interest, care and skills. As pointed to by Warwick et al (2018), assessing reptile welfare may be difficult for unskilled owners. They report that it is a growing concern that unwanted exotic pets are handed over to animal care centres because they have needs the owners cannot fulfil, and they suffer from abuse. A main cause of abuse in the reptile trade, as well as in the bird trade, is the caging that follows from the captivity. An inescapable factor that dramatically and negatively impacts on the biological suitability of reptiles to captivity is that, unlike dogs and cats, reptiles will almost universally be 'life-restricted' in small, arbitrarily and poorly conceived vivariums maintained by non-professionals (Warwick et al 2013). Warwick and colleagues' assessment of the animal welfare of captive reptiles, even those who are bred in captivity, is thus that they are unfit as 'pets' and suffer as a consequence of being put in this position.

With the introduction of the positive list, the Norwegian authorities created conditions for the victimization of reptiles as a result of exposing them to unskilled owners, of the kind that exotic birds have been victims of for decades. Engebretson (2006: 263) states, for example, that 'in general, their [parrots'] presence in the pet trade has resulted in serious animal welfare and conservation challenges for parrots, indicating that these animals may be unsuitable as human companions'. To expand the wildlife species that are permitted in trade is a deterioration rather than an improvement.

Even under the current positive list regime in Norway, where reptiles should supposedly have access to veterinary care, other issues remain. For example, failing skills among reptile keepers may prevent them from seeking veterinary care, since they may be unaware of their reptiles' suffering. An example of neglect appeared in a post on the *reptilforum* Facebook page. A person shared an advertisement she had found on the website *Finn.no*, advertising for sale a pearl lizard (*Timon lepidus*). The woman complained about the evident animal abuse, writing: 'The lizard looks thin, there are both live and dead crickets around and the terrarium is small.'[17] While this

---

[17] www.finn.no/bap/forsale/search.html?category=0.77&q=reptil

woman observed the abuse, it did not appear as if she had reported the owner of the lizards for animal abuse, which is easy through the FSA's reporting system.[18] Even though the FSA states[19] that reptile owners must ensure they are aware of the reptiles' needs, there are no requirements to document such knowledge, as there are no requirements for bird owners, or for owners of other typical 'pets' such as rabbits, dogs and cats.

The risks of wildlife laundering

Although it is forbidden to import reptiles for commercial reasons, there is no limit to the number of reptiles one person may import, as long as they are imported from the EU/EEA.[20] While there is a requirement for a certificate[21] from the breeder or 'pet' shop where the reptile was sold, this document can easily be forged, since it is based upon trust. For example, a person selling reptiles on the internet or at the Hamm reptile fair in Germany may state the reptiles are locally bred, while in fact they have been trafficked from nature. As long as the animal is trafficked from Germany, the document is produced and the animal is on the positive list, the import will be legal if the buyer obeys the other rules, such as how to transport the animal, and registers the import with customs and the FSA at the airport.

According to interviews with customs and the FSA, it is very hard to assess whether a reptile that is on the positive list, but which lives naturally in faraway countries, is bred within the EU or is wild caught. If, for example, an import of reptiles from China has been accepted in an EU/EEA country, then the rest of the journey would be allowed. The interviewees told of packages with Chinese stamps containing animals, such as fish used in aquaria, suggesting they did not originate in the Netherlands as claimed (Sollund, forthcoming).

Although it is stated on the website of the FSA that reptiles shall not be sent in packages, this does not mean it does not happen. For example, a veterinarian from the FSA and a custom's inspector at Oslo airport told me about a case of reptiles being sent from the Netherlands. On arrival in Oslo all the snakes were dead (Sollund 2021). Such shipments are clearly against the rules, but had they arrived safely, they could have been laundered into the legal market in Norway, provided they were on the positive list.

According to §11 of the Norwegian CITES regulation, if a person can document or justify that they were the owner of a CITES-listed 'specimen' before the species was listed (pre-convention), the NEA can issue an owner

---

[18] 'Varsle om dyr', www.mattilsynet.no
[19] 'Reptilene som er lovlige i Norge', www.mattilsynet.no
[20] The European Union/The European Economic Area
[21] 'Arts- og opprinnelsesdokument for eksotiske dyr', mattilsynet.no

certificate. An owner certificate can also be issued according to §8, for 'specimens' who were in Norway before 1 July 2018, but the owner must provide an owner certificate before 1 July 2023.

This may be read as an amnesty to people who knowingly or unknowingly have participated in the wildlife trade. I can use my own experiences to exemplify this. I have been the owner of parrots. Three of them naturally belonged in South America, and one in Africa (see Sollund 2017). I suspected at least two of them, possibly three, were wild caught and trafficked to Norway, due to their different (hysterical) reactions to thread and sticks, items that may have been used to capture them. They had had many owners, judged by the number of voices and sounds they made, particularly Kåre and Line, but I do not know where and how their journey began. They came to me in different ways; my home was a rescue home. Keeping parrots was legal; yet as a 'consumer' of wildlife; as an owner and recipient of parrots, provided they were really abducted from nature, I may unwillingly have been a contributor to the wildlife trade. Had they still been alive, I could perhaps have provided proof they had been in my care before 2018 by means of veterinary receipts or through witness declarations, but I had no CITES documents, since they had already been in Norway for a long time when they came to me (if they were not born in Norway).

Some kind of 'proof' can likely be produced in most cases, and in this way, people may be pardoned even if they have contributed wilfully to wildlife trafficking. For example, parrot breeders who sold parrots on the internet also went abroad to acquire parrots, who could be laundered into their business (Sollund 2019). Owners, who may be pardoned from their involvement in the wildlife trade, can have contributed to this intentionally or unintentionally.

Of course, the paperwork may make little difference for the CITES-listed live individuals who are already in the country, their legitimation is important foremost for their owners. However, a stricter regulation, which sets demands for owner documentation, may be positive to reduce future trade and reduce animal abuse, although the problem of forged certificates and laundering related to parallel legal and illegal markets remains. (See also Dominguez et al this volume in regards to laundering). The more illegal animals who are detected, the greater is, however, the risk that more animals who are victims of wildlife trade will die in the hands of the authorities.

The revised CITES regulation includes a new requirement for tagging of CITES individuals which may serve to reduce the laundering of illegal wildlife and wildlife products into the legal market. 'Specimens' that are listed on Appendix I (A), in addition to a number of species listed on Appendix II (B), must be tagged. Table 3.1 shows which species are included from Appendix II.

Table 3.1: Animal species that require tagging

Popular name	Scientific name
Wolf	Grey wolf, *Canis lupus*
All cat species	Felidae
All species of bears, including polar bears	Ursidae spp., incl. *Ursus maritimus*
All primates	Primates
Elephant	Elephantidae spp.
All diurnal birds of prey	Falconiformes
Jungle cock	*Gallus sonnerati*[24]
All species of owls	Strigiformes
All species of turtles	Testudinidae
All species of tortoises	Cheloniidae

It deserves mentioning that grey wolves, brown bears and polar bears,[22] as well as lynx, exist in Norwegian territory and are also listed on the Bern Convention's[23] appendices (see Lie, this volume).

The demand for tagging (chipping) of individuals on Appendix I (A) and those in Table 3.1, concerns both dead and live individuals. Individuals who are imported must be tagged within four weeks. Individuals listed on Appendix I (A) who are bred in captivity are subject to the same rules as individuals listed on Appendix II (B). It must be proven that the individual and their parents are born in captivity, in correspondence with CITES' decisions, according to the rules of the FSA and as documented by a veterinarian certificate. When an individual of Appendix I is born, the owner must apply to the NEA for an owner certificate. This may be an important measure to reduce the number of exotic CITES-listed 'pets' in Norway, however this again will depend on the ways in which it is actually enforced.

Conclusion

The revision of the CITES regulation in Norway with stricter demands for documentation, may potentially be an improvement for the enforcement of CITES. That the NEA with the revision of the CITES regulation

---

[22] Such tags may also be forged and Liodden (2019) documents there has been quite extensive laundering of polar bear skins through the Norwegian Arctic island Svalbard where there is no border control from Canada and Greenland.
[23] The Bern Convention on the Conservation of European Wildlife and Natural Habitats, www.coe.int
[24] The overview of confiscations from customs (2017–20) shows an increase in confiscations of Jungle cock feathers used for binding fishing flies.

increases enforcement measures such as through owner certificates, tagging and through attempts to save at least the trafficking victims of Appendix I, is a positive development. However, the risk still exists that illegal wildlife may be laundered into the legal market. This risk has increased with the lifting of the reptile ban and the introduction of a positive list. The partial legislation also entails that more animals are put at risk of abuse and neglect.

The positive list generally means that more pressure is put on reptiles in the form of trade exploitation, which directly and indirectly may impact upon the survival of reptile species in the wild; directly, because more animals are subjected to trade and illegal animals are laundered into the legal trade, indirectly because the lifting of the ban legitimates wildlife trade generally and the reptile trade specifically. This may lead to increased demand, rather than the opposite, which should be the goal. While the legal species are now traded openly on the internet, illegal species may still be traded under the radar of the enforcement agencies, entailing a combined pressure. The introduction of the positive list of legal reptile species in Norway has been a negative development, both in terms of law enforcement and animal welfare.

To improve the welfare of exotic species (as well as other species kept as 'pets'), the FSA should introduce a certification system through which potential 'pet' owners must prove they have the necessary skills to take care of the animal in a proper way, responding to this animal's species condition and individual needs. For example, in order to buy an exotic bird or a reptile, people should take a course organized by the FSA where they could learn how to care for these animals, rather than simply buying them on the internet or in a 'pet' shop.

Finally, the enforcement authorities should make far more effort to create transparency and awareness about wildlife trafficking in Norway, in order to dissuade people from participating in this evil. One first step would be to create registration codes for the different wildlife crimes. CITES products of plants and animals should have different codes, as should live CITES animals and plants and as should wildlife crimes, such as breaches of the Nature Diversity Act, when somebody kills an individual of an endangered species.

References

Altherr, S., and Lameter, K. (2020). The rush for the rare: reptiles and amphibians in the European pet trade. *Animals*, *10*(11), 2085. https://doi.org/10.3390/ani10112085

Altherr, S., Lameter, K., and Cantú Guzman, J. C. (2019). The trade in nationally protected lizards from Australia, Cuba, and Mexico and the EU's role as a main destination. *Traffic Bulletin*, *31*(2), 59.

Assou, D., Elwin, A., Norrey, J., Coulthard, E., Megson, D., Ronfot, D., et al (2021). Trade in African grey parrots for belief-based use: insights from West Africa's largest traditional medicine market. *Frontiers in Ecology and Evolution*, 29.

Auliya, M., Altherr, S., Ariano-Sanchez, D., Baard, E. H., Brown, C., Brown, R. M., and Hintzmann, J. (2016). Trade in live reptiles, its impact on wild populations, and the role of the European market. *Biological Conservation*, 204, s. 103–19.

CITES (n.d.) 'What is CITES?', https://cites.org/eng/disc/what.php (accessed 2 November 2021).

Engebretson, M. (2006). The welfare and suitability of parrots as companion animals: a review. *Animal Welfare*, 15(3), 263–76.

Frank, E. G., and Wilcove, D. S. (2019). Long delays in banning trade in threatened species. *Science*, 363(6428), 686–8.

Goyes, D., and Sollund, R. (2016). Contesting and contextualising CITES: wildlife trafficking in Colombia and Brazil. *International Journal for Crime, Justice and Social Democracy*, 5(4), 87.

Hedley, J., Johnson, R., and Yeates, J. (2019) 'Reptiles (*Reptilia*)', in J. Yeates (ed) *Companion Animal Care and Welfare: The UFAW Companion Animal Handbook*, John Wiley and Sons Ltd, pp 371–94.

Lavorgna, A. (2014). Wildlife trafficking in the Internet age. *Crime Science*, 3(1), 1–12.

Liodden, O. J. (2019). Polar Bears and Humans. Oslo: Naturfokus.

Maher, J. H., and Pierpoint, H. (2011). Friends, status symbols and weapons: the use of dogs by youth groups and youth gangs. *Crime, Law and Social Change*, 55(5), 405–20.

Marshall, B. M., Strine, C., and Hughes, A. C. (2020). Thousands of reptile species threatened by under-regulated global trade. *Nature Communications*, 11, 4738. https://doi.org/10.1038/s41467-020-18523-4

Mulà Arribas, A. (2015). *Protection of animals in the Convention on International Trade in Endangered Species of Wild Fauna and Flora (CITES)* (Master's thesis, Universidad Internacional de Andalucía).

Pepperberg, I. M. (2009). *The Alex Studies: Cognitive and Communicative Abilities of Grey Parrots*. Harvard University Press.

Reeve, R. (2014). *Policing International Trade in Endangered Species: The CITES Treaty and Compliance*. Routledge.

Robinson, J. E., Griffiths, R. A., John, F. A. S., and Roberts, D. L. (2015). Dynamics of the global trade in live reptiles: shifting trends in production and consequences for sustainability. *Biological Conservation*, 184, 42–50.

Scheffers, B. R., Oliveira, B. F., Lamb, I., and Edwards, D. P. (2019). Global wildlife trade across the tree of life. *Science*, 366, 71–6.

Sollund, R. (2011). Expressions of speciesism: the effects of keeping companion animals on animal abuse, animal trafficking and species decline. *Crime, Law and Social Change*, 55(5), 437–51.

Sollund, R. (2013). Animal trafficking and trade: abuse and species injustice. In R. Walters, D. Westerhuis, and T. Wyatt (eds) *Emerging Issues in Green Criminology* (pp 72–92). Palgrave Macmillan.

Sollund, R. (2017). Doing green, critical criminology with an auto-ethnographic, feminist approach. *Critical Criminology*, 25(2), 245–60.

Sollund, R. A. (2019). *The Crimes of Wildlife Trafficking: Issues of Justice, Legality and Morality*. Routledge.

Sollund, R. (2021). The development of enforcement of CITES in Norway: discretionary omissions and theoricides. *Revista Catalana de Dret Ambiental*, 12(1).

Sollund, R. (forthcoming). *Wildlife Trade: Parallel Harms and Crimes*. Routledge.

Sunde, S. (2010). Ett av tusen ulovlige reptiler i Norge blir beslaglagt? Miljøkrim. Ett av tusen ulovlige reptiler i Norge blir beslaglagt? *Miljøkrim. Tidsskriftet for miljøkriminalitet*, 3(13), 18–21.

Toland, E., Bando, M., Hamers, M., Cadenas, V., Laidlaw, R., Martínez-Silvestre, A., and van der Wielen, P. (2020). Turning negatives into positives for pet trading and keeping: a review of positive lists. *Animals*, 10(12), 2371.

van Uhm, D. P. (2016). *The Illegal Wildlife Trade: Inside the World of Poachers, Smugglers and Traders*. Springer.

Warwick, C., Arena, P., Lindley, S., Jessop, M., and Steedman, C. (2013). Assessing reptile welfare using behavioural criteria. *In Practice*, 35(3), 123–31.

Warwick, C., Steedman, C., Jessop, M., Arena, P., Pilny, A., and Nicholas, E. (2018). Exotic pet suitability: understanding some problems and using a labeling system to aid animal welfare, environment, and consumer protection. *Journal of Veterinary Behaviour*, 26, 17–26.

Wyatt, T. (2021). *Is CITES Protecting Wildlife? Assessing Implementation and Compliance*. Routledge.

Wyatt, T., Miralles, O., Massé, F., Lima, R., da Costa, T. V., and Giovanini, D. (2022). Wildlife trafficking via social media in Brazil. *Biological Conservation*, 265, 109420.

4

Online Illegal Trade in Reptiles in the Netherlands

*Isabella Dominguez, Marjan Hindriks,
Jordi Janssen and Daan van Uhm*

Introduction

In recent years, the illegal wildlife trade has received increasing attention. In the political debate, the focus is mainly on iconic species such as elephants, rhinoceroses, and tigers, but reptile populations are also seriously harmed by the illegal reptile trade. For example, reptiles are an easy target for criminal groups because they can often survive for a long time under poor transport conditions, reptiles are quiet, and they can easily be transported in suitcases or postal parcels (Altherr 2014). It has been determined that between 2010 and 2014, approximately 64,000 live wild vertebrates with protected status were seized; 95 per cent of these seized animals were reptiles (D'Cruze and Macdonald 2016).

Even though the illegal trade in reptiles is often associated with Asian origin countries, Europe is one of the biggest markets for illegal reptiles. This has been illustrated by research showing that the majority of all live animal seizures in the European Union (EU) over a ten-year period were reptiles (van Uhm 2016a). Sometimes the seizures concern reptile species from Europe, but many reptile species do not occur naturally within the EU. In fact, the majority of the illegal reptiles is first being imported from outside the EU and then the reptiles are freely traded within the EU borders (Gussow 2009; Sollund and Maher 2016; Mărginean et al 2018; van Uhm et al 2019; Sollund, this volume).

The Netherlands is an important player in the illegal reptile trade, both as a transit country and a destination country (van der Grijp 2016; van

Uhm 2016b; Janssen and Leupen 2019).[1] For example, the Netherlands is in the top ten of EU countries that import endangered reptile species, but a substantial part of the legal trade actually has an illegal origin (Janssen and Leupen 2019).[2] In addition to many live reptiles for the pet market, reptile products are on the market as belts, boots, bags, meat, medication, shields, skulls, skeletons, teeth and taxidermy (Auliya et al 2016; Harvey 2017). The more scarce, attractive and expensive some rare endangered reptiles become, the more interesting they are on the reptile black market (van der Grijp 2016).

The trade in wildlife, including endangered reptiles, is regulated by the Convention on International Trade in Endangered Species of Wild Fauna and Flora (CITES). CITES is an international legal framework that regulates wildlife trade through CITES permits. The 184 parties, including the EU, are obliged to comply with the provisions of the convention and more than 30,000 species are listed in CITES. CITES is implemented in the EU through a set of regulations known as the EU Wildlife Trade Regulations (European Commission 2015). These regulations also apply in the Netherlands, and the Netherlands ratified CITES in 1984 (van Uhm 2012). However, many reptile species are not listed in CITES and can therefore be traded freely (Marshall et al 2020; Janssen and Leupen 2019).

Since the growth of the internet, the activities of reptile traders have increasingly expanded online. Today, a wide variety of species are traded on digital fora and marketplaces (IFAW 2008, 2012; Interpol 2013, 2017; Hastie and McCrea-Steele 2014; Hinsley 2016). The most recent report from the International Fund for Animal Welfare (IFAW) (2018) found that the turtle and tortoise are the most popular in internet commerce. Turtles and tortoises make up 45 per cent of the total. Traditionally, there has been a large illegal trade in spur-thighed tortoises (*Testudo graeca*) in Europe, which, according to EU seizures, still comprise the largest group of live reptiles intercepted, mainly from Morocco (van Uhm 2016b). Other commonly seized reptiles are lizards, crocodiles, alligators and snakes (Hastie 2018).

The Dutch trade in reptiles via the internet is increasing, for both legal and illegal trade (Janssen and Blanken 2016). In fact, the internet is one of the most important channels for Dutch trade in reptile species today. Trading

---

[1] The Netherlands is an important player in the international illegal reptile trade due to its geographically central location in Western Europe, the national economic and logistic infrastructure, including major airport Schiphol and harbour Rotterdam, but also because of its historical trading position in Europe and strong ties with former colonies in Africa, Southeast Asia and Latin America (van Uhm 2016a).

[2] Only a small number of European reptile species are trade regulated under CITES (CITES; Robinson et al 2015) or under the EU Wildlife Trade Regulations (EU WTR; Auliya 2003). However, most reptile species are covered by protective legislation (Temple and Cox 2009).

takes place on Dutch websites of providers such as Marktplaats. In addition, social media platforms, such as Facebook, are increasingly used for illegal trade as well as shielded forums providing secret opportunities for Dutch reptile traders (CITES Intervention Strategy, 2013–17).

In this chapter we discuss how digital developments play a key role in the illegal reptile trade and how this complicates enforcement in the Netherlands. We start this chapter with our methodology, then we will discuss our empirical results, including the nature, actors, modi operandi and organization of the networks involved, and we conclude with a brief discussion about the bottlenecks for enforcement.

Methodology

This chapter is based on empirical data collected for two research projects between 2016 and 2018. In these research projects, police files were analysed, experts were interviewed, and a network analysis was conducted. Police files were collected for the period 2008 to 2018; cases of illegal reptile trade and cases with an 'internet component' were selected for this research. In addition, a total of 17 experts were interviewed, including specialists from the Netherlands Food and Consumer Product Safety Authority (NVWA), various police officials, internet investigators, criminologists and biologists, and employees of conservation organizations, including the RAVON Foundation, Herpetofauna Foundation, IUCN/SSC Tortoise and Freshwater Turtle Specialist Group, IFAW, the Wildlife Justice Commission (WJC), CITES Netherlands and the International Union for Conservation of Nature (IUCN). By using semi-structured interviews, it was possible to adjust the questions related to the different topics covered during the interview (Davies et al 2011). The interviews added to the police files and literature and provided more depth to the topic (Fylan 2005; Maesschalck 2016).

In order to get insights on how criminal networks behave and collaborate in a distinctive way via the internet, we performed a network analysis on a case of illegal trade in turtles and tortoises in South East Asia with a link to the Netherlands. Data used for this case study were provided by the Wildlife Justice Commission based on multiple investigations into criminal networks active in illegal trade of CITES Appendix I and II turtle and tortoise species. The network analysis scheme aimed to map out the partnerships between different key figures online and offline; the relationships between the key figures were weighed here. The degree of these relationships is based on the degree of criminal involvement and the certainty of this involvement (Morselli 2009). In addition, where possible, we present the role of a relevant key figure in the illegal trade in turtles and tortoises in the association scheme. The focus was on identifying central key figures that are important for the communication flow within the network, and the existence of smaller, tight-knit groups within the network. This provided information on the dynamics, structures and organizations of the illegal reptile trade networks.

Results

The illegal reptile trade

The reptile trade is characterized as trend sensitive (van Doorne 2007). For example, influenced by movies and social media, new reptile species become popular. Sometimes reptile species that are going to be included on the CITES list are popular in the illegal trade; when a potential CITES listing is announced, traders try to obtain as many animals as possible, illegally or not, before the stricter regulations come into effect (Rivalan et al 2007; Janssen and Krishnasamy 2018). Species that have recently been discovered are popular in the illegal reptile trade as well. Not incidentally, traders focus on trading them immediately after discovery.[3] A description of a new species in a publication with the exact coordinates where a population is located can provide sufficient information for this.[4] Other targeted species are those that are in high demand but are almost impossible to breed in captivity or are very expensive to breed, or those that do well in captivity but suffer from inbreeding and 'new blood' would be needed to revive these species (Altherr et al 2016). An example is the African spurred tortoise (*Centrochelys sulcata*), since breeding this tortoise to a significant size will take several years, which makes it unprofitable for traders.[5] In addition, it can be difficult to identify the difference between captive-bred reptiles and wild ones, providing opportunities for laundering illegal trade. An example of this is the illegal trade in the European pond turtle (*Emys obicularis*) (Auliya et al 2016).

The harms of the (illegal) reptile trade are diverse. First, the trade in reptiles can result in the extinction of reptile species, leading to a reduction in biodiversity (Hinsley et al 2016). About 45 per cent ($n = 4,669$) of all reptile species in the world have been assessed for the IUCN Red List: 180 reptile species are critically endangered; 361 reptile species are threatened; and 403 reptile species are vulnerable (Puritz and Weller 2018). Second, the trade disrupts habitats as a result of the capture of the animals since reptiles can play an important role in the ecosystem (Schlaepfer et al 2005). Third, the trade in reptiles has a serious impact on the welfare of the animals during capture, captive breeding, transportation, sale or use (Sollund 2019).

---

[3] Interview with NVWA Inspector, Nature team on 7 May 2018.
[4] Interview with Specialist reptiles, NVWA, on 4 May 2018.
[5] Interview with NVWA Inspector, Nature team on 29 May 2018 in The Hague.

Fourth, invasive reptile species can pose a serious threat to humans, through fungi, viruses and bacteria (Magalhães and São-Pedro 2012); a well-known example is Salmonella (Gilbert et al 2014). Fifth, the illegal reptile trade can pose a threat to native species, for example, native European tortoises are threatened because exotic red-eared sliders are released into the wild and they compete for food (Silva et al 2009; D'Cruze and Macdonald 2016). Another example is the barred grass snake (*Natrix helvetica*). This is the only grass snake that occurs naturally in the Netherlands. Research has shown that a subspecies of the eastern grass snake has been released in the Netherlands. Because these species are closely related, the chance of hybridization is high. Hybridization can be accompanied by 'genetic pollution' if genetic material from a native species is replaced by that of an exotic species. Due to the loss of local variants of genes, this is actually a form of extinction (van Riemsdijk et al 2020).

The actors

In the illegal online reptile trade in the Netherlands, a distinction can be made between three offender types: the organized trader, the professional trader and the enthusiast. First, there are well-organized Dutch criminal networks involved in the online reptile trade (Kuijer-Slobbe 2016; Wildlife Justice Commission 2016).[6] High profits in particular attract these criminal networks (Puritz and Weller 2018; Bennett 2011). Such crime groups consider the reptiles as just another form of contraband, without taking into account regulations, such as CITES. The crime groups are involved in trading on a large scale on internet platforms, which requires a certain knowledge of the reptiles to be able to trade. These criminal networks are increasingly using the internet for their illegal business practices.[7]

Second, professional online traders refer to the regular traders who partially engage in illegal activities (Gussow 2009). It is relatively easy for the legal traders to enter the illegal territory, since they have the necessary knowledge, trade routes and sales market (Kuijer-Slobbe 2016). The professional online trader often has a company, they have solid knowledge of the legislation and transport rules and have the necessary social skills to maintain international trade contacts (Vinke 2001; van Uhm 2018a, 2018b). In other words, the legitimate business structure in the Netherlands is used for illegal online reptile trade. For example, reptiles are laundered via breeding farms by tampering with the underlying number calculations and consequently offered for sale online (Janssen and Leupen 2019).

---

[6] Interview with NVWA Inspector, Nature team on 7 May 2018 and interview with Specialist reptiles, NVWA, on 4 May 2018.
[7] Interview with Specialist reptiles, NVWA, on 4 May 2018.

Third, there are private traders who are crossing the line by taking or shipping undocumented reptiles and keeping them for themselves or selling them (Gussow 2009; Sollund 2019). The enthusiast has the knowledge about where the reptiles are and how to catch them. A number of well-known Dutch reptile smugglers are known to let local residents do the trapping work for a small fee, in other cases they select the reptiles themselves and smuggle them, or let couriers smuggle the reptiles for a fee.[8] For this group, the internet offers the opportunity to enter the market without the need for high technical skills; online potential buyers and sellers can find each other via online forums, Facebook and similar social media (Lavorgna 2014; Wyatt et al 2022; Sollund, this volume).

Among the three groups, social ties established online seem to play a major role in the illegal reptile trade in the Netherlands (Kuijer-Slobbe 2016). There are many niche markets in the reptile trade; for example, one crime group is concerned with monitor lizards, another group is concerned with chameleons. They are specialist groups with their own target group and their own social network online. Therefore, the role of trust is sometimes an explanation for this connection, which plays an essential role in criminal cooperation due to a lack of legal protection (Kop et al 2012; van Uhm and Wong 2019). While the online social networks are important in the organized trade and professional trade network, the enthusiast can operate completely independently as a 'lone wolf'. On the Dutch internet forums, suppliers, wholesalers, intermediaries and traders have direct contact with each other. However, they often have a cross-border character, extending the Dutch borders, and research has shown that the same people are often behind multiple advertisements online, even if they use different names (NVWA 2013).[9]

The internet has a significant influence on the activities of the three offender types and has increased by lowering barriers and facilitating access to the online reptile underworld (Lavorgna 2014; van Uhm 2016a). The online reptile trade is carried out by a couple of well-known key offenders (Schneider 2008).[10] An internal Interpol report at the end of the 1990s already emphasized that a small group of Dutch people, some of them diversified from the drug trade into the illegal reptile trade, play a major role in the international reptile trade (Interpol 1996; van Uhm 2016b). In the first decade of the 21st century, this small group of Dutch people was still identified as important actors in the global illegal trade in reptiles and became active in the online reptile trade (Kuijer-Slobbe 2016). A number

---

[8] Interview with NVWA Inspector, Nature team on 7 May 2018.
[9] Interview with NVWA Inspector, Nature team on 7 May 2018.
[10] Interview with Specialist reptiles, NVWA, on 4 May 2018.

of the key traders of illegal reptiles have left the Netherlands and are now active in source countries, such as Indonesia.[11] However, the reptiles in which these people trade online do end up in the Netherlands (NVWA 2013).

Modi operandi

After agreements are made online, different methods are used to illegally trade reptiles depending on the different locations, seasons, quantities and destinations. Smuggling small quantities of reptiles by air is a common method, as it often involves live animals that need to be transported quickly.[12] Reptiles are, in this case, hidden in hand luggage, checked luggage or hidden under the smuggler's clothes.[13] Dutch criminal networks take advantage of the massiveness of tourism and ensure that the reptiles arrive at an airport where they know that the control methods are underdeveloped or that there is little attention to illegal wildlife trade.[14] From the EU's external borders, reptiles, such as the Egyptian tortoise (*Testudo kleinmanni*), are smuggled into the EU by trucks of transport companies.[15] Once in Europe, they are transported further to other countries, including the Netherlands, by (lorry) cars.[16]

In addition, the granting of licences to trade farmed reptiles offers opportunities for Dutch criminal groups. This is because the use of permits results in loopholes in the law. Often dubious breeding reports are produced, so that reptile species can still be traded to the Netherlands under certain permits.[17] For example, protected reptile species of wild origin that normally fall under CITES Appendix I and are prohibited from trading can be traded under source code D if they are bred in captivity (van Uhm 2016c). A Dutch inspector revealed this in a large shipment of African spurred tortoises. The African spurred tortoises had been reported as captive-bred, but the animals' physical appearance proved otherwise in the Netherlands.[18] These African spurred tortoises had a much larger carapace than would be plausible for captive-bred African spur tortoises; it would take many years to have a shell

---

[11] Some of these people have since passed away.
[12] Interviews with Wildlife Justice Commission Senior Investigation Manager on 25 May 2018 in The Hague; NVWA Inspector, Nature team on May 29, 2018 in The Hague; and biologist and co-founder Pro Wildlife on 31 July 2018 via email.
[13] Interviews with Wildlife Justice Commission Senior Research Manager on 25 May 2018 in The Hague; Zoologist and Deputy Chair of IUCN Tortoise and Freshwater Turtle Specialist Group on 25 June 2018; and specialist of Ecojust on 19 June 2018 in The Hague.
[14] Interview with NVWA Inspector, Nature team on 29 May 2018 in The Hague.
[15] Interviews with CITES wildlife crime consultant on 25 June 2018.
[16] Interview with NVWA Inspector, Nature team on 29 May 2018 in The Hague.
[17] Interview with founder of Herpetofauna foundation on 11 June 2018 in Tilburg.
[18] Interview with NVWA Inspector, Nature team on 29 May 2018 in The Hague.

of such a large size, resulting in higher prices for the tortoises than they were being sold for.[19]

Dutch criminals also benefit from the fact that some countries are not members of the CITES treaty and wild-caught reptiles can easily be sourced (Nijman and Shepherd 2011). Law enforcers regularly lack the expertise to identify reptile species, and some countries give low priority to tackling the illegal trade in reptiles (Sollund 2019).[20] A reptile expert explained that there are many suspicions that animals from the wild are being laundered as captive-bred by using a third country as a stopover. This is possible because some authorities have no idea what species they are dealing with and write down everything the trader in question says (Sollund 2022a).[21] The Netherlands also plays a role here as transit hub. For example, reptiles from Indonesia, destined for the United States, make a detour via the Netherlands, after which they are indicated as captive-bred reptiles and offered for sale online.[22]

Once the reptiles are in the Netherlands, often they are traded online, even though offline trading takes place at large reptile fairs, or in the parking lots of the relevant reptile fairs. A reptile fair that is central to this is the one in Houten in the Netherlands. However, a large number of the illegal reptiles are often already sold in advance via online forums before the fair takes place.[23] In other words, during the fair the illegal trade takes place, but the deal and payment have been made via the internet in advance (Sonricker Hansen et al 2012; Interpol 2013). This facilitates reptile parcels from all over the world to be delivered to Dutch customers without any problems and relatively cheap (Spapens 2016).

Going online

Even though reptiles are often offered in small batches online, they can be linked to large batches. In practice, if a Dutch trader indicates that he has 'a couple for sale' and ten people respond, the trader can sell a couple ten times. In this case, the trader has only one advertisement online and can therefore claim to have sold only one pair.[24] Therefore, it is difficult to determine

---

[19] Today, limits are set for reptile species in which this plays a role. This means that reptile species entering the EU with a cultured origin (origin code C) may not exceed a certain size. This is usually the size reached after a maximum of one year.
[20] Interview with founder of Herpetofauna foundation on 11 June 2018 in Tilburg and zoologist and deputy chairman of IUCN Tortoise and Freshwater Turtle Specialist Group on 25 June 2018.
[21] Zoologist and Deputy Chairman of IUCN Tortoise and Freshwater Turtle Specialist Group on 25 June 2018.
[22] Interview with a criminologist on 28 July 2018 in Amsterdam.
[23] Interviews with CITES wildlife crime consultant on 25 June 2018.
[24] Interview with Specialist reptiles, NVWA, on 4 May 2018.

what is behind one online advertisement; in several Dutch investigations, enforcers have found exceptionally large numbers of reptiles linked to such internet advertisements.

In addition, web design or maintenance developers, bitcoin exchangers, internet service providers and suppliers of legal products and postal services may play a part either willingly or unintentionally in the online illegal reptile trade in the Netherlands (Kruithof et al 2016). The internet can be seen as a bridge builder for the illegal reptile trade in the Netherlands. Internet enables contact with facilitators, for example contacts with Dutch criminals who are specialized in forging documents (Lavorgna 2014). Dutch cases show that they offer reptiles via the internet on different platforms, from public auction and sales sites such as Marktplaats, to online forums, corporate websites, classified ad sites and social media websites (Hinsley 2016).[25] However, the online marketplaces are still the main avenue for the illegal reptile trade, but the use of social media is increasing in the Netherlands (see also: Yu and Jia 2015; Hinsley 2016; Cuevas and McCrea-Steele 2017). Social media as a communication channel allows easy and private communication (Krishnasamy and Stoner 2016). Moreover, social media is flexible; by closing one channel, then reptile traders go to another, explained informants. For example, if Facebook becomes stricter, it will shift to WhatsApp, Signal or WeChat. New platforms are also being set up by the illegal reptile traders themselves. One of the advantages of using Facebook over commercial trading platforms is that it is free to use. Within Facebook there are 'Facebook groups', which provide a place for people with similar hobbies and interests to come together. Live reptiles are advertised and key figures in the reptile business post photos on Facebook for the purpose of selling them; social media not only serves as a means of communication between key figures, but also functions as an advertising platform.[26]

In particular, the speed with which reptiles can be advertised and sold using Facebook is of great importance to Dutch illegal reptile traders, as they often involve live reptiles destined for the exotic pet market. There is no longer a need for a physical store in the Netherlands, because illegally obtained animals can be traded directly on the platform.[27] Previously, it could take years before a Dutch buyer could track down a specific species, but with

---

[25] Interview with Specialist reptiles, NVWA, on 4 May 2018.
[26] Interviews with Wildlife Justice Commission Research Specialist on 11 June 2018 in The Hague; Zoologist and Deputy Chair of IUCN Tortoise and Freshwater Turtle Specialist Group on 25 June 2018; and with NVWA Inspector, Nature team on 29 May 2018 in The Hague.
[27] Interviews with a criminologist on 28 July 2018 in Amsterdam and founder of Herpetofauna foundation on 11 June 2018 in Tilburg.

the advent of the internet, buyers can now find out within a day where they can buy the animal species, even if this is sometimes on the other side of the world.[28] This has resulted in Facebook being completely flooded with advertisements of live reptiles.[29] Facebook has also had a significant impact on reptile markets. Dutch traders are trying to identify which species are most in demand by placing advertisements where people can place orders in advance. Moreover, Facebook is used to create new demand markets. According to a reptile expert, 'egging' is used. This happens when a merchant posts an ad online and advertises it as something very special. This creates a feeling of envy among the buyers, creating a new market for the reptile species that did not exist before.[30]

Reptile case: the organization behind the network

In order to better understand the organizational structure of the illegal reptile networks and the role of the internet and social media, a network analysis was performed (Figure 4.1). The network analysis revealed that the respective illegal reptile network, with a link to the Netherlands, was organized in a star structure. Key figures active in a star-structured organization play a central role in (online) communication and have a high degree of visibility within a network (Arquilla and Ronfeldt 2001; Clifton and Rastogi 2016). A high degree of visibility means that the relevant key figures are more exposed to law enforcement oversight (Morselli 2009). In addition, the presence of a star structure implies the absence of a hierarchy (Arquilla and Ronfeldt 2001). In a hierarchically structured network, key figures have a low degree of visibility and are in contact with as few others in the network as possible (Morselli 2009).

Three key figures emerged in the network analysis as intermediaries with the most direct (online) contacts with other key figures and traders in the network. This is in line with the growing evidence that key figures in a criminal network no longer only have an authoritative role, but act as intermediaries (Morselli 2009).

---

[28] Interviews with Wildlife Justice Commission Senior Research Manager on 25 May 2018 in The Hague; a criminologist on 28 July 2018 in Amsterdam; Zoologist and Deputy Chair of IUCN Tortoise and Freshwater Turtle Specialist Group on 25 June 2018.
[29] Interview with Wildlife Justice Commission Investigation Specialist on 11 June 2018 in The Hague.
[30] Interview with zoologist and deputy chairman of IUCN Tortoise and Freshwater Turtle Specialist Group on 25 June 2018.

Figure 4.1: Organization of a network

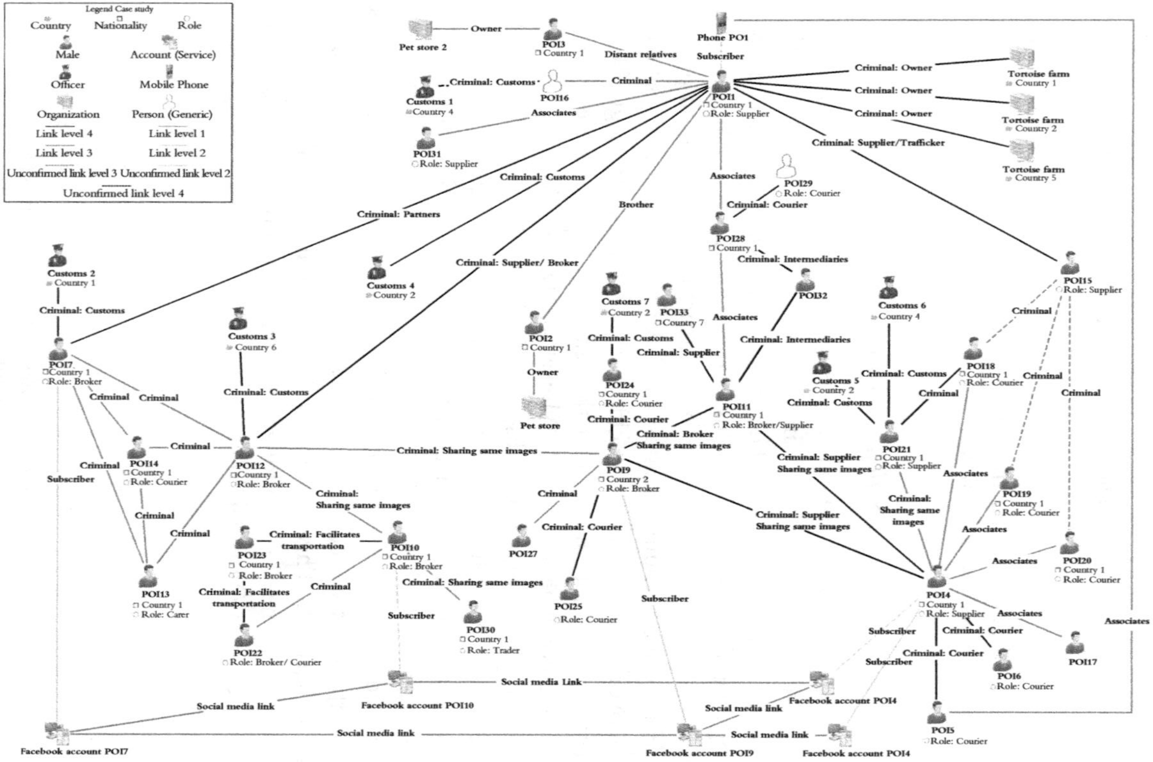

In the illegal reptile trade, the role of an intermediary to ensure rapid communication and money flows is of great importance. Money is often an important motive for organized illegal reptile traders active in the trade, but for enthusiasts economic interests play a subordinate role.[31] Therefore, the respective reptile trade network is driven by capital need efficiency in direct communication because there is a short time span between actions (Duijn et al 2014). Social media and internet perfectly facilitate this communication within the analysed network.

To facilitate fast communication flows, the illegal reptile traders take advantage of the security and speed of the internet. The network analysis shows that these communication flows were extensive, with several merchants across the world interacting through social media. In several cases, these traders advertised the same photos of turtles, tortoises and other reptile species on Facebook, suggesting a partnership between these traders.[32] The network analysis also revealed that on online platforms, such as Facebook, it is possible for illegal reptile traders to handle not only the sale but also the advertising of live reptiles. This may be an indication of a shift in the distribution of criminal activities whereby it is possible for them to take on multiple roles. In other words, the network analysis has shown that the internet facilitates international cooperation between illegal reptile traders and that by taking on multiple roles, a criminal network involved in reptiles can gain more control over the entire trade chain and thereby also gain more control over the illegal trade.

Bottlenecks for enforcement of online reptile trade

The Netherlands' role in the international reptile trade is intrinsically linked to the EU. The implementation of CITES in the EU – as one party – ensures that the EU Single Market facilitates internal trade in illegal reptile species. Even though the enforcement authorities in the Netherlands act within the respective national, European and international legislation, as soon as the reptiles have been illegally smuggled from the country of origin, they can be traded legally within the EU (van Uhm 2016a). Moreover, the EU Wildlife Trade Regulations currently do not prohibit the trade in several

---

[31] Interviews with Wildlife Justice Commission Senior Research Manager on 25 May 2018 in The Hague; founder of Herpetofauna foundation on 11 June 2018 in Tilburg; zoologist and deputy chair of IUCN Tortoise and Freshwater Turtle Specialist Group on 25 June 2018; Wildlife Justice Commission Research Specialist on 11 June 2018 in The Hague; and biologist and co-founder of Pro Wildlife on 31 July 2018 via email.

[32] This can also be a form of fraud. Similarly, photos of other traders are used to get people to transfer an advance, but they do not actually own the animals. An indication is if large numbers of rare animals are offered outside the country of origin.

reptile species that enjoy a protected status in their countries of origin, which makes the EU a major player in the illegal trade in such reptile species (Janssen and Leupen 2019).

In addition, it is not always mandatory for online reptile traders in the Netherlands to include proof that the seller meets the requirements of legislation; it can be difficult to ensure, together with a website owner, that the legislation is enforced or policies are developed to prevent illegal trade (Interpol 2013). The online marketplaces that have developed a strong policy show that this leads to a decrease in illegal trade via these sites, but the illegal trade is displaced to other fora (Cuevas and McCrea-Steele 2017).

Distinguishing legal reptile trade from illegal reptile trade via the internet presents another major challenge for Dutch law enforcement. Reptiles cannot be personally examined and there is usually little or no supporting CITES documentation proving legal trade (Cuevas and McCrea-Steele 2017). In the Netherlands, the internet is often still monitored manually per advertisement and expertise is needed for monitoring the online trade, which makes it a tedious, time-consuming and expensive task (Hernandez-Castro and Roberts 2015).

Moreover, online Dutch illegal reptile traders are rapidly adapting and moving to new platforms (Hinsley 2016). In particular, social media platforms mainly focus on communication and are not specifically made for online commerce. The communication on these platforms can take different forms with different privacy settings which complicates detection via the various platforms (Cuevas and McCrea-Steele 2017).

Finally, the Dutch authorities could develop policies to improve the transparency and awareness about illegal reptile trade, since many buyers and sometimes traders of reptiles are not aware of the illegal background of reptiles (Sollund 2022b). Together, these bottlenecks pose significant challenges to law enforcement and complicate preventing and tackling the online illegal reptile trade in the Netherlands.

References

Altherr, S. (2014). *Stolen Wildlife: Why the EU Needs to Tackle Smuggling of Nationally Protected Species*. Munich: Pro Wildlife.

Altherr, S., Schuller, A., and Fischer, A. C. (2016). *Stolen Wildlife II: Why the EU Still Needs to Tackle Smuggling of Nationally Protected Species*. Munich: Pro Wildlife.

Arquilla, J., and Ronfeldt, D. (2001). Networks and Netwars: The Future of Terror, Crime, and Militancy. Santa Monica, CA: Rand Corporation.

Auliya, M. (2003). Hot trade in cool creatures: a review of the live reptile trade in the European Union in the 1990s with a focus on Germany. *TRAFFIC Europe*, Brussels.

Auliya, M., Altherr, S., Ariano-Sanchez, D., Baard, E. H., Brown, C., Brown, R. M., et al (2016). Trade in live reptiles, its impact on wild populations, and the role of the European market. *Biological Conservation, 204*: 103–19. doi:10.1016/j.biocon.2016.05.2017.

Bennett, E. L. (2011). Another inconvenient truth: the failure of enforcement systems to save charismatic species. *Oryx, 45*(4): 476–9. doi:10.1017/S003060531000178X

Clifton, K. L., and Rastogi, A. (2016). *Curbing Illegal Wildlife Trade: The Role of Social Network Analysis*. Washington, DC: International Union for the Conservation of Nature.

Cuevas, F., and McCrea-Steele, T. (2017). IFAW Study on E-Commerce and Wildlife Crime: Effective Policies and Practices to Stem the Growth of Illicit Trade, 5th OECD Task Force meeting on Countering Illicit Trade. London: Public Governance and Territorial Development Directorate.

Davies, P., Francis, P., and Jupp, V. (2011). *Doing Criminological Research*. London: Sage Publications.

D'Cruze, N., and Macdonald, D. W. (2016). A review of global trends in CITES live wildlife confiscations. *Nature Conservation, 15*: 47–63. doi:https://doi.org/10.3897/natureconservation.15.10005

Duijn, P. A. C., Kashirin, V., and Sloot, P. M. A. (2014). The relative ineffectiveness of criminal network disruption. *Scientific Reports, 4*: 1–15. doi:10.1038/srep04238

Fylan, F. (2005). Semi-structured interviewing. In J. Miles and P. Gilbert (eds) *A Handbook of Research Methods for Clinical and Health Psychology* (pp 65–78). Oxford: Oxford University Press.

Gilbert, M. J., Kik, M., Timmerman, A. J., Severs, T. T., Kusters, J. G., Duim, B., and Wagenaar, J. A. (2014). Occurrence, diversity, and host association of intestinal *Campylobacter*, *Arcobacter*, and *Helicobacter* in reptiles. *PLoS ONE, 9*(7): e101599. https://doi.org/10.1371/journal.pone.0101599

Gussow, K. (2009). *Market Exploration Reptiles and Amphibians*. Utrecht: General Inspection Service, Department of Investigation, Information and Analysis.

Harvey, M. (2017). Wildlife-Friendly Online Trade 2017: A harmonized policy for e-commerce and social media companies. TRAFFIC, WWF, IFAW.

Hastie, J. (2018). Disrupt: Wildlife Cybercrime. Report. London: IFAW.

Hastie, J., and McCrea-Steele, T. (2014). Wanted: Dead or Alive – Investigating Online Wildlife Trade. Report. The Hague: IFAW.

Hernandez-Castro, J. C., and Roberts, D. L. (2015). Automatic detection of potentially illegal online sales of elephant ivory via data mining. *PeerJ Computer Science, 1*(10): 1–11. doi: http://doi.org/10.7717/peerj-cs.10

Hinsley, A. E. (2016). *Characterizing the Structure and Function of International Wildlife Trade Networks in the Age of Online Communication*. Kent: University of Kent.

Hinsley, A., Lee, T. E., Harrison, J. R., and Roberts, D. L. (2016). Estimating the extent and structure of trade in horticultural orchids via social media. *Conservation Biology, 30*(5): 1038–47. doi:10.1111/cobi.12721

IFAW (2008). Killing with Keystrokes: An Investigation of the Illegal Wildlife Trade on the World Wide Web. Yarmouth Port, MA: IFAW.

IFAW (2012). Killing with Keystrokes 2.0: IFAW's Investigation into the European Online Ivory Trade. Yarmouth Port, MA: IFAW.

IFAW (2018). Disrupt: Wildlife Cybercrime. Uncovering the Scale of Online Wildlife Trade. The Hague: IFAW.

Interpol (2013). Project Web: An investigation into the ivory trade over the internet. Lyon: Environmental Crime Programme.

Interpol (2017). Illegal Wildlife Trade in the Darknet. Research report. 2016/018/R/IGCI/IC/CI.

Janssen, J., and Blanken, L. (2016). Going Dutch: An analysis of the import of live animals from Indonesia by the Netherlands. Petaling Jaya, Selangor, Malaysia: TRAFFIC, South East Asia Regional Office.

Janssen, J., and Krishnasamy, K. (2018). Left hung out to dry: how inadequate international protection can fuel trade in endemic species – the case of the earless monitor. *Global Ecology and Conservation, 16*: e00464.

Janssen, J., and Leupen, B. T. C. (2019). The Role of the Netherlands in the Reptile Trade. Monitor Conservation Research Society.

Kop, N., van der Wal, R., and Snel, G. (2012). *Investigation in the Spotlight: On Strategies in Investigative Practice.* The Hague: Boom Lemma Publishers.

Krishnasamy, K., and Stoner, S. (2016). Trading Faces: A Rapid Assessment on the Use of Facebook to Trade Wildlife in Peninsular Malaysia. Report. Petaling Jaya, Selangor, Malaysia: TRAFFIC.

Kruithof, K., Aldridge, J., Décary Hétu, D., Sim, M., Dujso, E., and Hoorens, S. (2016). *Internet-facilitated Drugs Trade: An Analysis of the Size, Scope and the Role of the Netherlands.* Santa Monica, CA and Cambridge UK: RAND Corporation.

Kuijer-Slobbe, D. (2016). The Netherlands participates in wildlife trade. *Blue*, 12–15.

Lavorgna, A. (2014). Wildlife trafficking in the internet age. *Crime Science, 3*(5): 1–12.

Maesschalck, J. (2016). Methodological quality in qualitative research. In T. Decorte and D. Zaitch (eds) *Qualitative Methods and Techniques in Criminology* (3rd edn) (pp 132–60). Culemborg, NL: Acco.

Magalhães, A. L. B., and São-Pedro, V. A. (2012). Illegal trade on nonnative amphibians and reptiles in southeast Brazil: the status of e-commerce. *Phyllomedusa, 11*(2): 155–60.

Mărginean, G. I., Gherman, E., and Tibor, S. (2018). The illegal internet based trade in European pond turtle *Emys orbicularis* in Romania: a threat factor for conservation. *North-Western Journal of Zoology, 1*(1): 64–70.

Marshall, B. M., Strine, C., and Hughes, A. C. (2020). Thousands of reptile species threatened by under-regulated global trade. *Nature Communications*, 11: 4738.

Morselli, C. (2009). *Inside Criminal Networks*. New York: Springer.

Nijman, V., and Shepherd, C. R. (2011). The role of Thailand in the international trade in CITES-listed live reptiles and amphibians. *PLoS One*, 6(3): e17825.

NVWA (2013). CITES Intervention strategy. Utrecht: NVWA.

Puritz, A., and Weller, C. (2018). *Illegal Wildlife Trade and the EU: Legal Approaches*. London: ClientEarth.

Rivalan, P., Delmas, V., Angulo, E., Bull, L. S., Hall, R. J., Courchamp, F., et al (2007) Can bans stimulate wildlife trade? *Nature*, 447: 529–30.

Robinson, J. E., Griffiths, R. A., John, F. A. S., and Roberts, D. L. (2015). Dynamics of the global trade in live reptiles: shifting trends in production and consequences for sustainability. *Biological Conservation*, 184: 42–50.

Schlaepfer, M. A., Hoover, C., and Kenneth Dodd, C. (2005). Challenges in evaluating the impact of the trade in amphibians and reptiles on wild populations. *BioScience*, 55(3): 256–64. doi:https://doi.org/10.1641/0006-3568(2005)055[0256:CIETIO]2.0.CO;2

Schneider, J. L. (2008). Reducing the illicit trade in endangered wildlife: the market reduction approach. *Journal of Contemporary Criminal Justice*, 24(3): 274–95. doi:10.1177/1043986208318226

Silva, J. P., Toland, J., Jones, W., Eldridge, J., Hudson, T., and O'Hara, E. (2009). *Life and Europe's Reptiles and Amphibians: Conservation in Practice*. Luxembourg: European Communities.

Sollund, R. (2019) *The Crimes of Wildlife Trafficking: Issues of Justice, Legality and Morality*. London: Routledge.

Sollund, R. (2022a). Wildlife trade and law enforcement: a proposal for a remodeling of CITES incorporating species justice, ecojustice, and environmental justice. *International Journal of Offender Therapy and Comparative Criminology*, 66(9): 1017–35.

Sollund, R. A. (2022b). A gendered case file analysis of reptile trafficking and illegal keeping in Norway. In H. U. Agu and M. L. Gore (eds) *Women and Wildlife Trafficking: Participants, Perpetrators and Victims* (pp 143–60). Abingdon: Routledge.

Sollund, R., and Maher, J. (2015). The Illegal Wildlife Trade. A Case Study Report on the Illegal Wildlife Trade in the United Kingdom, Norway, Colombia and Brazil. Oslo and Wales: University of Oslo and University of South Wales.

Sonricker Hansen, A. L., Li, A., Joly, D., Mekaru, S., and Brownstein, J. S. (2012). Digital surveillance: a novel approach to monitoring the illegal wildlife trade. *PLoS One*, 7(12): e51156. doi:10.1371/journal.pone.0051156.

Spapens, T. (2016). *Environmental Crime Handbook: For Education and Practice*. Amsterdam: Reed Business.

Temple, H. J., and Cox, N. (2009). *European Red List of Reptiles*. Amsterdam: IUCN.

van Riemsdijk, I., Struijk, R. P. J. H., Pel, E., Janssen, I. A., and Wielstra, B. (2020). Hybridisation complicates the conservation of Natrix snakes in the Netherlands. *Salamandra, 56*(1): 78–82.

van der Grijp, N. (2016). Wildlife Crime in the Netherlands, In-depth Analysis. Brussels: Policy Department A: Economic and Scientific Policy, European Parliament.

van Doorne, B. (2007). *A Dive into Cyberspace? Exploring the Trade in Protected Animals and Plants over the Internet*. Utrecht: General Inspectorate (Nature Team).

van Uhm, D. P. (2012). De illegale handel in beschermde diersoorten. In *Justitiële Verkenningen, 28*(2): 91–100.

van Uhm, D. P. (2016a). *The Illegal Wildlife Trade: Inside the World of Poachers, Smugglers, and Traders* (Volume 15). New York: Springer.

van Uhm, D. P. (2016b). Illegal trade in wildlife and harms to the world. In A. C. M. Spapens, R. White and W. Huisman (eds) *Environmental Crime in Transnational Context* (pp 59–82). Farnham: Ashgate Publishing.

van Uhm, D. P. (2016c). De verwevenheid tussen de onder- en bovenwereld in de wildlife handel. *Cahiers Politiestudies, 38*(1): 41–54.

van Uhm, D. P. (2018a). Wildlife and laundering: interaction between the under and upper world. In T. Spapens, R. White, D. P. van Uhm and W. Huisman (eds) *Green Crimes and Dirty Money* (pp 197–214). Abingdon: Routledge.

van Uhm, D. P. (2018b). Wildlife crime and security. In P. Reichel and R. Randa (eds) *Transnational Crime and Global Security* (pp 73–96). Santa Barbara, CA: Praeger.

van Uhm, D. P., and Wong, R. W. Y. (2019). Establishing trust in the illegal wildlife trade in China. *Asian Journal of Criminology, 14*(1): 23–40.

van Uhm, D. P., Pires, S. F., Sosnowski, M., and Petrossian, G. A. (2019). A comparison of seizures of illegal wildlife between the US and the EU. In M. J. Lynch and S. F. Pires (eds) *Quantitative Studies in Green and Conservation Criminology: The Measurement of Environmental Harm and Crime* (pp 127–45). Abingdon: Routledge.

Vinke, C. M. (2001). Trade in exotic animals: organizational structures and practices. *Judicial Explorations: Animal and Law, 27*: 94–103.

Wildlife Justice Commission (2016, September 15). *Vietnam wildlife crime investigation: Public hearing announced*. Retrieved from wildlifejustice.org: https://wildlifejustice.org/viet-namwildlife-crime-investigation-public-hearing-announced/

Wyatt, T., Miralles, O., Massé, F., Lima, R., da Costa, T. V., and Giovanini, D. (2022). Wildlife trafficking via social media in Brazil. *Biological Conservation,* *265*: 109420.

Yu, X., and Jia, W. (2015). *Moving Targets: Tracking Online Sales of Illegal Wildlife Products in China.* Cambridge: TRAFFIC

5

Countering Wildlife Crimes in Italy: The Case of Bird Poaching

Lorenzo Natali, Ciro Troiano, Sara Zoja and Anita Lavorgna

Introduction

With 60,000 animal species and 12,000 vegetable species, Italy is one of the European countries with the richest biodiversity and with extremely high levels of endemism (ISPRA 2020). However, this heritage is considered at risk for many species of flora and fauna. Wildlife crimes, and particularly poaching in its various manifestations, are currently considered one of the main threats to the survival of rare or endangered species (Ministry of Environment, Land and Sea Protection of Italy 2017; ISPRA 2020).

Notably, wildlife crime can cause severe social and environmental harms – ranging from the loss of biodiversity and the potential transmission of zoonoses or other diseases, to abuse or cruelty towards animals and even security threats (see, for example, Benton 2007; White 2011; Sollund 2012, 2013a, 2013b; Wyatt 2013a, 2013b; Lynch and Stretesky 2014; Lavorgna 2015; Gore et al 2016; Haenlein 2016; van Uhm et al 2021). Nonetheless, and despite the relevance of many types of wildlife crimes in Italy, overall wildlife crime has received limited attention by researchers, activists and policy makers in the country, with a few notable exceptions (first and foremost the annual 'Zoomafia' reports published by the NGO LAV – see Troiano (2022) for the latest one at the time of writing – or the activities promoted by the public research institute *Istituto Superiore per la Promozione e Ricerca Ambientale* ISPRA; see Lavorgna (2022) for a recent academic book focusing on wildlife trafficking in Italy).

This review chapter will focus, in particular, on the analysis of criminal phenomena linked to animal poaching (*bracconaggio*) in the Italian context, broadly defined as the act of hunting or abducting animals illegally (in line with Sollund 2011). As poaching can manifest itself very differently depending on the animal poached, for the sake of brevity we will mostly use bird poaching as a case study. Currently, 67 species of birds (about 25 per cent of those surveyed) are considered at risk of extinction in Italy, ten of which are at a critical level (IUCN 2020). The situation slightly improved over the last decade (for example, from IUCN 2012); but overall it remains problematic, especially considering the impact of climate change on wildlife populations. After having presented an analysis of the major trends, phenomenology and characteristics of bird poaching and the related wildlife markets in Italy, and their impact on wildlife conservation, we will present a brief overview of the relevant national legislation and its implementation, suggesting how the system currently in place is not always adequate to confront a diffuse and socially embedded phenomenon the social and environmental harms of which are too often yet not fully recognized.

Phenomenology of (bird) poaching in the Italian context

Italy is a country affected by a number of wildlife crimes, impacting both flora and fauna, and crimes against (non-wild) animals, ranging for instance from wildlife trafficking (with Italy being a country of origin, transit and destination – see Lavorgna 2022) and nest disturbance to dog fighting and other types of animal abuse (Troiano 2020). In this panorama, poaching is only a portion of broader problems, those of wildlife crimes and animal abuse. Yet, poaching is a very interesting issue to discuss in the Italian context, as in this country it is possible to retrieve important data from both primary and secondary documentary sources; indeed, poaching has traditionally received (scarce but comparatively more than other forms of wildlife crimes and animal abuse) attention in the Italian context, possibly because it is more clearly reflected in the regulatory framework.

On average in Italy, in the last few years, about 1,500 confirmed cases of poaching have been recorded yearly, with more than 1,300 people being reported for violations of the relevant criminal legislation (Troiano 2021) which, as we will see later, mostly addresses illegal hunting. If we also consider the administrative infringements for hunting-related activities (in Italy, administrative law is considered a distinct branch of the law, aimed at regulating the relationship between citizens and public administration), the number of annual reported offences rises to about 7,000 (Legambiente 2021), even excluding CITES-related violations. Unsurprisingly, the dark number is extremely high.

In Italy, in line with the typology offered in Sollund (2019), we can distinguish among three different manifestations of poaching, which tend to rely on a different social organization of the actors involved: (1) professional poaching, carried out by specialized offenders, who mostly target very sought after animals for their trade as both live or dead specimens (for instance, the Golden Eagle, the Sardinian Mouflon or the Abruzzo Chamois are generally destined for the clandestine trade in trophies or taxidermized animals;[1] many parts of edible species are requested for the food market[2]); (2) cultural poaching, a widespread illegal behaviour especially common in certain areas of the country and/or social groups, and that translates into a normalized violation of the legal framework regulating the capture or killing of wildlife[3]; and (3) other forms of illegal hunting, generally carried out by single individuals who, while exercising a permitted activity, do not hesitate to shoot a member of rare or protected wild species, or to hunt outside the hunting season, in prohibited areas, or without a permit and firearm licence.

Even if it is important to note that poaching (and, more generally, wildlife crimes) are not always linked to organized crime in the country (Lavorgna 2022), it is nonetheless crucial to recognize that anecdotal evidence shows some links between poaching and major Italian organized crime groups. In the area of Caserta (in the Campania region), for instance, a series of law enforcement operations (*Volo Libero* ['Free Flight']) from 2001 to 2005 evidenced how fowling of water birds was carried out in lands controlled by, and enabled by, Camorra clans, in areas where stolen and otherwise illegal weapons were hidden (LIPU 2021).

Poaching, as briefly noted above, can be a very heterogeneous phenomenon. For the sake of brevity, we will now focus more in detail on bird poaching and fowling (that is, a subtype of bird poaching involving the capture of live birds with nets, cage-traps, loops, birdlime or mistletoe). Birds are generally captured to be used or sold as live decoys in hunting (as in the case of skylarks) or for falconry; for pleasure or ornamental purposes;

---

[1] While taxidermy is allowed and regulated by law, it can only be practised within certain limitations (for example, where the animal has been lawfully hunted, or it had regular ownership). Even if taxidermy is rarer than in the past, the illegal traffic of taxidermized species and trophies still occurs, both within the internal Italian market, and with Italy involved as a destination or transit country (for example, exotic animals killed during a safari), as emerges from law enforcement investigations and seizures (Troiano 2017).

[2] For instance, small birds, thrushes, pheasants, partridges and ducks together with mammals such as wild boar, roe deer, deer, rabbits, hares, porcupines, badgers and marmots are all victims of poaching for their meat, which is greatly appreciated especially in certain areas for local cultural traditions. From a folkloristic perspective, the case of the dormouse (*Glis glis*), a small rodent, provides an interesting example, as reportedly its meat is eaten during 'Ndrangheta meetings (*La Repubblica* 2008).

[3] At times, cultural poaching has direct economic motivations. Consider, for instance, the poaching of small migratory birds (for example, in the Brescia and Bergamo Prealps, and in the south of Sardinia). The birds, caught with little effort and in a short time, are then sold to restaurants. In some areas these activities are also carried out by unemployed people.

or as food. These activities are rooted in many parts of Italy,[4] and remain overall highly problematic (Barca et al 2016; ISPRA 2016; Ministry of Environment, Land and Sea Protection of Italy 2017; LIPU 2018), as demonstrated by several law enforcement operations in recent years. Some notable examples are provided by the 'Robin' operation of 2020, where 106 individuals were criminally charged, 400 illegal capture devices were seized, and more that 2,000 birds (800 alive and 1,200 dead) were also seized; among them, there were many protected and endangered species, all captured or killed illegally. More recently, in the course of the *Anello mancante* ['Missing ring'] operation in 2022, 104 persons were criminally charged and 44 administrative penalties for a total of 32,000 euros were also imposed; about 2,500 live birds were found and seized, some of which (to be used as decoy birds) had a value, on the illegal market, of up to 500 euros each (*Il Gazzettino* 2022).

It is important to note that the harms to the animals do not relate only to the loss of life or of freedom, but also to the suffering linked to some of the (forbidden) means used by poachers (for example, modified or handcrafted weapons, gauges, shotgun tubes, traps and snares), some of which can also put at risk other hunters and hikers who may unknowingly run into booby traps. Consider, for instance, how walking sticks or umbrellas transformed into single-barrel shotguns with a single cartridge – a trick to disguise the weapon and make it look like a harmless common object – have been seized during police operations (as detailed in Troiano 2018). Other illegal instruments are electronically or digitally operated acoustic calls, for instance those reproducing bird calls or songs to deceive wild species; they are concealed among the vegetation and connected to amplifiers, at times with connections to moulds or silhouettes of birds, especially during the migration period. Some traditional means, such as the bow trap used mainly in the valleys of Brescia and Bergamo to catch robins and other small birds, can cause hours of agony: a stick or a metal rod is inserted in the ground with a loop at the other end (made of nylon – originally a horse's hair); bait is placed near the loop and held firm by a bit of wood that keeps the stick on the ground. When a robin or a blackbird tries to take the bait and

---

[4] There are at least seven areas in Italy where bird poaching is most intense: the Lombard-Venetian Prealps; the Delta of the river Po, the Pontine-Campania coasts, the coasts and wetlands of Puglia, southern Sardinia, western Sicily and the Strait of Messina. To these hotspots can be added others where bird poaching is frequent, such as Liguria, the coastal strip of Tuscany, and the Romagna, Marche and Friuli-Venezia Giulia regions. In the Lombard Prealps (particularly near Brescia and Bergamo), illegal trapping is widespread in the autumn, through the use of nets, bow traps, mistletoe traps and other bird traps. The same kinds of activities, using nets and decoys, are also common in the Venetian Prealps and in Friuli (ISPRA 2016).

moves the bit of wood, the stick snaps upwards and the bird is caught and, generally, its legs are broken (for more details, see Troiano 2018, 2021, 2022).

The poaching of goldfinches and other *Fringillidae*: a closer look

The songbird family *Fringidillae* encompasses a broad number of small to medium-sized birds, some of which have colourful plumage and are considered among the best songsters; as such, some species (for example, the domestic canaries, the European goldfinches and other birds commonly called 'finches') are caged or bred in captivity as companion animals.

European goldfinches (*Carduelis carduelis*), small birds of the finch family found throughout the national territory, of which hunting is forbidden, are particularly paradigmatic of the problem. They are generally captured for pleasure or ornamental purposes, and are among the most illegally traded species in Italy: their beauty and elegance, their pleasant singing, and even their symbolism. Due to their facial plumage, goldfinches have become a symbol of the Passion of Christ; according to the legend, a goldfinch was wounded while trying to pull out the thorns from Christ's crown, becoming stained by blood. This made them not only a favourite subject in artistic representations (see Figure 5.1), but also prime targets for fowlers and traffickers (see Figure 5.2).

To capture a goldfinch, fowling practices are generally based on nets, causing stress and frequent injuries to the bird. Generally, a piece of ground is prepared with thistles, and covered in bird food and a source of water. Then a horizontal net, called *prodina*, is positioned on the ground, connected to some ropes that the fowler, hiding in a hut about ten metres away, uses at the opportune moment. To attract the wild birds, both caged birds and tied ones are used; for instance, in a method called *camicia* [shirt], some goldfinches are tied to a wooden wand with strings, so that they can move and flap their wings and attract others but not fly away, until they fall to the ground exhausted. Of course, this practice is illegal as it is considered animal abuse.

The *presicci* (that is, the recently captured birds) are confined in large numbers of very small cages (*ricevitori* [those receiving]) to prevent them hurting themselves when trying to escape, which would reduce their economic value. It is calculated that only about one-third of the captured birds survive the shock of the capture, while those surviving are destined for a very long period of captivity in the dark, to teach them to sing in captivity (Troiano 2000). Some birds are used to artificially create hybrids of canaries and goldfinches (so-called *incardellati*), all ending up in illegal wildlife markets. These markets can be held in very traditional settings (for example, especially in southern Italy there are still places and streets where illegal wildlife markets are improvised, mostly on Sundays, albeit to a much

Figure 5.1: *The Madonna del Cardellino* (Madonna of the goldfinch), oil on wood by the Italian Renaissance artist Raffaello Sanzio, 1506

lesser extent compared to the past), through the facilitation of legal pet shops, or, increasingly, online (Lavorgna 2014, 2022).

Overall, the poaching of *Fringillidae* is still thriving in Italy, as exemplified in a large-scale law enforcement operation that was completed in late 2020 under the coordination of the Public Prosecutor's Office of Santa Maria Capua Vetere (in the Campania region), and some specialized *Carabinieri* forces from Naples and Latina (respectively, in the Campania and Lazio regions). Overall, the investigative activities allowed the uncovering of a broad system of illegal trades of protected species that were systematically and indiscriminately captured using illegal methods (for example, traps and natural or artificial acoustic lures) by members of a criminal network with branches supplying illegal markets in various parts of the country. The birds were then kept in improvised depots, in conditions of extreme discomfort that caused them evident suffering, and finally sold in clandestine markets both to private individuals and to commercial traders, including in the Northern regions. From the investigations, the connivance and support of professional enablers (breeders and veterinarians)

Figure 5.2: A rescued goldfinch, which had been stuck to a branch and used as a decoy by poachers

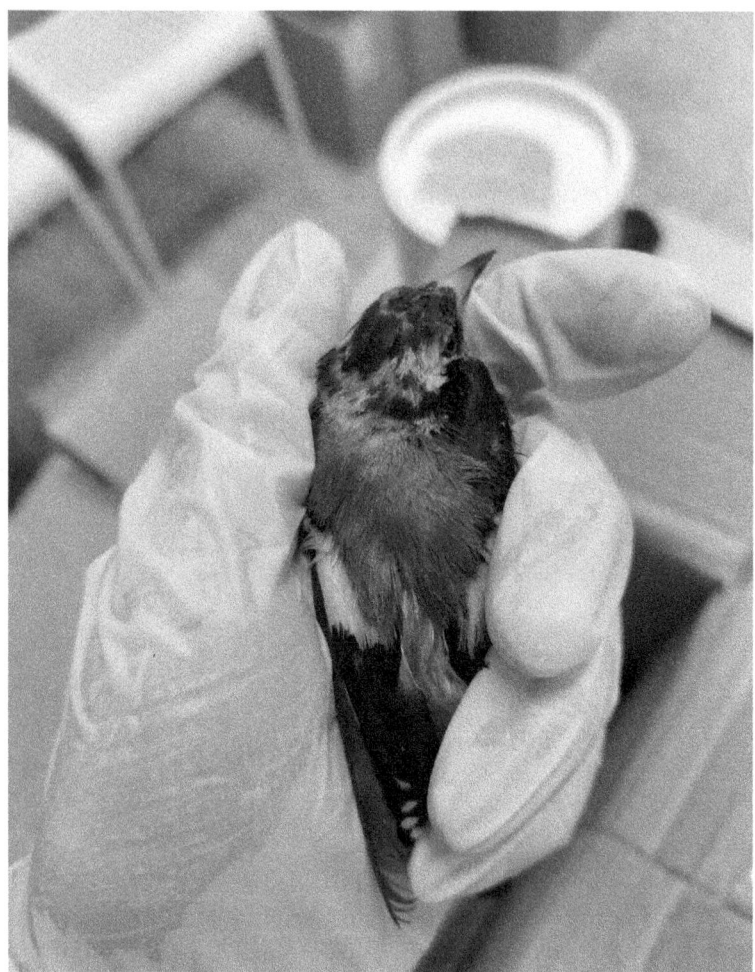

Source: *La Repubblica* 2021.

for the ringing of the wild animals and the creation of documentation accompanying subsequent sales was also demonstrated (Tribunale Santa Maria Capua Vetere 2018; *CasertaNews* 2020). As such, the poached birds fed both the legal and the illegal markets of lures and ornamental birds at the national level, producing severe harms in terms of loss of biodiversity and environmental patrimony, and causing changes in the relationship between living species and their habitats due to illegal anthropogenic activities, in addition to animal abuse and death. The economic advantages deriving from poaching were immediate and direct, favouring and consolidating illicit enrichment, with a turnover of about 350,000 euros per year (*Latinatu* 2020). Also, from the investigative activities and, in particular, from searches, seizures and interceptions, the presence of a relatively sophisticated and professional criminal organization could be observed; the organization demonstrated particular care and foresight during the transportation and storage stages, for instance by using relay cars and courtyards sheltered from sight and easily kept under control. Wiretapping also demonstrated the importance of creating an articulated network of suppliers and buyers and the establishment of a plurality of groups; rivals but also capable of cooperation. Some of the individuals involved had a criminal past linked to poaching, but also to the receiving of stolen goods, usury, fraud, extortion, robbery, slander, and even belonging to mafia-type associations (Tribunale Santa Maria Capua Vetere 2018).

The legal framework

In Italy, as briefly mentioned earlier, we have legal provisions relevant to wildlife crimes, and specifically poaching, in both criminal and administrative law. In this section we will briefly introduce some of the most relevant ones in this regard, without pretending to provide an exhaustive coverage of the legalistic approach to wildlife crimes in the country, which would exceed the scope of our short contribution. It is worth noting that traditionally, in the country, administrative law has been mostly used to regulate the matter (see Lavorgna 2022: 40); after all, it is relatively rare for a state to use coercive power in environmental matters, where most interventions generally focus on harm mitigation (EFFACE 2016; Nurse 2016). Of course, if we adopt a harm prevention and mitigation approach, the political and symbolic distinction on whether to intervene in the matter with criminal or administrative law might seem of scarce importance, as both these approaches should aim to reduce risks and therefore environmental and social harms (Hall 2015; Lavorgna 2022). Nonetheless, it is worth noting how, especially over the last decade, there has been a tendency in Italy to define new environmental crimes, especially in response to EU legislative input. Consider, for instance, the Legislative Decree 121/2011, implementing the EU Directive 99/2008 by amending the Criminal Code to insert articles 727*bis*[5] and

---

[5] '(1) Unless the fact entails a more serious crime, everyone who – with the exception of cases allowed by law – kills, captures, or otherwise holds specimens belonging to protected wildlife [animals] is punished with the arrest from one to six months, or with a fine up to EUR 4.000, unless the act targets a negligible amount of protected wildlife and has a negligible impact on that species conservation'. Please note that the second part of the article has similar provisions regarding endangered plants. As clarified by the Italian Supreme Court in 2020 (Cass.Sez.III Pen. 24 September 2020, n.26579), the interpretative key lies on the effects of the action on wildlife conservation: as such, for a highly endangered species, even the killing or capture of a single 'specimen' might be sufficient to intervene through criminal law instruments.

733*bis*,⁶ which lay down the penalties to be applied in case of violation of rules concerning the protection of habitats and the conservation of wildlife species (for a further discussion, see Pistorelli and Scarcella 2011; Scarcella 2011; Lo Monte 2015; Lavorgna 2022).

A key legislation intervening on the matter from both a criminal and administrative law perspective is Law 157/1992 and its further amendments, making provisions for the protection of wildlife and restrictions on hunting. This law, among other things, provides the (late) implementation to the 1979 Bern Convention on the Conservation of European Wildlife and Natural Habitats, ratified with Law 503/1981. It is important to note that this law provides some general rules at a national level, but then each administrative region applies local rules (determining, for instance, the areas where hunting is permitted, and the duration of the hunting season). At the core of the Italian approach is the idea that wildlife is considered an 'unavailable State asset'; as such, hunting is not an individual right, but rather a concession by the State, which manifests itself through the provision of hunting permits under certain circumstances. Similarly, the legal possession of each individual breed has a number of requirements; in the case of birds, for instance, each single animal needs to be equipped with an irremovable metal ring, which represents a 'State seal' the non-use or counterfeiting of which is a crime (Santoloci et al 2002; Troiano 2021). Wildlife, together with the agricultural productions in hunting areas, are the assets to be protected; as such, the legislation forbids the use of a number of hunting tools or means that, for instance, would cause suffering to the animal, such as the ones exemplified earlier in this chapter.

The readers are certainly aware of the Washington Convention on International Trade in Endangered Species of Fauna and Flora, more commonly known as CITES, the international agreement, which aims to protect plants and animals at risk of extinction, regulating and monitoring their trade, that is, export, re-export and import of live and dead animals, plants, as well as parts and derivatives. Considering the links between poaching and trafficking, of course CITES-related/adjunct legislation and its implementation matter in this context. In Italy, the CITES Convention was ratified with the Law 874/1975 and is currently also regulated by Council Regulation (EC) 338/97. In this context, we also need to mention Law 150/1992 and its later modifications (up to 2015), as it was only through the 1992 legislation that Italy came to govern the offences relating to the CITES implementation, leading to sanctions ranging from a fine to arrest in the most serious cases (prison sentence for repeat

---

⁶ '(1) Everyone – with the exception of cases allowed by law – who destroys a protected habitat or otherwise deteriorates it impacting on its conservation status, is punished with the arrest up to 18 months and with a fine of at least EUR3.000'.

offenders from three months to one year), and involving the seizure and confiscation of the animal, plant, or derivative product. Currently, the Ministry of the Ecological Transition (formerly known as the Ministry of the Environment and of the Protection of the Territory and the Sea) is the Management Authority primarily responsible for the execution of the CITES legislation (this ministry also acts as coordinating Scientific Authority), in collaboration with the Ministry of Economic Development (focusing on permits and certificates), and the Ministry of Agricultural, Food and Forestry Policies. There are currently three main Enforcement Focal Points, linked respectively to the Ministry of Defence (the *Arma dei Carabinieri*, and specifically its CITES team), and to the Financial Police (one to its International Cooperation Department, and one to its Operation Department) (see also Lavorgna 2022: 39ff).

Conclusion

By offering some insights from the Italian context, mainly focused on bird poaching, this contribution aims to foster more academic attention to this country's situation, and to further the core green criminology debate on the connection between environmental, ecological and inter-species justice regarding environmental harms and crimes, as it is particularly evident with respect to many forms of wildlife crimes.[7] Most importantly, crimes against wildlife cannot be simply seen as a kind of violence 'justifiable' exclusively by causes of an economic nature. In every form of abuse against animals there are overlapping causes of social, material, psychological and moral nature that are difficult to disentangle. Rob White (2011: 95) reminds us that, on the methodological and analytical level, the study of environmental crimes normally requires the investigation of 'chains of harm'. Indeed, those are often complex phenomena, and in order to understand them and to develop adequate harm prevention and mitigation strategies, we need to know the links between the different actors, at different levels, and their modus operandi; to comprehend the dynamics of supply and demand causing the circulation of these 'products'; but also to grasp the underlying cultural aspects enabling and fostering these behaviours.

---

[7] In line with White (2011: 106), who underlines the importance of those theoretical proposals that place the issues of harm to animals within a wide philosophical frame linking directly with interspecies justice concerns. The connection between environmental, ecological and inter-species justice would imply a philosophical reflection on the complexity of the ontological relationship between human and 'non-human' animals (consider, for instance, Parks and Roberts 2006; Schlosberg 2007; White 2008, 2015; Okereke and Charlesworth 2016; Moulton et al 2019; Sollund 2019).

As such, in the Italian context it would be important to renew the present juridical apparatus and, more generally, the entire system of prevention and criminal protection of animals, especially as regards its sanctioning aspects, to achieve more efficient and dissuasive penalties targeting those who currently consider poaching a low-risk, high-gain type of activity. Also, it would be pivotal to add more investigative tools and more operative personnel to the authorities involved in the fight, and to practise a correct and deeper training of the personnel, mindful of the severity of the offence in terms of both social and environmental harms. But this would not be enough. In terms of criminal policy, it would be necessary to abandon the misleading belief that, in order to arrest 'the alliances, personal habits and institutional routines that sanction a more generalized mode of environmental decay, it would be enough to capture the "environmental criminals"' (Halsey 2004: 837; see also Natali 2015, 2017).

This is largely because criminal law and criminal justice systems, while useful, suffer from some limitations when facing the specific problems and features of environmental 'offending' and 'victimisation' (Hall 2014: 99): 'the idea that any law (much less criminal law) can or should constitute the sole solution to the problems of environmental harm is surely wrong' (Hall 2014: 98). Along these lines, the socio-legal debate, while recognizing the importance of effective criminal law interventions, should also focus on 'what combination of civil, administrative, mediation-based, criminal justice or other legal—versus extra-legal—approaches to the issue of environmental harm will minimize the risk of such harm occurring or reoccurring' (Hall 2014: 103). Additionally, in the context of wildlife crime, also restorative justice and empathy-based interventions can play a crucial and innovative role in reducing reoffending, and repairing the harm done to victims and the community (see Wyatt et al 2022b). However, as the authors remark, focusing on the Scottish context, 'there are a number of barriers which would hinder using restorative justice and empathy-based approaches for animal-related crimes. These include who would speak for the animal, who would be involved in the approach, and identifying when to use such interventions depending on the nature of the offence' (see Wyatt et al 2022b: 4).

If in the short and medium term it is necessary to ameliorate the effective application of the laws and their implementation and, at the same time, to re-image our way to respond to the phenomenon, in the long run it is necessary to work on the educational and cultural level[8] to sensitize and increase the sense of responsibility of the consumers (see Wyatt 2013a: 314).

---

[8] On this point, it is worth mentioning the first Museum of Environmental Crime in Europe was opened in Rome in 2014.

Crimes against wildlife, in fact, bring to the fore an apparent total denial (Cohen 2001) towards a vital dimension that does not only concern the animal itself but also the human being (see Sollund 2013c).[9] More or less consciously, one chooses *not to* listen, *not to* know, *not to* understand and, above all, *not to* respond. The consideration of this psycho-social process could contribute to explain the apparent lack of foresight of human beings with regard to the survival of their own species and of others. To re-orient this attitude, the concept of *biophilia* could be appropriate. The term was coined by psychoanalyst Erich Fromm and successively reintroduced by American biologist Edward Wilson in his book *Biophilia* (1984). Wilson defines biophilia as 'the innate tendency to concentrate our attention on life forms and on all that recalls them and, in some circumstances, to become emotionally affiliated with them' (Wilson 2002: 134). As such, the need of human beings to live in constant integration and harmony with the natural world, conserving its other animal species, could be given further incentive through dedicated projects of sensitization and awareness-raising in the educational context and in the society as a whole. Finally, the challenge will be that of recognizing the relationships of inequalities, domination and racism that exist and operate where human beings and the more widespread non-human world meet (Zaffaroni 2012), and to continue promoting the (mostly) lacking but increasingly needed dialogue between species justice, ecojustice, environmental justice and animal rights (Sollund 2022; Wyatt et al 2022a).

References

Barca, B., Lindon, A. and Root-Bernstein, M. (2016) Environmentalism in the crosshairs: perspectives on migratory bird hunting and poaching conflicts in Italy. *Global Ecology and Conservation* 6: 189–207.

Benton, T. (2007) Ecology, community and justice: the meaning of 'green'. In P. Beirne and N. South (eds) *Issues in Green Criminology: Confronting Harms against Environments, Humanity and Other Animals* (pp 3–32). Cullompton: Willan Publishing.

---

[9] We can understand 'denial' also by resorting to a psychoanalytic perspective. In this sense, denial is a psychological defence mechanism that stops certain data of reality, potentially painful and traumatic, from reaching the emotional sphere. To deny oneself our (human) dependence upon the environment can hide the deepest fear of human beings: death. The denial allows it to be exorcized through a dangerous anthropocentric interpretation of life. On this, see Jung (1964).

CasertaNews (2020) Scoperto il 'mercato nero' degli uccelli: 7 indagati. Accordi coi commercianti: giro d'affari di 350mila euro [Bird 'black market' discovered: 7 suspects. Agreements with traders: turn over of 350,000 euros]. Available at: www.casertanews.it/cronaca/arresti-cattura-uccelli-caserta-latina-mercato-illegale.html?fbclid=IwAR2Gg5EVLdFDPqGeO1m6jK-KTBt3ohD7YsReXfQKKHH0Ijgi1HMHuwbsHms

Cohen, S. (2001) *States of Denial: Knowing about atrocities and suffering*. Cambridge: Polity Press.

EFFACE (2016) *Conclusions and Recommendations (Deliverable 7.4)*. European Union Action to Fight Environmental Crime. Available at: www.efface.eu/sites/default/files/publications/EFFACE_Conclusions_recommendations/index.pdf

Gore, M. L., Lute, M. L., Ratsimbazafy, J. H. and Rajaonson, A. (2016) Local perspectives on environmental security and its influence on illegal biodiversity exploitation. *PLoS One*. DOI: https://doi.org/10.1371/journal.pone.0150337

Haenlein, C. (2016) *Poaching, Wildlife Trafficking and Security in Africa: Myths and realities*. London: RUSI.

Hall, M. (2014) The roles and use of law in green criminology. *International Journal for Crime, Justice and Social Democracy* 3(2): 96–109.

Hall, M. (2015) *Exploring Green Crime: Introducing the legal, social and criminological context of environmental harm*. New York: Palgrave.

Halsey, M. (2004) Against 'green' criminology. *British Journal of Criminology*, 44(6): 833–53

Il Gazzettino (2022) Sequestrati 55 uccelli da richiamo con anelli alterati, denunciato il gestore dell'allevamento: stroncato business illecito. Available at: www.ilgazzettino.it/nordest/padova/sequestro_uccelli_richiamo_anelli_alterati_allevamento_curtarolo_denunciato_titolare_carabinieri_forestali-6586888.html#:~:text=PADOVA%20%2D%20I%20carabinieri%20forestali%20hanno,carabinieri%20Cites%20di%20tutta

ISPRA (2016) Lotta al bracconaggio. Comunicato stampa [Fight against poaching. Press release]. Available at: www.isprambiente.gov.it/files/comunicati-stampa/2016/Comunicato_stampa_bracconaggio.pdf

ISPRA (2020) *Annuario dei Dati Ambientali* [Environmental data yearbook]. Rome: Istituto Superiore per la Protezione e la Ricerca Ambientale [Higher Institute for Environmental Research and Protection]. Available at: https://development.isprambiente.gov.it/it/news/annuario-dei-dati-ambientali-2020

IUCN (2012) *Lista Rossa italiana sugli uccelli nidificanti* [Italian Red List on nesting birds]. Rome: Comitato Italiano IUCN.

IUCN (2020) *Lista Rossa italiana sugli uccelli nidificanti* [Italian Red List on nesting birds]. Rome: Comitato Italiano IUCN. Available at: www.iucn.it/dettaglio.php?id=61639

Jung, C. G. (1964) *Man and His Symbols*. Garden City, NY: Doubleday and Co.

La Repubblica (2008) E gli affari si trattano alle cene dei ghiri [And business is done at dormice dinners]. Available at: https://ricerca.repubblica.it/repubblica/archivio/repubblica/2008/09/18/gli-affari-si-trattano-alle-cene.html

La Repubblica (2021) Brescia, l'Enpa denuncia: 'Cardellino incollato a un ramo da bracconieri e usato come esca' [Brescia, Enpa denounces: 'Goldfinch glued to a branch by poachers and used as bait']. Available at: https://milano.repubblica.it/cronaca/2021/09/10/news/cardellino_denuncia_enpa_brescia-317143258/

Latinatu (2020) Il mercato nero degli uccelli arriva anche a Formia: giro da 350mila euro [The black market for birds also reaches Formia: turn over of 350,000 euros]. Available at: https://latinatu.it/il-mercato-nero-degli-uccelli-arriva-anche-a-formia-giro-da-350mila-euro/

Legambiente (2021) *Rapporto Ecomafia 2021* [Eco-mafia report 2021]. Rome: Legambiente.

Lavorgna, A. (2014) Wildlife trafficking in the Internet age. *Crime Science* 3(1): 1–12.

Lavorgna, A. (2015) The social organization of pet trafficking in cyberspace. *European Journal on Criminal Policy and Research* 21(3): 353–70.

Lavorgna, A. (2022) *Il traffico di specie protette. Prospettive critiche e interdisciplinari* [The trafficking of protected species. Critical and interdisciplinary perspectives]. Milan: FrancoAngeli.

LIPU (2018) Comunicato stampa [Press release]. Available at: www.lipu.it/news-natura/notizie/16-comunicati-stampa/1192-da-comacchio-un-allenza-contro-il-bracconaggio

LIPU (2021) Le origini di Volo libero: intervista col ministro Sergio Costa [The origins of free flight: interview with Minister Sergio Costa]. Available at: www.lipu.it/news-natura/notizie/10-caccia-e-bracconaggio/1541-le-origini-di-volo-libero-intervista-col-ministro-sergio-costa

Lo Monte, E. (2015) Considerazioni sulla (in)applicabilità delle fattispecie di cui agli artt. 772*bis* and 733*bis* c.p. [Considerations on the (in)applicability of the cases referred to in articles 772*bis* and 733*bis* of the Criminal code]. *Diritto Penale Contemporaneo* 1: 220–30.

Lynch, M. and Stretesky, P. (2014) *Exploring Green Criminology: Toward a greed criminological revolution*. Farnham: Ashgate.

Ministry of Environment, Land and Sea Protection of Italy (2017) Agreement on the National Action Plan to Combat Offences against Wild Birds [Accordo sul Piano d'azione nazionale per il contrasto degli illeciti contro gli uccelli selvatici], on initiative of the Ministry of Environment, Land and Sea Protection of Italy, to implement the National Strategy on biodiversity (Repertorio n. 37/CSR, 17A03562, GU Serie Generale n.120 del 25-05-2017). Available at: www.regioni.it/news/2017/05/26/accordo-3730-03-2017csr-uccelli-selvatici-accordo-su-piano-nazionale-contrasto-illeciti- 515578/.

Moulton, D. J., Van Sant, A. A. and Williams, L. (2019) Anthropocene, Capitalocene, ... Plantationocene? A manifesto for ecological justice in an age of global crises. *Geography Compass* 13: e12438.

Natali, L. (2015) *Green Criminology: Prospettive emergenti sui crimini ambientali* [Green Criminology: Emerging perspectives on environmental crimes]. Turin: Giappichelli.

Natali, L. (2017) The Contribution of Green Criminology to the Analysis of Historical Pollution. In F. Centonze and S. Manacorda (eds) *Historical Pollution: Comparative legal responses to environmental crimes* (pp 21–55). Cham: Springer International Publishing.

Nurse, A. (2016) *An Introduction to Green Criminology and Environmental Justice*. London: Sage.

Okereke, C. and Charlesworth, M. (2014) Environmental and Ecological Justice. In M. M. Betsill, K. Hochstetler and D. Stevis (eds) *Advances in International Environmental Politics* (2nd edn) (pp 328–55). London: Palgrave Macmillan.

Parks, B. C. and Roberts, J. T. (2006) Environmental and Ecological Justice. In Betsill MM, Hochstetler K and Stevis D (eds.) *Palgrave Advances in International Environmental Politics* (pp 329–60). London: Palgrave Macmillan.

Pistorelli, L. and Scarcella, A. (2011) Sulle novità di rilievo penalistico introdotte dal decreto egislative di recepimento delle direttive CE in materia di ambiente (d. lgs. 7 luglio 2011, n. 121) [On the novelties of criminal law introduced by the legislative decree transposing the EC directives on the environment]. *Diritto Penale Contemporaneo*, 4 August.

Santoloci, M., Fantilli, P. and Fioravanti, S. (2002) *La disciplina della caccia* [The Regulatory Framework of Hunting]. Piacenza: La Tribuna.

Scarcella, A. (2011). Nuovi 'ecoreati' ed estensione ai reati ambientali del D. Lgs. n. 231/2001 sulla responsabilità degli enti [New 'eco-crimes' and extension to environmental crimes of Legislative Decree no. 231/2001 on the liability of institutions]. *Ambiente and Sviluppo*, 10.

Schlosberg, D. (2007) *Defining Environmental Justice: Theories, movements, and nature*. Oxford: Oxford University Press.

Sollund, R. A. (2011) Expressions of speciesism: the effects of keeping companion animals on animal abuse, animal trafficking and species decline. *Crime, Law and Social Change* 55(5): 437–51.

Sollund, R. A. (2012) Speciesism as Doxic Practice Versus Valuing Difference and Plurality. In R. Ellefsen, R. A. Sollund and G. Larsen (eds) *Eco-global Crimes: Contemporary problems and future challenges* (pp 333–46). Farnham: Ashgate Publishing.

Sollund, R. A. (2013a) The Victimization of Women, Children and Non-Human Species Through Trafficking and Trade. In N. South and A. Brisman (eds) *Routledge International Handbook of Green Criminology* (pp 72–93). London: Routledge.

Sollund, R. A. (2013b) Animal Trafficking and Trade: Abuse and Species Injustice. In R. Walters, D. S. Westerhuis and T. Wyatt (eds) *Emerging Issues in Green Criminology: Exploring power, justice and harm* (pp 75–96). London: Palgrave Macmillan.

Sollund, R. A. (2013c) Causes for Speciesism: Difference, Distance and Denial? In R. White (ed) *Transnational Environmental Crime*. London: Routledge.

Sollund, R. A. (2019) *The Crimes of Wildlife Trafficking: Issues of justice, legality and morality*. London: Routledge.

Sollund, R. A. (2022) Wildlife trade and law enforcement: a proposal for a remodelling of CITES incorporating species justice, ecojustice, and environmental justice. *International Journal of Offender Therapy and Comparative Criminology* 66(9): 1017–35.

Tribunale Santa Maria Capua Vetere (2018) Ufficio del Giudice delle Indagini Preliminari, Ordinanza di applicazione di misura coercitiva [Court of Santa Maria Capua Vetere (2018) Office of the Preliminary Investigation Judge, Ordinance for the application of coercive measures], N. 8344/2018 R.G.N.R.; N. 7888/2018 R.G.I.P.

Troiano, C. (2000) *Zoomafia. Mafia, camorra and gli altri animali* [Zoomafia. Mafia, Camorra and the other animals]. Turin: Cosmopolis.

Troiano, C. (2017) *Rapporto Zoomafia 2017* [Zoomafia report 2017]. Rome: LAV.

Troiano, C. (2018) *Rapporto Zoomafia 2018* [Zoomafia report 2018]. Rome: LAV.

Troiano, C. (2020) *Il maltrattamento organizzato di animali – Manuale contro I crimini zoomafiosi* [The organized abuse of animals. Manual against zoomafia crimes]. Rome: LAV.

Troiano, C. (2021) *Rapporto Zoomafia 2021* [Zoomafia report 2021]. Rome: LAV.

Troiano, C. (2022) *Rapporto Zoomafia 2022* [Zoomafia report 2022]. Rome: LAV.

van Uhm, D. P., South, N. and Wyatt, T. (2021) Connections between trades and trafficking in wildlife and drugs. *Trends in Organised Crime* 24: 425–46.

White, R. (2008) *Crimes Against Nature: Environmental criminology and ecological justice*. Abingdon: Routledge.

White, R. (2011) *Transnational Environmental Crime: Toward an eco-global criminology*. London: Routledge.

White, R. (2015) Environmental Victimology and Ecological Justice. In D. Wilson and S. Ross (eds) *Crime, Victims and Policy* (pp 33–52). London: Palgrave Macmillan.

Wilson, E. O. (1986) *Biophilia*. Cambridge, MA: Harvard University Press.

Wilson, E. O. (2002) *The Future of Life*. New York: Knopf.

Wyatt, T. (2013a) Uncovering the Significance of and Motivation for Wildlife Trafficking. In N. South and A. Brisman (eds) *Routledge International Handbook of Green Criminology* (pp 319–32). London: Routledge.

Wyatt, T. (2013b) The security implications of the illegal wildlife trade. *CRIMSOC: The Journal of Social Criminology. Special Issue: 'Green Criminology'*, Autumn: 130–58.

Wyatt, T., Maher, J., Allen, D., Clarke, N. and Rook, D. (2022a) The welfare of wildlife: an interdisciplinary analysis of harm in the legal and illegal wildlife trades and possible ways forward. *Crime Law and Social Change* 77: 69–89.

Wyatt, T., Weedy, A. and Walling-Wefelmeyer, R. (2022b) Restorative justice and empathy-based interventions for animal welfare and wildlife crimes. Published by the Scottish Government. Available at www.gov.scot

Zaffaroni, E. R. (2012) *La Pachamama y el humano*. Buenos Aires: Ediciones Madres de Plaza de Mayo.

6

Analysis of Social and Legal Factors Influencing the Effectiveness of Tackling the Illegal Killing of Wolves in Poland

Piotr J. Chmielewski and Agnieszka Serlikowska

Introduction

In this chapter, we aim to answer three main research questions concerning the social and legal factors that affect the fight against the illegal killing of wolves in Poland: What factors influence the jurisprudence of this country's courts in cases concerning these theriocides? What social factors entail that the illegal killing of wolves may be tolerated by the general public in Poland? Finally, what are the greatest difficulties facing law enforcement agencies in effectively counteracting the illegal killing of wolves in this country?

The data obtained for this study were acquired from a scientific literature review, and analysis of law and court judgments published in the Commercial Law Information Systems mostly used in Poland (Grobelny and Wysocki 2018) as well as on the portal of Polish common courts' judgments (http://orzeczenia.ms.gov.pl) and websites of wildlife foundations that monitor such cases (that is, Stowarzyszenie 'Z Szarym za Płotem', Fundacja WWF Polska, Stowarzyszenie dla Natury 'Wilk'). The current standardized texts of legal Acts were obtained via access to the Internet Legal Acts System (ISAP). It should be noted that there are no official statistics for crimes related to protected species of wildlife, including wolves, in Poland, but wolf theriocides reported by the general public to the law enforcement authorities in Poland every year are significant and increasing (Paquel 2016).

Research conducted by Nowak et al (2021) showed that between 2002 and 2020 there were 91 cases of slain wolves, of whom 54 (59.3 per cent) were shot and 37 (40.7 per cent) trapped. The illegal shooting occurred in the geographical ranges of all wolf populations that are present in Poland: Central European, Baltic and Carpathian. These figures are not reflected in official statistics, and even less in the outcomes of proceedings involving prosecutions or court judgments. According to studies conducted in 2017, the number of people convicted each year by criminal courts for crimes against animals (both domestic and wild) has remained at a similar, low level since 2010. For example, in 2017, 1,869 people were convicted for crimes against animals; in 2016 the number was 1,673; in 2015 it was 1,846 (Czarna Owca Foundation 2018). When it comes to the crime of possessing, producing or collecting tools used for poaching (irrespective of whether they were used to kill an individual of a species that it is permitted to hunt or a protected animal such as a wolf) only nine people were convicted in 2019 in Poland (Polish Ministry of Justice statistics).[1]

Methodology

To decipher the arguments of judges, prosecutors and police officers regarding the low conviction rates, we searched the above-mentioned law information systems, using keywords such as culling [in Polish language: *zabicie zwierzęcia*], poaching [Polish *kłusownictwo*] and wolf [Polish *wilk*], analysing published rulings or at least credible references to them. The study was conducted on a sample purposely selected by searching judgments and decisions to prosecute not only by the aforementioned key terms and all crimes against animals in external legal databases, but also on the webpages of wildlife foundations active in Poland that monitor such cases (WWF Poland, Stowarzyszenie dla Natury 'Wilk'). In Poland there is no legal obligation to publish all judgments, and because of that we had to select the judgments deliberately among those published. First, we analysed records about rulings in commercial and public law information systems or at least credible references to them in the timeframe from 7 July 1922 to 6 April 2022. At the beginning we enlisted 58 rulings and decisions that could be related to illegal killings of wolves in Poland. After the preliminary analysis, we identified six cases of illegal killings of wolves (including two at a preliminary – police and prosecution – stage), one case of destroying wolves' prey base, two cases concerning transporting or trading of wolf

---

[1] Polish Ministry of Justice statistics, received on 11 April 2022 (motion based on act on access to public information).

trophies and 22 involving general, unspecified 'poaching acts' (aimed generally towards wildlife that could include wolves), mostly breaches of the hunting law or damage to the natural environment according to the Polish Penal Code (Art 182).[2] It should be noted that because of the formal character of crimes described in the Polish Hunting Law and the vague definition of 'environment' in the Polish Penal Code, it was impossible to assess which animals could have fallen victim to those crimes.[3] By formal crimes, we refer to crimes consummated by mere attempt or proposal/ overt act. If somebody is charged with a crime of possessing, producing or collecting tools used for poaching, nobody is checking whether they wanted to use them to kill a wolf or a deer. They are punished only because they have tools to do that. Because of environmental factors and the general descriptions of the crimes in these court rulings, it is possible that these crimes also were related to wolves. That is why those cases were also included in our study.

When it comes to identifying social factors, we focused on the results of public opinion polls, literature, NGO workshops and expert panel discussions.

The legal status of wolves in Poland

Wolves in Poland have a long and rich history of population changes. The first historical writings on livestock damage caused by wolves and attacks on man may be found in the archives of the Grand Duchy of Poznań in the first half of the 19th century (Okarma 2015). This period was a time when wolves were systematically eradicated (a situation that lasted during the partitions of Poland) via various methods (mass hunting, poisoning, and so on). Later, it is worth mentioning the Tsar's decree of 1846 on the extermination of wolves. Similarly to Norway (Sollund and Goyes 2021; Lie, this volume), under the provisions of this Act, *poviat* (county) tax offices paid bonuses for killed wolves, and the required proof was the submission of the tail and wolf ears to the relevant authority (Okarma 2015; Hedemann 1936).

Despite their mass and often organized eradication, during the First World War, wolves extended their geographical range westwards and grew more abundant in the Polish part of the Carpathians (Okarma 2015; Świętorzecki 1926). After the First World War and the proclamation of Polish independence, according to the new Polish hunting law of 3 December 1927, wolves were defined as a huntable species. This enactment allowed

---

[2] Polish Penal Code (Act of 6 June 1997 Penal Code, consolidated text, *Journal of Laws of 2022*, item 1138, as amended).

[3] Polish Hunting Law (Act of 13 October 1995 Hunting Law, consolidated text, *Journal of Laws of 2023*, item 1082, as amended).

hunting for wolves throughout the year. The aforementioned hunting law defined the wolf as an absolute 'pest' that could be hunted with various kinds of traps (Okarma 2015).

During the Second World War, wolves in Poland again managed to rebuild their population and extend their range beyond the Vistula River (Okarma 2015). Due to increased injury to farm animals in Poland, a resolution of the Council of Ministers regarding the start of extermination of wolves was issued in 1955. Under its provisions, an obligation was imposed on Voivodeship National Councils to take steps to exterminate this species. A catalogue of monetary rewards for specific forms of killing wolves was introduced (that is, PLN 1,000 for killing a wolf during an individual hunt, PLN 500 for killing a wolf during a group hunt, and PLN 200 for a wolf pup taken from the den) (Okarma 2015).

Wolves were excluded from the list of huntable species, pursuant to the Ordinance of the Minister of Forestry of 26 February 1955, on the implementation of Resolution No. 75 of the Government Presidium of 29 January 1955 on the extermination of wolves. At that time, they were neither under the status of huntable nor legally protected species, meaning that wolves could be hunted freely without any regulations of the hunt. Subsequently, in January 1956, the Regulation of the Ministry for Forestry and Timber Industry was published establishing commissioners for the extermination of wolves. In the following years the rewards for killing wolves grew (Okarma 1992, 2015).

Due to the aforementioned extermination policy, the number of wolves in Poland decreased drastically to around 100 individuals by 1970 (Okarma 2015; Śmietana 2019). Many statements emerged from various scientific sources about the need to introduce a protective period for the wolf, otherwise this species might have been completely eradicated in Poland (Sumiński 1973; Buchalczyk 1972; Klarowski 1973; Okarma 2015). In the first phase of the wolf eradication programme, the extermination of wolves was mitigated by establishing a Regulation of the Ministry of Forestry and Timber Industry of 5 July 1973, regarding the reduction of wolves. The regulation established that the state forest authorities were responsible for the number of wolves (Okarma 2015).

The second phase included re-entering the wolf onto the list of huntable species under the Regulation of the Ministry of Forestry and Wood Industry of 17 November 1975. The regulation introduced a hunting season running from 1 August to 31 March, except for the Krosno, Nowy Sącz and Przemyśl voivodeships, where all-year hunting was allowed. A protective period was introduced in 1981 under the provisions of the Regulation of the Ministry of Forestry and Wood Industry of 30 December 1981 (Okarma 2015).

Wolves became a protected species for the first time in 1992 in the Poznań voivodeship thanks to the Regulation of Poznań Voivode on 13 April 1992 and the Polish Act on Nature Conservation from 1991. During the same year, wolves gained the status of protected species in the Gorzów Wielkopolski and Piła voivodeships (Figura and Mysłajek 2019; Bereszyński 1998). It was also influenced by the introduction of two international conventions in Poland – the Convention on Biological Diversity (CBD) and the Convention on the Conservation of European Wildlife and Natural Habitats (Bern Convention). In March 1995, the government signed the Bern Convention but with a reservation that in Poland wolves would not be 'strictly protected', although they are listed in the convention's Appendix II of 'strictly protected fauna species' (Niedziałkowski and Putkowska-Smoter 2020).

Nevertheless, wolves in Poland became a strictly protected species in 1998, under the Regulation of the Ministry of Environmental Protection, Natural Resources and Forestry of 2 April 1998 (Okarma 2015). In the justification for this decision, the positive role of wolves in maintaining the ecological balance in forests was emphasized. The current legal status of the wolf is regulated by the Nature Conservation Act and the Regulation of the Minister of the Environment of 16 December 2016, on the protection of animal species.[4] According to these, wolves are strictly protected. It is forbidden to kill, mutilate, capture, keep, destroy the burrows and abduct puppies from them, as well as to store and sell pelts and other fragments of dead individuals without proper permission. Any violation of the rules governing the voluntary and involuntary acquisition of protected species is punishable by from three months' up to five years' imprisonment (Art 127a), with additional punitive measures related to damages for animal protection purposes (Art 129).

In addition, protection zones can be created for them around breeding sites (dens) in the period from 1 April to 31 August. The above prohibitions do not apply to situations where it is necessary to capture wounded and weakened animals in order to provide them with veterinary assistance and move them to a rehabilitation centre, or when it is necessary to catch an animal that has strayed near human settlements and return it to where it usually lives. In special cases, deviations from the above prohibitions are possible on the basis of a permit issued by the General Director for Environmental Protection.

A thorough analysis of the Polish legal system shows that these are not the only regulations related to wolf protection. As for Polish criminal regulations, we can distinguish four different types of statutes as sources of legislation that should be considered as factors influencing the efficiency with which the illegal killing of wolves is prosecuted: the above-mentioned Nature Conservation Act, the Polish Criminal Code, the Animal Protection

---

[4] Regulation of the Polish Minister of the Environment of 16 December 2016 on the protection of species animals (*Journal of Laws of 2022*, item 2380, with further amendments).

Act, and the Hunting Law Act (a multitude of regulations is also followed by a lack of consistency between them regarding illegal wolf killings). The fact that wolves are supposedly protected under all these different Acts is a possible source of confusion regarding which should be applicable when it comes to wolf theriocides or other human activities that harm these animals.

For example, according to the Polish legal framework, it is forbidden to hunt wolves (Kosierb 2021). However, as mentioned, actions that are considered crimes in the Hunting Law, such as possessing, producing or collecting tools used for poaching, can also concern wolves. In case of those Acts, trying to poach is sufficient to be sentenced. This also means that there is no need to prove what animals one was planning to poach or did poach. As a result, the regulation of poaching in the Hunting Law can also be aimed at wolves (which it is forbidden to hunt), even though theoretically wolves are not protected by the Hunting Law because they are not a huntable species. On the other hand, the Animal Protection Act is the basic legal framework concerning animal welfare in Poland. It clearly states that no animals are things; they are living beings, capable of feeling pain, and therefore humans owe them respect, protection and help (Art 1.1). This Act defines wildlife as undomesticated animal species independent of human activity (Art 4, p 21) that are a national good and (therefore) should be provided with conditions for development and free existence (Art 21). This is the basic Act when it comes to describing crimes of killing animals. A stipulated penalty for this kind of behaviour is imprisonment for up to three years, and when it comes to particularly cruel violations – from three months up to five years (Arts 35.1 and 2).

Last, but not least there is another regulation in Polish law that is used for the illegal killing of wolves. This is Art 181 of the Polish Penal Code that deals with crime that causes (undefined) environmental damage concerning both fauna and flora. The penalty for such actions is from six months up to eight years imprisonment or a fine, restriction of liberty or imprisonment from three months up to three years in the event of destruction or damage caused to protected plants or animals.

This basic description of regulations related to the illegal killing of wolves leads to preliminary conclusions. The system of crimes concerning wildlife in Poland is complicated and vague. It is difficult to predict which type of Act will be applicable when it comes to potentially punishable acts concerning a particular animal, especially when it is under the special protection of the law. Based on our analysis of court and prosecution rulings, the base still seems to be the Polish Penal Code. As noticed by Kulik, as a rule, it should be assumed that the provisions from Art 181 of this Act excludes the application of regulations from the Hunting Law, the Animal Protection Act, and so on. The actual coincidence and cumulative qualification occur between the commented provisions on wilful damage to nature and the provision of Art 288 of the Polish Penal Code (crime against property). The latter protects property and its hallmark is damage to property, which does not occur under Art 181 of the Polish Penal Code. What is more, a cumulative overlap of the provision of Art 181 §3 (destruction or damage to an organism under protection) under Art 288 §1 in connection with Art 294 §2 of the Polish Penal Code (destruction or damage to an item constituting a good of special importance for culture) is also possible in cases of wolf theriocides. It seems that a valuable 'individual' of nature, such as a wolf, can be considered such a good (Kulik 2022). There is a double qualification by prosecutors and courts in which there is a combination of Art 181 and Art 288, which concerns property and property damage – and it happens that this also applies to wolves, that the financial damage to the State Treasury is calculated in connection with the killing of an animal. The 'property aspect' can be crucial when it comes to further considerations related to legal factors that affect the effectiveness of the enforcement of legal provisions related to wildlife crime. Kuszlewicz and Kulik point out that coincidence and cumulative qualification within many regulations related to animal law is an extremely complex matter (Kuszlewicz 2021; Kulik 2022). As Kuszlewicz noted,

> all of the above-mentioned legal acts protect animals, but are of different qualitative natures and, in principle, each time they require consideration of whether, in a given situation, there will be a real and appropriate confluence of criminal provisions, implying a cumulative criminal classification of the act, or whether, based on specialty or consumption, one provision will be excluded by the second. (Kuszlewicz 2021)

The implementation of CITES and the Bern Convention in Poland

Somewhere between those four above-mentioned Acts, is the Convention on International Trade in Endangered Species of Wild Fauna and Flora – CITES Washington Convention. In Poland, CITES entered into force on 12 March 1990, and was ratified on 12 December 1989. However, some of the provisions of the convention were implemented in the Polish legal system through the Act of 16 April 2004 on nature conservation[5] at the same time as Poland's accession to the European Union (1 May 2004). Some of

---

[5] Polish Nature Conservation Act (Act of 16 April 2004 on nature conservation, consolidated text, *Journal of Laws of 2023*, item 1336, as amended).

the regulations were applicable earlier, while others still do not have a direct reference in Polish law, and others still are dispersed throughout different Acts (Kepel and Kala 2016). These tasks of Management Authorities are assigned to the Customs Service, the Border Guard and the police. Designated officers, referred to as 'CITES coordinators' operate within the police and customs structures (Duda 2021).

The Ministry of Environment is the national authority responsible for wolf management. There is no official legal hunting of wolves, but the Ministry can issue permits for the lethal control of some wolves in areas where they cause excessive damages to livestock (Salvatori and Linnell 2005). There is also a provision in the Nature Conservation Act (Art 56(1)(1)), which allows the General Director for Environmental Protection to issue administrative permissions for the killing of wolves that pose a significant threat to human health or livelihood or cause significant damage to livestock. A small number of such permits are issued annually. Permits may be issued in the absence of alternative solutions, if they are not harmful to the preservation of the wolf population at the level of a favourable conservation status, as demanded by the Habitats Directive, and the applied livestock protection methods have proven ineffective. Applications for such derogations from bans in the field of species protection are always considered individually.

The anthropocentrism in regards to the concept of animal welfare is salient in all Polish regulations related to wolves as well as those implemented through the European Regulation on CITES. It is particularly visible in the already mentioned legal references to damage to property when it comes to causing harm to the environment. The killing of an animal is perceived as a financial loss for the nation that possessed it. According to the Polish Animal Protection Act, an animal is not a thing, yet in matters not covered by the Act, the legislation concerning property shall apply accordingly to animals.[6] This approach is particularly visible in the jurisprudence we have analysed. However, it should be noted that this does not change when it comes to individual species like wolves. Political discussion in Poland is mainly focused on animals that yield high profit, such as fur animals (Rejowska 2021) or those that are subjects of ritual slaughter (Mroczek 2021). In answers to parliamentary questions, the Polish Ministry of Environment consequently outlines the importance of preserving the wolf population in Poland and the rare issuance of permits derogating from the prohibition against the wilful killing of wild wolves.[7] It should be noted though, that the number of these permits seems to be increasing, but the lack of official statistics makes

---

[6] Polish Animal Protection Act (Act of 21 August 1997 on the protection of animals, consolidated text, *Journal of Laws of 2023*, item 1580, as amended).

[7] Polish Ministry of Environment interpellation answers – 30580, 31549, 21523.

it difficult to prove. In the years 2000–12, at least 49 wolves were affected by issuing such permits (10 were killed) (Reinhardt et al 2013). In the years 2012–14, eight such permits to kill wolves were issued and in four cases applications for such permits were dismissed. In the time period 2014–15, another seven decisions (permits) were issued regarding 17 wolves (six were killed). In 2016, a permit was issued to kill two wolves causing damage in Lutowiska (Subcarpathian Province). From January to April 2019, as many as seven permits were issued by the General Director of the Environmental Protection (GDEP) (Polish Ministry of Environment interpellations).

Jurisprudence of courts in cases related to the illegal killing of wolves

Of the nine rulings related to the wolf crimes (six illegal killings, one destroying wolves' prey base, two transporting or trading of wolf trophies), seven were made at the court level and two at the preliminary 'police and prosecution' stage. Both cases at the preliminary level concerned illegal killings and did not end up with charging somebody with a crime because of lack of evidence or knowledge about the potential perpetrators. All of the six killings were well known in local communities and condemned by the media (for example, the 'Kosy' case and the 'Miko' case').

One ruling involved the destruction of protected areas of wolf habitat, another – causing significant harm to animals' habitat by breaking up a wolf pack when killing a dominant male (the 'Kosy' case). Both acts were qualified as a crime of causing damage to the environment (Art 181 of Polish Penal Code). However, in the first, the accused was acquitted because of a lack of proof of actual damage (II Ka 374/13 from 24 October 2013), while in the second, the accused was acquitted but the reason is unknown (Kojzar 2023).[8] Another two cases were related to the same case (first instance and appeal) of a theriocide (shooting) of a two-year-old female wolf. Two perpetrators were found guilty of this act and sentenced, respectively, to eight and ten months' imprisonment suspended for a two-year probation period, fined 3,000 PLN and 8,000 PLN and given additional punitive measures (the forfeiture of weapons, ammunition, wolf pelts and making the judgment public) as well as having to pay 2,200 PLN in compensation for punitive damages. Most important here is the prosecution and courts' legal decision in regards to what Act should be applied in a case of shooting a female wolf, taking her pelt and disposing of the body – the perpetrators were found guilty of stealing property from the Regional Directorate for Environmental Protection and causing damage to the animal environment (Art 278.1 and 181.3 of Polish

---

[8] Media information from 28 September 2023 and final judgment.

Penal Code). What is more, the sentence mentions the financial value of a female wolf estimated at 'at least 2,200 PLN' which was explained by the second instance court as follows:

> If it [a wolf] cannot be obtained legally in Poland, then some measurement method had to be adopted and reasonably justified. The choice of prices in neighbouring countries [there is no information which ones] and adopting the lowest possible value is included in the postulate described in Art. 5 § 2 of the Polish Criminal Code. The value could be higher, but it could not be lower, so its definition is correct.

In another case, the killing of two wolves (of unknown sex) was qualified only as a crime of causing damage to the environment (Art 181 of the Polish Criminal Code); the defendants were found guilty and sentenced to three months of imprisonment (which was conditionally suspended for three years), a fine of 20,000 PLN and punitive damages for the National Fund for Environmental Protection and Water Management in the amount of 8,000 PLN. The court had the possibility to assess actual damage to the environment (not the financial value of the wolf as in the above-mentioned case) by using the opinions of environmental organizations as expert witness statements, but refrained from doing so (Nowak et al 2021). The two last cases that we identified concerned the import of wolf pelts where the alleged perpetrator was eventually found innocent (VI Ka 489/15 from 1 September 2015),[9] and possession of trophies from animals including a wolf where the accused was found guilty and sentenced to one year of imprisonment (II K 3/15 from 12 January 2015).[10]

The analysis of the collected judgments of courts in Poland showed that cases concerning the illegal killing of wolves are few compared to all cases of related crimes committed against wild animals (both those protected by law as endangered species and covered by a different legal regime), in particular concerning illegal killing and breaching prohibitions associated with protected animal species. An important factor related to the effectiveness of combating crimes against wolves (and other protected wildlife) is the lack of information available to the general public on the number of such cases and the outcome of related court decisions. Public knowledge about the number and nature of court decisions related to wildlife crimes can serve as a deterrent. If potential offenders are aware that these crimes are being taken seriously by the legal system and that there are severe consequences for

---

[9] https://sip.lex.pl/orzeczenia-i-pisma-urzedowe/orzeczenia-sadow/i-cgg-15-15-wyrok-sadu-okregowego-w-gliwicach-522376340

[10] https://orzeczenia.wabrzezno.sr.gov.pl/content/$N/151025300001006_II_K_000003_2015_Uz_2015-12-01_001

engaging in such activities, they may think twice before committing wildlife crimes. This can help prevent offences by instilling fear of punishment and increasing the perceived risk of getting caught. Lack of public information on wildlife crime cases can also hamper law enforcement efforts. When there is no centralized system to track and document these offences, it becomes difficult for authorities to identify patterns, allocate resources and prioritize investigations. Having a comprehensive database can aid law enforcement agencies in allocating resources effectively and investigating crimes more efficiently.

Data on crimes against wolves (and wildlife crime in general) are collected only for specific purposes (for example, Nowak et al 2021) and constitute only a fragment of the actual scale of this type of crime in Poland (Paquel 2016).

As mentioned at the beginning of this chapter, to broaden our scope of research we have also selected 22 court rulings concerning general poaching acts mostly breaching the Hunting Law, and crimes described in Art 182 of the Polish Penal Code (causing undefined damages to the environment), including cases where perpetrators used tools (such as snares), or where the area or crime scene could have been related to the presence of wolves, however in the judgments there was no specific information about the animal victims of those acts.

It should also be noted that there are single cases of involvement of environmental NGOs in court proceedings that deal with crimes against wolves in Poland. There are, for example, complaints brought by the WWF Poland and the 'Z Szarym za Płotem' Association in the preparatory proceedings regarding the shooting of a wolf near Wenecja near Morąg, and active participation of Stowarzyszenie dla Natury 'Wilk' in the initial proceedings in the cases of the poisoned wolves Kosy (a wolf that lived in the Roztoczański National Park) and Miko (shot in the forests near Kluczbork).

While NGOs can play a supportive role, including raising awareness, providing expertise and advocating for stronger policies, they typically rely on the authorities to enforce laws and prosecute offenders. If the relationship between NGOs and the authorities is not well established or if there is limited cooperation, it can hinder NGO participation in the prosecution of individual cases of illegal wolf killings. When engaging in legal action in such cases, NGOs may face challenges related to gathering evidence, navigating legal systems and ensuring the safety of their staff and volunteers. These factors can discourage some NGOs from actively participating in cases of wildlife crimes, including illegal shooting of wolves.

Court proceedings regarding the illegal killing of wolves are also characterized by the sporadic participation of experts in the field of wolf biology and ecology. What is more, the training in the legal protection of wild animals offered to specific groups – judges and assessors adjudicating in criminal departments, prosecutors and prosecutor's assessors – is too general and insufficient when it comes to wildlife crimes. The 'Legal protection of animals' course is the most well-known training coordinated by the National School of Judiciary and Public Prosecution. However, it does not cover the legal protection of wild animals (in particular those under species protection). It focuses on groups of animals with different legal statuses (pets, farm animals, animals used for entertainment, shows, films, special purposes) (National School of Judiciary and Public Prosecution 2022).

The lack of sources of information on Poland's participation in international cooperation (for example, information exchange and best practices) on counteracting the illegal killing of wolves (and other species under protection) is also worth mentioning. This applies to the work of bodies such as ENPE (European Network of Prosecutors for the Environment) and EUFJE (European Union Forum of Judges for the Environment). It is worth pointing out the involvement of the Customs and Tax Service and the Polish police in the fight against crime related to international trade in endangered species – including trophies from wolves and other large predatory mammals. An example is a workshop on counteracting wildlife crime against large predators, organized in October 2021 by the WWF Poland Foundation and the Białowieża National Park in Białowieża. One of the topics discussed was indeed the prevention of wolf poaching. Particular attention was paid to difficulties in identifying the perpetrators of such crimes, insufficient specialist training, lack of inter-institutional cooperation in counteracting wildlife crime, frequent staff rotation in the services involved, and the lack of a specialized formation to counteract wildlife crime in Poland (LIFE EuroLargeCarnivores 2021). (II K 121/16 from 8 June 2017, II Ka 338/17 from 7 November 2017).

Social factors and the general tolerance or intolerance of illegal killing of wolves in Poland

Illegal killing of wolves, apart from breaking the legal norms defined by criminal provisions, is also a significant social problem. This applies both to the issue of respecting the applicable legal norms as well as the social acceptance of the presence of wolves in a given area without potential conflicts. In Poland, the majority of the public is against the illegal killing of wolves, as confirmed in a survey conducted by Eurogroup for Animals (2020) which commissioned Savanta ComRes to conduct an opinion poll among six EU member states (France, Germany, Italy, Spain, Poland and Finland) to better understand public perceptions and attitudes towards wolf protection across Europe. Researchers interviewed 6,137 adults (aged 18+) in the aforementioned six European countries online between 11 and 17 February 2020 (Eurogroup for Animals 2020).

Regarding the possibility of killing wolves and its legality, respondents were asked to agree or disagree with this statement: 'Only the authorities should be able to issue permits and carry out the killing of wolves to protect farm animals where necessary'. In Poland, as many as 88 per cent of the respondents agreed with the above statement. This was the highest result compared to respondents from the other five countries. The same was the case of disagreement with this statement (8 per cent of respondents, the lowest result of all the countries) (Eurogroup for Animals 2020).

One of the question categories was also devoted to acceptance of killing wolves in various conflict situations. Table 6.1 presents the responses for Poland. It shows that based on this limited study, the majority of the general public in Poland is against the shooting of wolves in the country, even in conflict situations such as when a wolf attacks a farm animal. Only 5 per cent of respondents accept the shooting of a wolf for fur, and only 4 per cent of shooting a wolf for leisure (Eurogroup for Animals 2020).

Table 6.2 shows that in Poland a majority of the surveyed adult respondents say that it is rarely or never acceptable to kill wolves in any of the scenarios

Table 6.1: Acceptance of motivations for killing wolves

NET % Agree	Poland (n=1,049 persons)
Killing wolves that have attacked farm animals	38
Killing wolves to control their population size	37
Killing wolves to decrease the pressure on populations of other animals lower down the food chain (for example, deer or hares)	30
Killing wolves for their fur	5
Killing wolves for leisure	4

Table 6.2: Disagreement with motivations for killing wolves

NET % Rarely/never acceptable	Poland (n=1,049 persons)
Killing wolves that have attacked farm animals	57
Killing wolves to control their population size	57
Killing wolves to decrease the pressure on populations of other animals lower down the food chain (for example, deer or hares)	60
Killing wolves for their fur	92
Killing wolves for leisure	93

listed. The respondents also stated that they are the most likely to find it rarely/never acceptable to kill wolves for their fur (92 per cent) or leisure (93 per cent). This was similar to the responses from other countries (Eurogroup for Animals 2020).

A study by Gosling et al (2019) revealed that only 32 per cent of respondents – foresters and residents of rural areas of Augustów Forest, the Białowieża Forest, Bieszczady Mountains, Świętokrzyska Forest, Drawska Forest and Dolnośląskie Forest – thought that wolves should be under complete protection. Forty-seven per cent did not agree to the complete protection of this species. Over half – 55 per cent of the respondents – supported wolf hunting provided that it is seasonally limited, and 50 per cent of respondents believed that hunting should be limited to isolated areas. Only 11 per cent of the respondents were in favour of hunting wolves throughout the year. Foresters supported the total protection of wolves to a lesser extent than other residents and expressed greater support for seasonally and spatially limited wolf hunts (Gosling et al 2019).

Inhabitants of the areas located west of the Vistula had a more positive general attitude towards wolves than residents in areas located in the east of the country. An explanation of this might be that there are more farms in the east. Eastern Poland also has a longer history of human–wolf interaction. Factors negatively affecting opinions about wolf conservation are: living in the eastern part of the country, higher age of respondents, being a forester or hunter, and positive opinions about hunting. Eastern respondents and those with less knowledge about wolves were more afraid of these predators (Gosling et al 2019). A study by Olszańska (2012) has shown that over 80 per cent of hunters and almost 60 per cent of foresters were against the strict protection of wolves in Poland. Paradoxically, these groups had the most knowledge of wolf biology and ecology and the least fear of wolves. Groups with less knowledge of this species – teenagers and farmers – manifested greater fear of wolves. The aforementioned study shows that over 15 per cent of farmers and 11 per cent of teenagers believed that 'wolf attacks on humans are common' (Olszańska 2012).

The differences between the views of the general public (including representatives of urban centres) and smaller villages located in wolf areas are confirmed by meetings during workshops organized by the LIFE EuroLargeCarnivores project entitled 'Improving coexistence with large carnivores in Europe through communication, cross-border cooperation and knowledge exchange'. Inhabitants of smaller villages (in particular livestock farmers) said that 'they have nothing against wolves, but do not want to be harmed by them' (Berchi 2018). Another example is a conversation during one of the workshops on communicating on the topic of the cohabitation of people with wolves, which took place in Iłowa (Lubusz voivodeship) in October 2019, where one of the hunters explicitly admitted that he knew a person who illegally shot a wolf since he treated him as a competitor in killing 'game' (LIFE EuroLargeCarnivores 2019).

At a nationwide workshop on counteracting crimes against large predators in Białowieża (October 2021), the participants discussed, inter alia, the biggest problems in detecting these crimes. The workshop was attended by officers of the Customs and Tax Service and representatives of the Provincial Police Headquarters. In the plenary discussion, it was said that the key problem is the lack of cooperation between representatives of the local community and law enforcement authorities, and the existing 'conspiracy of silence' in cases of poaching, which is also often covered up because of local ties between different people who often play important roles in local communities (LIFE EuroLargeCarnivores 2021)

Conclusion

The main goal of this chapter was to answer three main research questions: What factors influence the jurisprudence of this country's courts in cases concerning these theriocides? What social factors entail that the illegal killing of wolves may be tolerated by the general public in Poland? Finally, what are the greatest difficulties facing law enforcement agencies in effectively counteracting the illegal killing of wolves in this country? The analysis leads to the conclusion that the Polish legal framework is not harmonized, but complicated when it comes to criminal regulations related to wolf protection, and that the courts have an anthropocentric approach to wolf theriocides. Legal standards for the protection of wolves are scattered among various types of Acts, and there is no uniform approach in the legislation. Moreover, penal sanctions for killing wolves are constructed in an anthropocentric way. Law, jurisprudence and the approach taken by the prosecutor's offices show a financial approach to killed animals, which means that it is valued as material damage to the State. An important factor is also the lack of coordinated activities from public authorities and official statistics concerning wolf killings, and rare court rulings that do not meet the basic rule of criminal law – the inevitability of punishment. A relatively small number of rulings strictly concerning wolf crimes translate into a lack of learning and specialization in these cases for law enforcement authorities and judges.

Social factors that influence whether illegal killing of wolves may be tolerated by the general public in Poland are the place of residence (influenced by the probability of interaction with a wolf), the possibility of a conflict situation (wolf depredation of farm animals) and socio-demographic characteristics – age, gender, level of education and occupation. However, as was stated previously, the majority of the general public in Poland is against the shooting of wolves in the country, even in conflict situations such as when a wolf attacks a farm animal.

The greatest difficulties facing law enforcement agencies in effectively counteracting the illegal killing of wolves in Poland confirms the findings of Paquel (2016), who argues that in terms of wildlife crime (although of a different kind, CITES-related cases), Polish courts close the cases in the early phase or impose low penalties in the final verdicts. Furthermore, such judicial action does not have a deterrent effect for the potential perpetrators of similar crimes (Paquel 2016). Analysis of the jurisprudence also confirms Paquel's findings of the insufficient knowledge and environmental awareness of Polish judges in terms of violations of nature conservation law in general. It needs to be noted again that we were analysing records about rulings that are available in commercial and public law information systems or at least credible references to them in the timeframe from 7 July 1922 to 6 April 2022, and we found only a few cases, including those that were made at the preliminary stage. This low number of published cases can create a false impression that crimes against wolves are something rare, niche in Poland, which can create a vicious circle. The small number of rulings creates an impression that these offences are not so important in comparison to other types of crimes, especially those concerning humans, business or state, therefore there are almost no experts on crimes against wolves among judges or prosecutors, because it seems that there is no 'need' for such expertise. This lack of prioritization and expertise subsequently leads to poor investigation and prosecution and few convictions in these cases.

References

Berchi, G. M. 2018. LIFE EuroLargeCarnivores: Improving coexistence with large carnivores in Europe through communication and transboundary cooperation. WWF Romania. Available at www.carpathianconvention.org/tl_files/carpathiancon/Downloads/03%20Meetings%20and%20Events/Working%20Groups/Biodiversity/10th%20WG%20Biodiveristy/presentations/2Gavril%20Marius%20Berchi-Life%20EuroLargeCarnivores%20Project.pdf

Bereszyński, A. 1998. *Wilk (Canis lupus Linnaeus, 1758) w Polsce i jego ochrona*. Wydawnictwo Akademii Rolniczej w Poznaniu.

Buchalczyk, T. 1972. O nowy stosunek do drapieżników i niektórych szkodników łowieckich. *Łowiec Polski* 9, pp 14–16.

Czarna Owca Foundation. 2018. Raport 'Osadzeni za zwierzęta. Monitoring wykonywania kar'. [Report 'Sentenced for the crimes against animals. The analysis of the execution of criminal penalties']. Available at https://czarnaowca.org/wp-content/uploads/CzarnaOwca-%E2%80%93-Osadzeni-za-zwierzeta.pdf

Duda, M. A. 2021. CITES crimes in Poland: causes, manifestations, counteracting. *Studia Prawnoustrojowe* 52, pp 67–83.

Eurogroup for Animals. 2020. Wolf Protection Research – Europe. Available at www.eurogroupforanimals.org/news/wolves-eu-risk-having-protection-downgraded

Figura, M., Mysłajek, R. W. 2019. Canis lupus politicus – dyskurs polityczny związany z ochroną wilka we współczesnej Polsce. *Zoophilologica. Polish Journal of Animal Studies* 5, pp 367–79.

Gosling, E., Bojarska, K., Gula, R., and Kuehn, R. 2019. Recent arrivals or established tenants? History of wolf presence influences attitudes toward the carnivore, *Wildlife Society Bulletin* 43(4), pp 639–50.

Grobelny, M., and Wysocki, R. 2018. A comparison of Polish law information systems. *Annales Universitatis Apulensis Series Jurisprudentia*, 21, pp 409–24.

Hedemann, O. 1936. Z dawnej Białowieży [:] O uszach i ogonach wilczych. *Echa Leśne* 13(1), pp 4–5.

Kepel, A., and Kala, B. 2016. *CITES w Polsce i Unii Europejskiej: podręcznik dla praktyków*. Poznań.

Klarowski, R. 1973. Wilkowi grozi wymarcie. *Chrońmy Przyrodę Ojczystą* 6, pp 66–7.

Kojzar, K. 2023. Kosy zginął od strzału z broni palnej. Myśliwy, oskarżony o zabicie wilka, został uniewinniony. OKO.Press, 29 September. Available at https://oko.press/wilk-zginal-od-strzalu-z-broni-wyrok

Kosierb, I. 2021. *Kodeks wykroczeń. Komentarz*, J. Lachowski (ed), Warsaw: Wolters Kluwer, art 165.

Kulik, M. 2022. *Kodeks karny. Komentarz aktualizowany*. M. Mozgawa (ed), Warsaw: Wolters Kluwer, art 181.

Kuszlewicz, K. 2021.*Ustawa o ochronie zwierząt: Komentarz*. Wolters Kluwer Polska.

LIFE EuroLargeCarnivores. 2019. Mejorar la convivencia con grandes carnívoros. Available at www.wwf.es/nuestro_trabajo/especies_y_habitats/grandes_carnivoros_europeos_/

LIFE EuroLargeCarnivores. 2021. Layman Report. Available at www.eurolargecarnivores.eu/fr/layman-report

Mroczek, R. 2021. Religious slaughter of animals in Poland. *Zagadnienia Ekonomiki Rolnej/Problems of Agricultural Economics* 1.

National School for Judiciary and Prosecution. Training programmes. Available at www.kssip.gov.pl/szkolenia

Niedziałkowski, Krzysztof, and Putkowska-Smoter, R. 2020. What makes a major change of wildlife management policy possible? Institutional analysis of Polish wolf governance. *PloS One* 15(4): e0231601. https://journals.plos.org/plosone/article?id=10.1371/journal.pone.0231601

Niedziałkowski, K., Konopka, A., and Putkowska-Smoter, R. 2021. To hunt or to protect? Discourse-coalitions in the Polish wolf management. *Conservation and Society* 19(2), pp 91–100.

Nowak, S., Żmihorski, M., Figura, M., Stachyra, P., and Mysłajek, R. W. 2021. The illegal shooting and snaring of legally protected wolves in Poland. *Biological Conservation* 264.

Okarma, H. 1992. *Wilk monografia przyrodniczo-łowiecka*. Białowieża.

Okarma, H. 2015. *Wilk. Biblioteka przyrodniczo-łowiecka*. Kraków: H_2O Publishing House.

Olszańska, A. 2012. Comparison of attitudes of the key interest groups toward the wolf (*Canis lupus*) and the Eurasian lynx (*Lynx lynx*) conservation in Poland. PhD thesis, Jagiellonian University, Kraków.

Paquel, K. 2016. Wildlife crime in Poland: In-depth analysis for the ENVI-Committee. European Parliament. https://data.europa.eu/doi/10.2861/706830

Reinhardt, I., Kluth, G., Nowak, S. and Mysłajek, R. 2013. *A Review of Wolf Management in Poland and Germany with Recommendations for Future Transboundary Collaboration*. Bundesamt für Naturschutz (BfN) Federal Agency for Nature Conservation.

Rejowska, A. 2021. Material culture as a tool of anthropological exploration: fur and the polarization of Polish society. *Cargo Journal* 17(1–2).

Salvatori, V., and Linnell, J. 2005. Report on the Conservation Status and Threats for Wolf (Canis lupus) in Europe. Available at www.euronatur.org/fileadmin/docs/arten/infl6e_2005_Conservation_Threats_Wolf1.pdf

Śmietana, W. 2019. Presentation at the seminar 'Pilotażowy monitoring wilka i rysia w Polsce realizowany w ramach Państwowego Monitoringu Środowiska'. Available at www.gov.pl/web/gios/poiis---monitoring-wilka-i-rysia

Sollund, R., and Goyes, D. 2021. State-organized crime and the killing of wolves in Norway. *Trends in Organanized Crime* 24, pp 467–84.

Sumiński, P. 1973. 'The wolf in Poland'. In *Proceedings of the First Working Meeting of Wolf Specialists and of the First International Conference on the Wolf, Stockholm, September*. Morges, Switzerland: IUCN, pp 44–52.

Świętorzecki, B. 1926. *Wilk monografia*. Warsaw.

7

CITES in Spain: Blueprints and Challenges of Spanish Practice on CITES and Welfare of Trafficked Victims

Teresa Fajardo

Introduction

Almost 50 years after its adoption, the Convention on International Trade in Endangered Species of Wild Fauna and Flora (CITES hereinafter) is much more than a treaty on wildlife trade. In 1973, the priority objective of its States Parties was not the protection of biodiversity, but 50 years later it is, as they have stated in their Strategic Vision 2021–30 (COP18 2019; COP19 2022). As its former Secretary General, John Scanlon, said: 'CITES is both a trade and a conservation convention that uses trade-related measures to achieve its conservation objectives. It is also the first, and possibly remains the only, global legal instrument to directly address animal welfare, albeit in relation to a limited number of issues' (2015). He also remarked that

> to date, States have considered that most animal welfare issues should be addressed through domestic law rather than international law and there is currently no global treaty governing either animal welfare or animal rights. It is perhaps partly for this reason that CITES often serves as a forum for the expression of a wide range of differing views on international trade in wild animals, including on particular trade transactions, whether all of the actions sought by various actors fall under the current mandate of CITES or not. (Scanlon 2015)

The project Criminal Justice, Wildlife Conservation and Animal Rights in the Anthropocene (CRIMEANTHROP project hereinafter) led by Professor Ragnhild A. Sollund is a groundbreaking example of academic research that opens a new debate on CITES. CRIMEANTHROP 'explores the regulation, rationale behind and enforcement of wildlife conservation, the normative and socio-legal messages of this enforcement, and their implications for wildlife conservation and individual animal welfare' (Sollund 2022). This chapter contributes to the debate led by Sollund with a reflection on the adaptability of this international treaty on trade to a vision constantly renewed at their Conferences of the Parties from 2000 up to now (COP hereinafter). It stands out that the CITES Vision Statement adopted by the COP16 urged States to 'Conserve biodiversity and contribute to its sustainable use by ensuring that no species of wild fauna or flora is or remains subject to unsustainable exploitation through international trade, thereby contributing to a significant reduction in the rate of biodiversity loss' (COP16, Bangkok 2013). This statement was renewed at the COP17, when the Strategic Vision was amended to refer to the Sustainable Development Goals and the targets of the 2030 Agenda for Sustainable Development (COP17, Johannesburg 2016). The current Strategic Vision 2021–30 affirms that 'CITES stands at the intersection between trade, the environment and development, promotes the conservation and sustainable use of biodiversity, should contribute to tangible benefits for indigenous peoples and local communities, and ensure that no species is threatened with extinction by entering into international trade' (COP18, Geneva 2019; COP19, Panama 2022). Based on this vision of CITES (established in COP18 and updated in COP19), this chapter presents the practice of CITES in Spain. Thus, this chapter will raise the matters of CRIMEANTHROP while acknowledging that some of them lie outside of the current remit of the Convention (Scanlon 2015) and the national legal frameworks that develop it. They are in any case the inspiration for the changes that can be achieved in CITES and the necessary requirements for the evaluation of their results.

The need to update and review the debate on the relationship between trade and environment in the CITES framework has led its State Parties to assume new priorities, within the broader framework of biodiversity conservation. Thus, the last CITES Strategic Vision 2021–30 states that the objective of the convention is to '[c]onserve biodiversity and contribute to its sustainable use by ensuring that no species of wild fauna or flora becomes or remains subject to unsustainable exploitation through international trade, thereby contributing to the significant reduction of the rate of biodiversity loss' (COP18, Geneva 2019; COP19, Panama 2022). This new vision updates the mandate from the convention text and its resolutions and decisions and will be further developed by next COPs of CITES and other biodiversity-related conventions, in particular, the Framework Convention of Biological Diversity (CBD).[1] CITES has responded over the last decade to biodiversity conservation challenges embracing CBD's strategies that were incorporated into CITES' compliance monitoring mechanisms and its biennial compliance questionnaires to be submitted by States Parties. An example of this can be seen in the latest reports and questionnaires submitted by the Spanish CITES authorities on the state of implementation and enforcement of the convention in Spain, as will be seen below.

Now that the CBD's Kunming-Montreal COP has adopted new targets and a Strategy for the post-2020 period (CBD 2022), CITES has also taken on these new commitments. Thus, in the CBD COP15 celebrated in Kunming-Montreal in 2022, the CITES Secretary General renewed 'the commitment of CITES Parties to contribute to the implementation of the post 2020 Global Biodiversity Framework (GBF), through the implementation of CITES' and promised 'stronger cooperation as well as effective and efficient implementation of the GBF [which] will allow us all to play our parts in achieving the 2030 Agenda for Sustainable Development and its Sustainable Development Goals, and ensure that by 2050, the shared vision of living in harmony with nature is fulfilled' (CITES 2022). In addition to strengthening cooperation for the implementation and enforcement of both conventions, CITES and CBD are jointly responsible for the new Target 5 of the Kunming-Montreal GBF that calls on States Parties to ensure that the use, harvesting and trade of wild species is sustainable, safe and legal. This Target 5 fits in with the CITES Vision Statement by 2030 that seeks that all international trade in wild fauna and flora is legal and sustainable, consistent with the long-term conservation of species, and thereby contributing to halting biodiversity loss, to ensuring its sustainable use, and to achieving the 2030 Agenda for Sustainable Development. This melting pot discourse on trade and wildlife conservation is not only the result of institutional cooperation between conventions but has also been supported by States Parties in these conventions. This is seen in a growing involvement of the countries of origin of trade, which is reflected in the leadership that African countries will take at upcoming meetings where they will call for increased funding for national biodiversity conservation plans in line with what has already been decided at CBD COP15 and CITES COP19 (African Union 2023).

In these documents, which formulate the strategic policies of both conventions for the next decade, no reference is made to animal welfare, just a general mandate for its Parties to 'improve the conservation status of CITES-listed specimens, put in place national conservation actions, support

---

[1] Framework Convention on Biological Diversity, adopted 5 June 1992, entered into force 29 December 1993, 1760 UNTS 79.

their sustainable use and promote cooperation in managing shared wildlife resources' (CITES 2022). Although the mandate only refers to species listed in the CITES appendices and their appropriate conservation status, this already implies the assumption of a new narrative in which the discourses on sustainable development goals and biodiversity strategies converge.

Despite the latest policy and regulatory developments, CITES and European Union regulations on CITES still reflect an anthropocentric approach to wildlife, in which the interests of animals are not yet taken into account. The new European Union Action Plan on Wildlife Trafficking, adopted in November 2022 (WAP 2022 hereinafter), only refers to animal welfare in a footnote. Accordingly, the scales on which the value of biodiversity conservation and trade are weighed only take into account the social and economic values associated with the needs of local communities and Indigenous peoples, the value chain of products that bring resources to developing countries, and the utilitarian interests of the pharmaceutical, food and luxury industries and collectors. Unfortunately, the weight of the lives lost and the pain experienced by individuals of wild animal species during their extraction, trafficking and captivity – whether legal or illegal – has not yet been added to this scale, as Sollund has so often proposed (Sollund 2019, 2022; Sollund and Wyatt 2022).

Relevant changes are taking place in the way international and European wildlife trafficking regimes are interpreted and applied by international institutions and States. The update of CITES depends on its States Parties, which must succeed in transposing the CITES obligations into their domestic legal systems and comply with them in a complex process in which national CITES authorities, the police, judges and prosecutors, and above all citizens, must participate and cooperate. The ultimate addressees of CITES obligations, with the intermediation of the States, are the citizens, who are the ones who ultimately keep wildlife trade alive with their demand.

Spain joined CITES in 1986 as one of the many necessary requirements to join the European Union. Since then, Spain has developed a regulatory framework that goes further in the degree of protection it offers. In its compliance with its international CITES obligations, Spain has also taken into account the new trends that lead to the incorporation of the wildlife conservation principle provided for in the CBD. In Spain, there have recently been important changes in the enforcement of CITES regulations with the aim of ensuring that wildlife trade is sustainable and promoting conservation in the countries of origin. However, the welfare of victims of wildlife trafficking and animal rights are not considered directly in the Spanish legislation on wildlife trafficking (WLT hereinafter). Although animals are now considered sentient beings in the Spanish Civil Code (Albiez Dohrmann 2022), they are still objects of commerce, albeit with the protection of the general principle of animal welfare enshrined in the Spanish constitutional jurisprudence (Alonso García, 2011) and in Article 13 of the Treaty on the Functioning of the European Union.

Methodology

Unlike most of the contributions to the CRIMEANTHROP project, theoretically, this research is not presented in the framework of green criminology, but in that of International and European law and examines CITES enforcement by Spain (Fajardo et al 2015; Fuentes and Fajardo, 2020). Spain's performance at the national level in complying with its International and European obligations, allows us to identify strengths and weaknesses not only at the level of its internal compliance, but also, ambitiously, it serves to identify gaps and areas for improvement in the CITES Convention, the EU CITES Regulations and the EU Action Plan on Wildlife Trafficking 2016 (WAP 2016 hereinafter). These legal instruments were first analysed for the European Union Action to Fight Environmental Crime Project (EFFACE) in 2016. In this sense, this chapter is a continuation of the research initiated in that project and the reports presented to the European Parliament in 2016 (Sina et al 2016; Fajardo 2016). These were used to draw up the WAP 2016. The WAP 2016 required Member States to adopt National Plans to implement and develop the Regulation EC 338/97 on the protection of species of wild fauna and flora by regulating trade therein (EU CITES Regulation hereinafter) and recommendations according to their national circumstances. The WAP 2016 and EU CITES Regulation have been further implemented in Spain through the Spanish Action Plan against illegal trafficking and international poaching of wildlife species of 2018 (TIFIES Plan hereinafter). This chapter reviews, based on analysis of crime statistics, judgments and expert interviews, the implementation of the TIFIES Plan over the past five years. This research also draws on previous work done with Juan Fuentes on the implementation of the Environmental Crime Directive in Spain for the LIFE Guardians for Nature project (Fuentes and Fajardo 2020). The first results of the analyses of the implementation of CITES in Spain (Fajardo 2016; Fuentes and Fajardo 2020) showed that despite the achievements made in CITES enforcement by the Spanish CITES authorities, the Spanish police unit for the protection of nature (SEPRONA hereinafter) and the specialized environmental prosecutor's office in Spain, there were problems regarding an uneven interpretation and application of CITES legislation that, for example, led to years of accepting the illegal capture, killing, possession and trade of birds as a cultural practice, and other reasons that would interpret the grounds for acquittal of wildlife trafficking liberally, as examined below (Fuentes and Fajardo 2022). They also showed that there were limited human and economic resources to enforce it. Many CITES infractions were not prosecuted or were resolved with insignificant fines, classified as administrative infractions and not as criminal offences, as had been the case in other CITES State Parties (Sollund et al 2018, Sollund and Maher 2015; Stefes, this volume). The analysis has revealed that in the fight against environmental crime in Spain, the most notable strength of the Spanish model is the specialization of law enforcement agencies, in particular, the environmental prosecutor's office and SEPRONA. They have developed a modus operandi of cooperation to fight WLT with the CITES authorities that could serve as a model for other CITES States Parties and for EU and CITES institutions; and so, it was noted in the UNEP report on the state of the environmental rule of law (UNEP 2019: 46). However, one of the weaknesses detected is that personnel in the judicial system had little or no CITES-related training, as judges are not specialized in the Spanish judiciary. However, this issue is now one of the priorities of the new WAP 2022.

For this chapter I have conducted qualitative interviews with the heads of the CITES Management Authority at the Ministry for Ecological Transition and the Demographic Challenge (MITECO), members of SEPRONA and ENVICRIMENET, the unit under EUROPOL combating environmental crime, the Environmental Prosecutor's Office, and the Council of State and experts of NGOs such as WWF Spain[2] and SEO-Birdlife.[3] Participating in LIFE programme activities and projects such as LIFE Guardians of Nature and LIFE Successful Wildlife Crime Prosecution in Europe (SWIPE), has allowed me to discuss the implementation and enforcement of environmental legislation with SEPRONA agents, judges and prosecutors, representatives of NGOs and rescue centres for animal victims of trade. I have also participated in the teaching of courses on environmental crime in the Spanish Judicial School and in the Academy of European Law in Germany (ERA), which has allowed me to know the opinion of judges and prosecutors on the regulatory framework of EU environmental law and its application in Spain and in other EU countries.

Despite the annual publication of statistics on the environmental crime reports by the environmental prosecutor's office, the data are not disaggregated according to offences, so that those relating to the application of the CITES Convention are not specified (Fajardo et al 2015; Fuentes and Fajardo 2020; Spanish Prosecutor's Office for the Environment and Urban Planning 2021).[4] The data are not processed according to criminological criteria. Data protection rules also prevent existing data platforms from

---

[2] WWF España, www.wwf.es/
[3] Seo-Birdlife, Sociedad Española de Ornitología, Spanish Society of Ornithology, https://seo.org/
[4] In the case of Norway, the same situation exists (Sollund and Maher 2015; Maher and Sollund 2018; Sollund 2018, 2021, this volume).

incorporating personal data that would make it possible to identify repeat offenders in different EU countries.

This chapter also analyses the Spanish judicial decisions of the last 15 years in which the CITES Convention is applied, distinguishing the decisions in which Art 334 of the Criminal Code or Arts 2 and 11 of the Smuggling Act 1995 are applied. The judicial decisions analysed were the result of a search of the jurisprudential database of the official database of the General Council of the Judiciary of Spain (CENDOJ).

Spanish legislation on CITES

The incorporation of CITES into the Spanish legal system has been through European legislation, in particular, the so-called CITES Regulations. Regarding the rules for complying with CITES regulations and sanctioning infractions thereof, Spain has adopted a stricter although fragmented legal framework composed of administrative law and criminal regulations of the Criminal Code and the Smuggling Act 1995. The sanctioning system combines the administrative and criminal sanctions foreseen in the Smuggling Act 1995 and those of the Criminal Code. The fragmentation of this regulatory framework and the difficulty of getting to know it for all those involved in its application results in limited compliance and enforcement in practice by customs, law enforcement agents, prosecutors and judges, and above all citizens. This problem is shared with other EU member states and has been highlighted in the proposal for a new environmental crime directive (European Commission 2021).

CITES authorities and law enforcement agencies in Spain

The considerable success of CITES enforcement in Spain lies in the cooperation between all enforcement authorities (UNEP 2019): CITES authorities, SEPRONA and the Public Prosecutor's Office. Their cooperation has also been adapted to the conservation and increasing trade limitation requirements of the CITES Strategic Vision, the WAP 2016 and the TIFIES Plan.

The CITES authorities in Spain have undergone a substantive change that is in line with the CITES Strategic Vision to prioritize the principle of biodiversity conservation when controlling wildlife trade. The CITES authorities in Spain, which until 2021 were located in the Ministry of Economy, have been moved to the Ministry of Ecological Transition (MITECO). From January 2022, the CITES Management Authorities in charge of administering the licensing system are now attached to the MITECO and the Scientific Authorities that are to advise them on the effects of trade on the conservation status of the species, to the Spanish

National Research Council (CSIC) depending on the Ministry of Science and Innovation. These authorities ensure compliance with the obligations set out in the CITES Regulations and in the Spanish laws that further develop them. One of the main changes is the centralization of the relevant national CITES authorities that continue processing (requests for) import, (re-)export and intra-EU trade documents in Madrid headquarters, instead of the decentralized centres.

The CITES Management Authority controls legal trade ensuring it responds to the two main prerequisites for legal international trade under CITES. First, the non-detriment finding, 'in which a scientific authority is required to certify that the export of a given Appendix I or Appendix II species will not be detrimental to the survival of the species in the wild' (Korwin et al 2019: 275). Then, it regards the verification of legal acquisition, which involves a wide range of authorities in the country of export and destination, with complex internal permit control operations. These operations are especially challenging when the animal victims, derivatives and parts of animals were imported or transferred as part of a sale or inheritance, in unreferenced or uncertified time periods.[5] This verification process also requires cooperation with the authorities of origin. This avoids the laundering of wild individuals with those bred in captivity and the laundering of protected species with those that are not, as in the case of timber, as exposed in Operation Quercus (SEPRONA 2020). This operation gathered intelligence on illegal timber trade by carrying out systematic checks on suppliers and facilities involved in the import and export of timber, furniture manufacture, sawmills, manufacture and distribution of parquet, manufacture of musical instruments or wooden pallets. In the course of Operation Quercus, SEPRONA cooperated with authorities from Brazil, Portugal, Italy and Romania, among other European countries, through the European Multidisciplinary Platform Against Criminal Threats (EMPACT). Spain has developed a tool which allows an initial in situ identification of the species of timber being traded, which is now also used by a large number of CITES States Parties. However, the use of this tool has not reached its full potential due to the lack of inspectors and the limited number of customs inspections, as stood out in interviews with law enforcement agents.

SEPRONA is an example of a specialized police force, where members are trained and specialized throughout their careers. Economic crises have limited their human and material resources, which are spread thin with no increase in their numbers in recent years. SEPRONA has 1,850 operatives distributed in a Central Operational Unit for the Environment (UCOMA), 60 investigation teams located at the headquarters of each province and 300

---

[5] SAP B 1932/2020 – ECLI:ES:APB:2020:1932

off-road patrols distributed throughout the national territory (SEPRONA 2022). Despite the stalled number of SEPRONA personnel, the number of cases brought before the courts has increased, as shown in the annual reports of the Public Prosecutor's Office. The capacity of intervention is founded on a consolidated practice based on prevention and on criminal intelligence acquired through periodic controls of stakeholders such as pet-shop owners and breeders. SEPRONA's cooperation with EUROPOL and its section ENVICRIMINET has led them to consider new trends in environmental crime and organized crime that have not yet reached Spain but are already being used in Europe (Fuentes and Fajardo 2020;, SEPRONA 2021; SWIPE 2022). In 2022, SEPRONA created the National Central Office for the analysis of information on illegal environmental activities, in collaboration with MITECO, linked to the TIFIES Plan, which will be discussed later in the next section.

Unlike the judiciary, the public prosecutor's office has been specialized since 2006. In a mixed system of prosecution, the prosecutor is responsible for the charge and the procedure is the responsibility of the judge or court. There is no possibility of plea bargaining in environmental cases, however offenders can accept an agreement with the prosecutor's office after accepting criminal responsibility in the so-called procedure of *conformidad*. In the prosecution of environmental crimes, the difficulty in proving certain elements of the offence and its complexity explains why the prosecutor has a strong interest in reaching agreements of *conformidad*. However, in WLT cases, it is not common to find acceptance of criminal responsibility, since, although this implies a reduction of the sanction, it does not limit the disqualifications for the exercise of activities related to animals, and the loss of hunting and gun permits.

The implementation of CITES in Spain through the TIFIES Plan

Spain's major contribution to compliance with CITES is the TIFIES Plan. It was adopted two years after the European Commission presented the WAP 2016,[6] and it adapts it[7] to the reality of Spain as a country of origin,

---

[6] See Communication from the Commission to the European Parliament, the Council, the European Economic and Social Committee and the Committee of the Regions, EU Action Plan against Wildlife Trafficking, *COM(2016) 87 final*, 26 February 2016.

[7] See Resolution of 4 April 2018, Directorate-General for Environmental Quality and Assessment and the Natural Environment, which publishes the Agreement of Council of Ministers of 16 February 2018, approving the Spanish Action Plan against illegal trafficking and international poaching of wildlife species, *BOE Núm 87*, 10 April 2018, Sec III, pp 37365–83.

destination and transit of wildlife trade (Fajardo 2016, 2018). It has three priorities that address the major challenges of achieving WLT prevention, the best possible compliance with its regulatory framework and improved cooperation with countries of origin and transit. I will now introduce and comment on these priorities and their fulfilment.

Priority 1: Prevent illegal trafficking and international poaching of wildlife and tackle its root causes by involving public administrations and civil society

The first objective of the TIFIES Plan has only been partially met, insofar as statistics show that illegal wildlife trade (IWT) has increased after the initial decline during the pandemic (TRAFFIC 2022). The prevention of illegal trafficking is a major pending issue that needs to be addressed by controlling and limiting the drivers of both illegal and legal wildlife consumption. As Peter Sand said, '[A] characteristic feature of the trade is its luxury orientation, in response to consumption patterns often ranging from the non-essential to the perverse' (Sand 1997: 29). This feature of the global IWT phenomenon is also manifest in Spain. The CITES Management Authority declared in the interviews that they have attempted to control the rising trend of an unjustifiable, unsustainable legal and illegal trade in exotic pets. Thus, tackling the root causes of illegal wildlife trafficking requires consideration of the motivations that lead buyers and sellers to take part in a criminal modus operandi (Wyatt 2013; Sollund and Maher 2015; Fajardo 2015; van Uhm 2016; Sollund 2019). The brokering carried out by a varied profile of smugglers and traders shows that illegal trafficking is still motivated by high profit and limited risk of detection, prosecution and conviction in Spain (SEO-Birdlife 2020) as much as it is in other CITES State Parties (UNODC 2020, 2021).

During the years of my data collection (2012–22), traditional information campaigns at airports warning that the import of protected species constituted wildlife trafficking, an administrative offence or an environmental crime depending on the economic value of what was seized, have been complemented by new channels of communication. The channels with the highest audience impact are television programmes, specialized courses for environmental journalists and awareness-raising courses run by rescue centres for victims of wildlife trafficking. These include television programmes such as *SEPRONA in Action* on the Discovery Max channel, and success stories on SEPRONA's website, which show the results of major operations to seize illicit trafficking from Africa and Latin America or destined for Asia. Spanish authorities are also committed to the awareness-raising work carried out by the NGOs such as SEO-Birdlife and WWF with which MITECO collaborates, as well as the activities carried out by the rescue centres to show the terrible reality of IWT victims.[8] In the development of the TIFIES Plan, MITECO as CITES Management Authority will designate and create a national network of rescue centres for seized CITES victims (MITECO 2021). They will be centres with 3Rs: rescue, rehabilitation and reintroduction. If reintroduction is not possible, MITECO will try to incorporate them into the recovery programmes of the European Association of Zoos and Aquaria. However, as the Spanish CITES authorities have also repeatedly stated, the success of the fight against IWT would in any case be reflected in the disappearance of the demand for wildlife. Only in that situation would rescue centres no longer be needed.

The new WAP 2022 has made it a priority to raise awareness among citizens to stop consuming wildlife, therefore, the Spanish authorities must continue to multiply their communication and awareness-raising efforts.

Priority 2: Implement and enforce existing rules, and combat related illegal activities, more effectively

The second priority of the TIFIES Plan is to implement and enforce existing IWT regulations more effectively, in line with the mandate of WAP 2016. This requires Spanish law enforcement agencies to increase the effectiveness of the implementation in Spain of the EU regulatory framework and, in particular, of the CITES Regulation.[9] As mentioned before, at the level of the national compliance of CITES, the legislative measures adopted by Spain create a too fragmented legal framework composed of administrative and criminal law with a sanctioning system that combines the administrative and criminal sanctions foreseen in the Smuggling Act 1995 and those of the Spanish Criminal Code. In addition, each of the 17 Autonomous Communities has also adopted its own administrative regulatory framework which makes it difficult for both citizens and public officials to know the applicable rules and the consequences of non-compliance. For this reason, it is common to find that, in practice, the cases opened do not lead to criminal sanctions, due to the fact that in criminal proceedings, the judges consider that, as the offenders are unaware of the applicable regulations, they cannot be convicted in criminal proceedings as there is no proof of malice and *mens rea*. Therefore, judges consider the lack of malice as one of the grounds for acquittal in 15 per cent of environmental crimes, which leads to exonerating

---

[8] See www.discoveryplus.com/es/show/seprona-en-accion
[9] See the above-mentioned Regulation and its subsequent amendments by EU Regulation No 57/2011, Council Regulation EC No 1224/2009 and Council Regulation EC No 1005/2008, and the Guide to these regulations produced by the European Commission and Traffic, the WWF spin-off NGO that investigates illegal wildlife trafficking, *Reference Guide to the European Union Wildlife Trade Regulations*, Brussels, 2020.

the offenders from their criminal conduct, despite evidence of illegal trade. However, the matter is then usually referred to the administrative jurisdiction (Fuentes and Fajardo, 2022: 7).

The case law shows the limitations of the provisions of the Spanish Criminal Code and the Smuggling Act 1995 due to the lack of clear distinguishing criteria (Fuentes and Fajardo 2020). Since there is a substantial coincidence between the administrative and criminal offences, it is necessary to clarify the structure of the offence against IWT. The Smuggling Act 1995 considers possession and trafficking of CITES and EU-listed species without the necessary CITES permit to be an administrative or criminal offence depending on the value of the confiscated victims. In the case of Art 334 of the Criminal Code, it considers as a crime the possession and trafficking of protected species, with the exception of trafficking of derisory and negligeable quantities – always measured with an anthropocentric and economic approach, considered just as administrative infractions. Thus, the analysis of the case law requires a comparison between the sentences in which the Smuggling Law 1995 and Art 334 of the Criminal Code are applied.

Even though the provisions of the Smuggling Act 1995 cover both trafficking and possession of wildlife, the 15 court decisions in the last five years applying them only refer to trafficking. In the same period, the 25 court cases applying Art 334 of the Criminal Code refer to both trafficking and possession of wild flora and fauna. However, in this group of sentences, there have been frequent acquittals resulting from the lack of *mens rea* when the offender has claimed ignorance of the protected or endangered nature of the species or of the need for a permit or certificate. Thus, the case law shows the different criteria used by judges in similar cases and how elements such as the lack of knowledge[10] of the status of protected species by sellers and collectors, or the time elapsed since importation, have been considered grounds for acquittal (Fuentes and Fajardo 2022). Other grounds for acquittal are when it is considered that a CITES permit was not provided because it was not required at the time of import in pre-convention times. This is a recurring argument when it comes to taxidermy, elephant tusks, snakeskin bags and fur coats that are considered antiques or part of a family inheritance. In order to prevent these types of disparities from occurring, clarification and better wording of the criminal offence of illegal trafficking in wildlife is needed.

In this regard, in the opinion of the judges with whom I have discussed environmental crime, the main problem is that Spanish criminal rules are not easy to apply given the blurring lines between administrative and criminal offences and the lack of dissuasive effects due to the very limited sanctions

---

[10] SAP B 5060/2022 – ECLI:ES:APB:2022:5060

they establish for wildlife crimes. In crimes against the environment, prison sentences do not exceed two years. Only exceptionally are longer sentences provided for in the aggravated types of crimes against natural resources, and in such cases, partial pardons are frequently granted to avoid serving the prison sentence (Fuentes and Fajardo 2022: 2). Moreover, the provision of evidence in criminal proceedings continues to be one of the most important obstacles in cases of WLT, especially when the permit system remains unreliable given that they are still paper-based. In CITES cases, permits and licences are frequently falsified or replaced by the documents of dead animals. Evidence of the antiquity of an elephant tusk is difficult and very costly to provide, even if the ivory can be dated.[11]

Priority 3: Strengthen the global partnership of origin, transit and destination countries against illegal trafficking and international wildlife poaching

In Spain, the Spanish Criminal Code and the 1995 Smuggling Law establish a maximum penalty for wildlife crime of two years' imprisonment. This makes it impossible, as in the case of most EU member states, to activate the international cooperation provided for in the Palermo Convention against Transnational Organized Crime, since its Art 2 requires that serious crimes punishable by at least four years' imprisonment are involved in order for it to be invoked. However, Spain has developed an important and extensive network of informal and formal cooperation with countries of origin, transit and destination, as well as with international organizations. International judicial cooperation has shown limitations that could be overcome by establishing a system of electronic permits. Currently, import and export permits are issued on paper, the originals of which are not yet allowed to be sent within the framework of European mutual legal assistance. The system of mutual recognition of both legislation and documents adopted by the EU Member States, however, does not apply to third states, which are refused an extradition order on the grounds that the principle of double criminality is not complied with. This principle holds that an act is not extraditable unless it constitutes a crime in both the requesting and requested countries, which in the case of CITES can only occur when species are listed in CITES annexes and wildlife trafficking is considered as a crime by all States concerned. This means that, in practice, those responsible for cases of trafficking in native species that are not on the CITES list cannot be extradited, or if they are, the trafficking is not considered a crime but an administrative offence by the States Parties. A dismissed case on trafficking of Peruvian toucans illustrates

---

[11] SAP B 5060/2022 – ECLI:ES:APB:2022:5060

this situation in a most striking way. In this case, a Spanish national had been convicted in absentia in Peru for trafficking in native birds protected under Peruvian law and some of them (cabezon toucan) by CITES (Annex III). The extradition request made to Spain was not granted because the facts do not constitute a crime in Spain. 'Under Peruvian law, the facts are to be considered as constituting an offence of illegal trafficking in species of wild flora and fauna under Article 308 of the Criminal Code, with application of the aggravated subtype of Article 309, since the animals in question are protected by national legislation, and the offence is punishable by a prison sentence of up to 7 years'.[12] However, under Spanish law, the facts must be analysed as a customs offence, in accordance with the provisions of Article 2.2. b) of the Smuggling Act 1995, and only as an administrative infraction because its economic value was less than 50,000 euros.

International cooperation has been developed by MITECO and SEPRONA to fight environmental crimes in targeted developing countries in Africa, Latin America and Asia, looking to identify best ways to prevent and respond to these crimes with initiatives and activities such as the training of national park guards. Thus, in Africa, Spanish CITES Management Authorities and MITECO have provided training courses for rangers from national parks and conservation areas in Tanzania, Uganda and Congo, with the main objective of improving their expertise in their fight against wildlife poaching and trafficking. Future research will need to compare whether there are initiatives that are more inclusive in terms of the participation of Indigenous peoples and local communities, NGOs and national authorities at state, regional and local levels. The European Parliament has discussed all these aspects in order to consider future cooperation to development aid (Sollund and Wyatt 2022).

Asia is the area of destination of the WLT in European glass eels of Spanish origin. SEPRONA's fight against international eel trafficking has uncovered the existence of organized criminal networks. These networks changed their routes and modus operandi after the success of the first operations launched in 2016 in Spain by SEPRONA with the collaboration of EUROPOL – Operations Askea I and II, Lake, Celacanto, Eel-ilicit, Suculenta and Ave Fenix. Ever since then, the EU-TWIX digital platform[13] has helped to reveal new modi operandi, including information on the type of suitcases used for

---

[12] Judgment of the Audiencia Nacional, National High Court, Criminal Chamber, 21 September 2021, AAN 6526/2021 - ECLI:ES:AN:2021:6526A.
[13] The acronym EU-TWIX stands for Trade on Wildlife Information Exchange, as its website explains, its database 'contains centralised data on seizures and offences reported by the 27 EU Member States, Bosnia and Herzegovina, Iceland, Montenegro, North Macedonia, Switzerland, Ukraine and the United Kingdom', www.eu-twix.org/

air transport, and enabled their detection at the airports where subsequent operations were carried out.

Spain has also been the country of origin of WLT of native species, such as amphibians and birds of prey (Fajardo 2016, 2018). In the interviews with CITES Management authorities, SEPRONA and NGOs such as SEO-Birdlife, they pointed out that Spain has also become a transit country for trafficking barbary macaques from Morocco (van Uhm 2016); for bushmeat trade, as evidenced by the confiscation of suitcases bound for Paris by the customs service, or for mixing animal victims with human trafficking (Quercus Editorial Team 2021).

Blueprints and challenges of Spanish practice on CITES and welfare of trafficked victims

Spain has adopted a blueprint practice regarding the fate of seized live animals at borders. The previous CITES recommendations on seized animals which stated that they should be euthanized were not followed in Spain, which adopted a policy based on recovery and reintroduction that goes beyond the new CITES recommendations (CITES Resolution Conf. 17.8).[14] Now CITES promotes the exchange of information on and cooperation with countries of origin in order to return trafficked victims when possible. Thus, the CITES Secretariat 'shall collect information on existing networks and resources on the management of seized and confiscated live animals and make it available to Parties' (CITES Decision 18.159).[15]

The Spanish authorities have facilitated the reintroduction of such individuals into the wild in the origin countries. Thus, a lioness was returned to South Africa (Quercus Editorial Team 2021). On other occasions, reintroduction of wildlife victims was not possible, due to the cost and impossibility of recovery. However, animals seized in relation to trafficking offences were re-homed in zoological gardens and rescue centres or the Museum of Natural Sciences in Madrid,[16] but due to lack of space in these facilities, some were also kept by the offenders (Fajardo 2018) as has happened in the UK (Sollund and Maher 2015). I visited a rescue centre in my hometown dedicated to birds and spoke with staff who lamented an aspect that cannot be addressed in this research but is equally important: the state of stress resulting from the abuse suffered by trafficked birds. Offenders cannot abandon animals anonymously in rescue centres in order to avoid

---

[14] Available at https://cites.org/sites/default/files/document/E-Res-17-08.pdf
[15] Available at https://cites.org/eng/imp/disposal_of_confiscated_specimen/disposal_of_live_specimens
[16] SJP 479/2020 – ECLI:ES:JP:2020:479

penalties and the centres cannot accept the animals without permits. In the opinion of the experts in the centre, this request for identity and permits exacerbates the state of deterioration in which the animals eventually arrive after being abandoned by the traffickers and offenders or after being confiscated by the authorities.

Conclusion

In conclusion, as the CITES Strategic Vision declares, 'a common vision of sustainable use and a transformative change in the human-nature relationship' is required to stop unsustainable and illegal trade in wildlife, yet the solutions that CITES State parties and the CITES authorities have proposed do not include an approach that takes into account the individuals – animals and plants – that are victims of trade and how it is conducted. In the new EU WAP 2022, animal welfare only appears as a footnote to consider cooperation with animal welfare authorities when seeking 'multi-agency cooperation and coordination to effectively prevent, detect, prosecute and sanction wildlife crime' (European Commission 2022). Attempts to update CITES with regard to sustainable use and the conservation principle have been the source of an interesting reform in Spain, including relocation of CITES authorities and the implementation of the TIFIES Plan.

With regard to the regulatory framework of wildlife, a change is needed to make the types of offences easier to understand and apply for both the various authorities responsible for their enforcement and citizens. The proposal for a new environmental crime directive recognizes the need for improvements such as a clear definition of wildlife crimes as well as criteria of distinction for criminal and administrative offences and sanctions in all EU member states.

Career-long specialization is also one of SEPRONA's blueprints. Close cooperation of specialized police with CITES authorities and prosecutors has resulted in the implementation of the TIFIES Plan, which calls for increased specialization of all authorities involved in CITES enforcement. In this regard, the new EU WAP 2022 recognizes the importance of this specialization and proposes to extend it to judges.

Spanish practice also shows that it is necessary to adapt to the new challenges posed by wildlife trafficking in the digital world. Thus, the introduction of digital permits and means of traceability will facilitate implementation and international cooperation but a digital revolution needs to be enforced in CITES governance.

The toucan case demonstrates that the external dimension of the TIFIES Plan, as with any other plan to improve CITES implementation, requires further international cooperation. It needs agreements 'with teeth' and legal tools for preventing, prosecuting and punishing environmental crime committed in developing countries of origin of wildlife destined for Europe. But the required action must always start at the level of citizens, as foreseen in the new WAP 2022 and the proposal of a new environmental crime directive. Only by getting citizens to stop being consumers of wildlife will it be possible to achieve animal justice.

References

African Union (2023) Notification to the Parties on the Africa, Caribbean and Pacific Conference on the implementation of the outcomes of the CBD COP15 and CITES CoP19, No 2023/055, Geneva, 26 April. Available at: https://cites.org/sites/default/files/notifications/E-Notif-2023-055.pdf

Albiez Dohrmann, J. (2022) 'Una nueva lectura de la compraventa de animales de compañía' [A new reading of the sale and purchase of pets], *Indret*, 4: 1–42.

Alonso García, E. (2011) 'El bienestar de los animales como seres sensibles-sentientes: su valor como principio general, de rango constitucional, en el derecho español' [Animal welfare as sensitive-sentient beings: its value as a general principle, of constitutional rank, in Spanish law], *La Ley Digital*, 1120: 1–50.

CBD (2022) Kunming-Montreal Global biodiversity framework Draft decision submitted by the President, 18 December, LIMITED CBD/COP/15/L.25. Available at: www.cbd.int/doc/c/e6d3/cd1d/daf663719 a03902a9b116c34/cop-15-l-25-en.pdf

CITES (2022) Secretary General's Statement on Cooperation at CBD CoP15, 8 December. Available at: https://cites.org/eng/news/sg/sgs-statement-on-cooperation-at-cbd-cop15

European Commission (2021) Proposal for a Directive of the European Parliament and of the Council on the protection of the environment through criminal law and replacing Directive 2008/99/EC, COM(2021) 851 final, 15 December 2021.

European Commission (2022) Communication from the Commission to the European Parliament, the Council, the European Economic and Social Committee and the Committee of the Regions Revision of the EU Action Plan Against Wildlife Trafficking, COM(2022) 581 final. Available at https://eur-lex.europa.eu/legal content/EN/TXT/PDF/?uri=CELEX:52022DC0581

Fajardo, T. (2015) 'The United Nations Convention on Transnational Organised Crime and the environment. Organised Crime and Environmental Crime: Analysis of International Legal Instruments'. Study in the Framework of the EFFACE Research Project. Granada: University of Granada, 2015. Available at https://efface.eu/sites/default/files/EFFACE_Organised%20Crime%20and%20Environmental%20Crime_International%20Level/index.pdf

Fajardo, T. (2016) 'Wildlife crime: the European Union's approach in the fight against wildlife trafficking: challenges ahead', *Journal of International Wildlife Law and Policy*, 19(1): 1–21.

Fajardo, T. (2018) 'El Plan de Acción Español contra el Tráfico Ilegal y el Furtivismo Internacional de Especies Silvestres', *Revista General de Derecho Animal y Estudios Interdisciplinares de Bienestar Animal / Journal of Animal Law & Interdisciplinary Animal Welfare Studies*, 1: 1–42.

Fajardo, T. (2021) 'Principles and Approaches in the Convention on Biological Diversity and Other Biodiversity-Related Conventions in the Post-2020 Scenario', in M. Campins Eritja and T. Fajardo del Castillo (eds) *Biological Diversity and International Law: Challenges for the Post-2020 Scenario*, Cham and New York: Springer Verlag, pp 15–34.

Fajardo, T., Fuentes, J., Ramos, I. and Verdú, J. (2015) Fighting Environmental Crime in Spain: A Country Report, Study in the framework of the EFFACE Research Project, 83 pp.

Fuentes, J. and Fajardo, T. (2020) Report prepared in the framework of the LIFE Guardians of Nature Project, financed by the European Commission: Study on the dissuasive, effective and proportional nature of criminal sanctions imposed in Spain and Portugal for crimes against the environment and their adaptation to Directive 2008/99/EC on the protection of the environment through criminal law (Study in Spain), SEO/BirdLife.

Fuentes, J. and Fajardo, T. (2022) 'Motivos de absolución en los delitos contra el medio ambiente: una comparación entre los delitos contra la fauna y contra los recursos naturales' [Grounds for acquittal in environmental crime: a comparison between wildlife and natural resource offences], *Revista Electrónica de Criminología* [Electronic Journal of Criminology], 4(3): 1–17.

Korwin, S., Denier, L., Lieberman, S. and Reeve, R. (2019) 'Verification of legal acquisition under the CITES Convention: the need for guidance on the scope of legality', *Journal of International Wildlife Law & Policy*, 22: 274–304.

Maher, J. and Sollund, R. (2018) 'Wildlife Trafficking: Harms and Victimization', in R. Sollund, C. Stefes and A. R. Germani (eds) *Fighting Environmental Crime in Europe and Beyond: The Role of the EU and Its Member States*, Palgrave Studies in Green Criminology.

MITECO (2021) Plan TIFIES. Available at https://sites.google.com/gl.miteco.gob.es/tifies

Quercus Editorial Team (2021) 'Lucha contra el tráfico ilegal de biodiversidad. Una oportunidad única' [Fighting illegal trafficking of biodiversity. A unique opportunity] *Quercus, Special Issue*. Available at www.revistaquercus.es/noticia/8126/especiales-quercus/plan-tifies-contra-el-trafico-ilegal-de-biodiversidad.html

Sand, P. H. (1997) 'Whither CITES? The evolution of a treaty regime in the borderland of trade and environment', *European Journal of International Law*, 1: 29–58.

Scanlon, J. E. (2015) 'CITES and wildlife trade – how CITES works and what it is and isn't', Secretary-General, CITES Secretariat Tbilisi, 20 October 2015. Available at https://cites.org/eng/news/sg/keynote_address_cites_secretary_general_Ilia_state_university_tbilisi_20102015

SEO Birdlife (2020) Nature Guardians Project. Available at https://guardianes.seo.org/en/

SEPRONA (2020) Quercus Operation. Available at www.miteco.gob.es/va/prensa/ultimas-noticias/2020/02/finaliza_con_exitoelprimeroperativorealizadoenespanacontraeltraf/jcr:content/root/container/container-main/container-content/press_release_form.html

SEPRONA (2021) Proyecto LIFE+SATEC Enfoque estratégico para hacer frente a los delitos contra el medioambiente. Available at www.envicrimenet.eu/proyecto-lifesatec/

SEPRONA (2022) Medio ambiente. Available at www.guardiacivil.es/es/institucional/Conocenos/especialidades/Medio_ambiente/index.html

Sina, S., Gerstetter, C., Porsch, L., Roberts, E., Smith, L. O., Klaas, K. and Fajardo del Castillo, T. (2016) *Study on Wildlife Crime*. Commissioned by the European Parliament, Brussels, 2016 (2016/2076(INI)). Available at www.europarl.europa.eu/RegData/etudes/STUD/2016/570008/IPOL_STU(2016)570008_EN.pdf

Sollund, R. (2019) *The Crimes of Wildlife Trafficking: Issues of Justice, Legality and Morality*. London and New York: Routledge.

Sollund, R. (2022) 'Wildlife trade and law enforcement: a proposal for remodeling of CITES incorporating species justice, ecojustice, and environmental justice', *International Journal of Offender Therapy and Comparative Criminology*, 66: 1017–35.

Sollund, R. and Maher, J. (2015) *The Illegal Wildlife Trade. A Case Study report on the Illegal Wildlife Trade in the United Kingdom, Norway, Colombia and Brazil*. A study compiled as part of the EFFACE project. University of Oslo and University of South Wales.

Sollund, R. and Wyatt, T. (2022) *In-depth analysis. Environmental criminality in developing countries*. Workshop requested by the DEVE Committee, European Parliament. Available at www.europarl.europa.eu/RegData/etudes/STUD/2022/702565/EXPO_STU(2022)702565_EN.pdf

Sollund, R., Stefes, Ch. and Germani, A. R. (2018) *Fighting Environmental Crime in Europe and Beyond: The Role of the EU and Its Member States*, Palgrave Studies in Green Criminology, Palgrave Macmillan.

Spanish Prosecutor's Office for the Environment and Urban Planning (2021) *Memoria 2020: Medio ambiente y Urbanismo* [Annual Report: Environment Urban Planning] 21 September. Available at: www.miteco.gob.es/es/ceneam/grupos-de-trabajo-y-seminarios/fiscalias-de-medio-ambiente/memoria2020fiscaliacoordinadorademedioambiente_tcm30-537060.pdf

SWIPE (2022) Successful Wildlife Crime Prosecution in Europe (SWIPE) LIFE project. Available at https://stopwildlifecrime.eu/

TRAFFIC (2022) *An overview of seizures of CITES-listed wildlife in the EU in 2020*. Available at www.traffic.org/publications/reports/an-overview-of-seizures-of-cites-listed-wildlife-in-the-eu-in-2020/

UNEP (2019) *Environmental Rule of Law*. Available at: https://wedocs.unep.org/bitstream/handle/20.500.11822/27279/Environmental_rule_of_law.pdf?sequence=1&isAllowed=y

UNODC (2020) *World Wildlife Crime Report*. Available at www.unodc.org/documents/data-and-analysis/wildlife/2020/World_Wildlife_Report_2020_9July.pdf

UNODC (2021) *Global Programme for Combating Wildlife and Forest Crime, Annual Report*. Available at www.unodc.org/documents/Wildlife/Annual_Report_GPWLFC2021.pdf

van Uhm, D. (2016) 'Illegal Wildlife Trade to the EU and Harms to the World', in T. Spapens, R. White and W. Huisman (eds) *Environmental Crime in Transnational Context*, Global Issues in Green Enforcement and Criminology, London and New York: Routledge, pp 59–82.

Wyatt, T. (2013) *Wildlife Trafficking A Deconstruction of the Crime, the Victims, and the Offenders*, Basingstoke: Palgrave Macmillan.

8

Paper Tigers and Local Perseverance: Wildlife Protection in Germany

Christoph H. Stefes[1]

Introduction

Germany is Europe's biggest import country and transshipment point of wildlife products, including live animals for the domestic pet market and hunting trophies (Altheer and Lameter 2020: 2; Fachtagung Artenschutzrecht 2021: 5). Germany is also signatory to numerous regional and international wildlife protection treaties, such as the Washington Convention on International Trade in Endangered Species of Wild Fauna and Flora (CITES), the Convention on the Conservation of Migratory Species of Wild Animals (CMS), and the Convention on the Conservation of European Wildlife and Natural Habitats (Bern Convention). Furthermore, as a member of the European Union (EU), Germany is bound by extensive EU regulations and directives for the protection of endangered species – namely, the various Wildlife Trade Regulations that transpose CITES into EU Law, as well as the Habitats Directive and the Birds Directive (BfN 2010: 15–17). Finally, Germany is an active participant in international meetings where its delegations regularly advocate for expanding the protection of endangered species (Interviews (Ints) 13, 17; Klaas et al 2016: 23). For all these reasons, we would expect Germany to be an exemplary protector of endangered wildlife at home. Alas, although Germany has faithfully incorporated international

---

[1] The author thanks Elizabeth Cox and Kayla Gabehart for their invaluable research assistance. He further thanks Irina von Maravić, Florian Distelrath, and Jürgen Hinzmann for many hours of insightful discussions.

treaties and European law into federal legislation, law enforcement is wanting and sentencing is routinely too lenient to have a deterring effect. Germany's wildlife protection legislation is thereby rendered into a paper tiger.

This chapter attempts to explain why Germany's actions at home so glaringly contradict its demonstrated ambitions abroad. Understanding this gap is crucial, as Ragnhild Sollund points out:

> The ways in which legislation is enforced is also an indicator of the human-animal relationship and can regulate humans' relationship to non-human animals. Analysis of enforcement (or lack of enforcement) can show the influence of general norms on legislation and vice versa and whether duties towards wildlife are respected. (Sollund 2016: 82)

The most obvious reason for lack of enforcement is the insufficient allocation of resources needed for the effective enforcement of wildlife protection laws. Germany's federal system further compounds insufficient resource allocation by adding inefficiency to the mix. The enforcement of nature protection laws is left to the 16 federal states (Glaser 2011: 7f). Some of these states further delegate responsibilities in varying degrees to the municipal level, imposing undue burden on Germany's municipal officials or, what I call, Germany's street-level bureaucrats (SLBs). German federalism thereby turns the country into a confusing patchwork of enforcement. Yet, by detailing the perseverance of local and state officials as custodians of endangered species, this chapter also shows that highly motivated SLBs can make a difference. It concludes with some recommendations for strengthening the enforcement of wildlife protection in Germany through the empowerment of these bureaucrats.

For this study, I combine the insights of 31 interviews I conducted with state and non-state actors at the federal, state and municipal levels with quantitative data gathered and made public by Germany's Federal Criminal Police Office (*Bundeskriminalamt*, BKA) and the Federal Agency for Nature Protection (*Bundesamt für Naturschutz*, BfN) to detail the consequences of insufficient and inefficient resource allocation in Germany's federalized enforcement system (BKA 2022; BfN 2022). The chapter begins with a discussion of the pros and cons of federalism, with a particular focus on Germany's 'administrative federalism' (Behnke and Kropp 2021). Considering the importance of SLBs in decentralized law-implementation regimes, the role of these bureaucrats is further highlighted. The next section summarizes the legal framework of Germany's wildlife protection legislation and its convoluted system of enforcement. The chapter continues by outlining the methodology used for arriving at the main findings. Thereafter, I will detail the general obstacles that hamper the enforcement of wildlife protection, followed by a more detailed exploration of the ways these obstacles are further compounded by Germany's federal administrative system, showing how motivated officials find various (in)formal ways to overcome these obstacles. The penultimate section connects the insights derived from the qualitative research with quantitative analysis. The chapter concludes with a summary of the findings and recommends reforms that could facilitate improving these enforcement efforts.

Germany's administrative federalism and the role of street-level bureaucrats

Federal and unitary systems have their specific advantages and disadvantages. Federalism is hailed for flexible governance, being able to adapt to unique, local circumstances. For instance, the challenges of running large, rural communities differ considerably from managing large, densely populated cities (Gabehart 2022). It brings government closer to the people, allowing for mutually beneficial cooperation between public administration and citizens. It thereby encourages public participation in policy making and implementation. Furthermore, states and municipalities serve as natural laboratories, as they compete in their attempts to attract new businesses and citizens. Ideally, a byproduct of this competition is more efficient governance. Finally, federalism adds checks-and-balances to a political system, circumscribing the role of central governments (Rozell and Wilcox 2019: chapter 6).

Federalism's guiding principle is subsidiarity which 'is intended to ensure that decisions are taken as closely as possible to the citizen and that constant checks are made as to whether action at Community level is justified in the light of the possibilities available at national, regional or local level' (Wouter 2020). Yet, how close to the citizens should decisions be taken and implemented? At which point do the costs outweigh the benefits? For instance, competition between municipalities and federal states might create a collective action problem, causing a race to the bottom and undermining the pursuit of collective goods. Businesses and citizens might relocate to states and municipalities with low taxes, few regulations and lax enforcement. The outcome might well be, what Garret Hardin (1968) famously called 'the tragedy of the commons', with wanting public resources, rudimentary environmental and labour regulations, and an insufficient administration.

Furthermore, the moment states and municipalities pass their own laws and regulations or amend federal laws, and implement these laws and regulations in diverging ways, they contravene the goal of creating equal living conditions across a country. In addition, a patchwork of incoherent policies and policy-implementation practices makes it difficult for sub-federal units to coordinate effective responses to problems that are not localized, but which transcend administrative boundaries. Finally, federal governments tend to 'pass the buck' to local and state governments whenever policies are unpopular. Federal governments thereby conveniently ignore that administrations at lower levels might not be sufficiently equipped and their officials not sufficiently experienced to handle the tasks (Rozell and Wilcox 2019: chapter 6).

Federal systems seem particularly problematic in societies in which uniformity of living standards across the country is considered a collective good, as outlined in Art 44 of Germany's Constitution (*Grundgesetz*). Germany's 16 states enjoy less policy making authority than, for instance, their counterparts in the United States and Switzerland. However, they enjoy considerable latitude in how they implement federal laws. And since most federal laws are implemented at the state level, the 16 federal states are granted co-legislative power through the Upper House (*Bundesrat*). Nathalie Behnke and Sabine Kropp (2021) succinctly summarize the two basic dimensions of this form of 'administrative federalism':

> On the one hand, it emphasizes that governments and administrations at all territorial levels are powerful actors in policymaking and implementation processes. On the other hand, compared to other federations, the German model implies that legislation predominantly takes place at the federal level, while the *Länder* (the relevant political sub-federal units) implement federal laws in their own right, through their own administration and at their own cost. (Behnke and Kropp 2021: 35)

Germany thereby exhibits an almost paradoxical federalism in which federal laws take precedence over state and municipal laws with little policy *making* authority at the lower levels of the federation. Yet, at the same time, wide latitude and diverging capacity in policy *implementation* contradicts the attempt to achieve uniform living standards. As Behnke and Kropp point out, 'administrative capacity and financial power are not evenly distributed among the German Länder. Not surprisingly, some of the smaller Länder and city-states face difficulties in drafting their own policy solutions or in implementing laws, even when exclusive jurisdictions, exit options and deviation rights are constitutionally provided' (Behnke and Kropp 2021: 47). This situation has consequences beyond the territory of the Federal Republic. As Art 25 of the German *Grundgesetz* states, international law 'shall take precedence over the laws and directly create rights and duties for the inhabitants of the federal territory'. In other words, administrative federalism might well cause an unequal application of international treaties and European law across Germany, contravening the spirit of Art 25.

Irrespective of the general debate concerning the pros and cons of federalism, decentralizing policy implementation enhances the role of bureaucrats at the lower administrative levels, namely the SLBs (sometimes called frontline workers). Simply defined, an SLB is a civil servant who is regularly in direct contact with ordinary citizens, such as police officers, teachers and rubbish collectors. For a long time, the agency of SLBs was downplayed. They were thought to simply execute clearly defined policies with little room for interpretation. Yet, Michael Lipsky (1980, 2010), who studied SLBs to arrive at a more thorough understanding of policy implementation, demonstrated that SLBs enjoy considerable administrative discretion and sometimes even circumvent official rules to serve their clients better or to pursue personal interests (for example, career advancement). And sometimes, SLBs overstep their discretion to make their jobs easier by shirking implementation responsibilities. Factors that influence the actions of SLBs are: (a) signals and guidance they receive from their superiors and politicians; (b) organizational discretion; (c) degree of professionalism, training, and knowledge that SLBs have about their clients and tasks; (d) budget, time and other constraints (May and Winter 2000). Thus, SLBs are actively constructing de facto policy on the ground. The performance of these SLBs often determines whether policies are implemented effectively, and their actions thereby compound the inevitable variability in policy implementation in federal systems (Brodkin and Marston 2013; Hupe et al 2015; Zacka 2017).

Studies that investigate the role of SLBs in the implementation of environmental policies are rare, but they generally emphasize the discretion environmental SLBs enjoy. For instance, Sara Rinfret and Michelle Pautz find that 'despite common presumptions of adversarialism in the environmental regulatory arena, the frontline environmental inspectors in [Ohio and Wisconsin] generally have positive attitudes regarding the regulated community, and they cope well with external contextual factors' (Rinfret and Pautz 2013: 112). Likewise, Mikael Sevä and Sverker Jagers (2013) find that Swedish SLBs exert high levels of discretion in different administrative structures. This study arrives at a similar conclusion. However, these studies also highlight the significant barriers and constraints that SLBs experience when enforcing wildlife laws in states that have decentralized full authority to the lowest level of governance, the municipal level.

Legal framework and patchwork enforcement

For Germany, as for all EU member states, wildlife protection legislation cascades from the international, to the EU, and finally to the national level. Figure 8.1 summarizes this dynamic.[2]

---

[2] This section is largely based on research previously published (Stefes 2021).

Figure 8.1: Outlining the legal framework

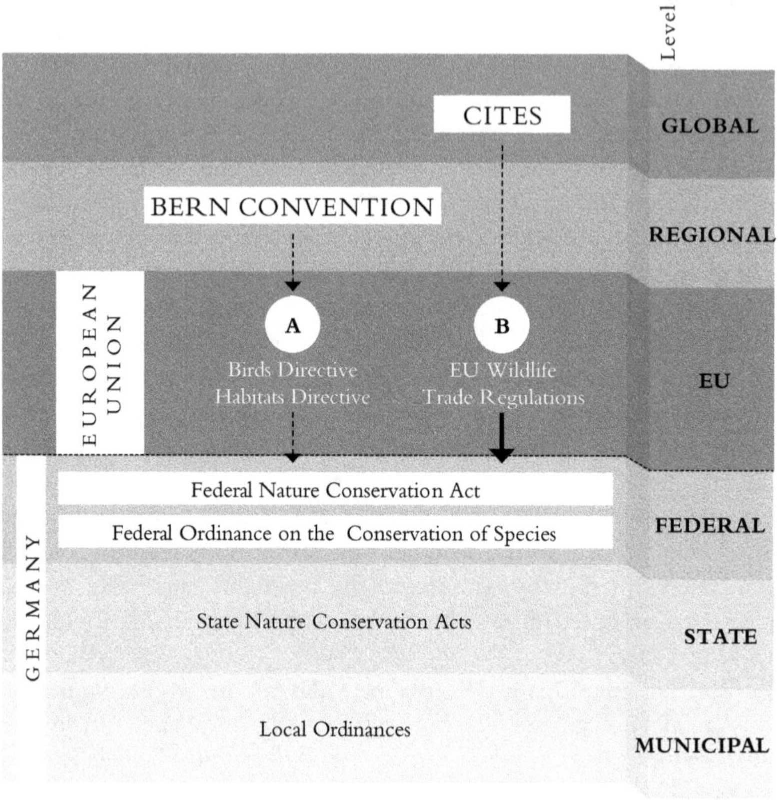

```
                                    CITES           GLOBAL
                    BERN CONVENTION                 REGIONAL
    EUROPEAN UNION
                    A              B
                    Birds Directive    EU Wildlife  EU
                    Habitats Directive Trade Regulations

    GERMANY
                Federal Nature Conservation Act
                Federal Ordinance on the Conservation of Species   FEDERAL

                State Nature Conservation Acts     STATE

                Local Ordinances                    MUNICIPAL
```

Level

CITES

Germany was one of the first countries that ratified the Convention. The EU only officially became a full party to CITES in 2015. Yet already in 1984, the EU began to pass regulations that applied CITES directly to all its member states. CITES aims at controlling the international wildlife trade. CITES classifies species into three groups, depending on the level of endangerment. Close to 40,000 species are listed in CITES (about 6,000 animals and 33,000 plants), representing roughly 2 per cent of currently known species in the world (CITES 2022a). CITES' appendices are updated every two to three years when the delegations of the parties to CITES meet (CITES 2022b).

The EU's Wildlife Trade Regulations have adopted the three CITES appendices. Appendices I–III are largely congruent with Annex A–C in Council Regulation (EC) No 338/97. Annex D has no equivalent in CITES, though it includes some species listed in CITES Appendix III. It is often referred to as the monitoring list. Species in Annex D are closely monitored for statistical purposes, allowing for a scientific assessment of whether a higher level of protection should eventually be recommended to CITES (Sina et al 2016: 23–5).

As the EU's Wildlife Trade Regulations are directly applicable, Germany has incorporated these regulations into its Federal Nature Conservation Act (*Bundesnaturschutzgesetz*, BNatSchG) and the Federal Ordinance on the Conservation of Species (*Bundesartenschutzverordnung*, BArtSchV). In Art 7, the Nature Conservation Act distinguishes between two groups of protected species: strictly protected (highest protection level) and specially protected (high protection level). All strictly protected species are also specially protected. No specially protected species may be killed. Moreover, these species and their derived products (for example, eggs, horns, skins) are not allowed to be captured, traded or commercially exhibited. All strictly protected species must not even be disturbed in their natural habitats. Import and export licences are required for all specially protected species. Exceptions are granted. For instance, the killing of individual animals is allowed under certain circumstances if the species itself is not threatened. Moreover, animals can be relocated to equally suitable environments (Art 44, BNatSchG).

All species listed in Annex A of the EU's Wildlife Trade Regulations are considered strictly protected under German law, and violations are subject to criminal prosecution, with punishments including fines (up to €50,000) and prison sentences (up to five years). German law considers all species listed in Annex B as specially protected. Harm done to these species does not fall under criminal law. Instead, these harmful acts are considered administrative violations, potentially leading to significant administrative fines (up to €50,000). The exact range of fines for specific infringements varies from state to state though (Arts 69, 71, BNatSchG).

The BNatSchG furthermore outlines the administrative implementation of the EU's Wildlife Trade Regulations in its territory. Germany's constitution (*Grundgesetz*) stipulates that the execution of nature protection legislation falls almost entirely under the jurisdiction of Germany's 16 federal states (BfN 2021). Nature conservation acts passed by the states therefore constitute an additional body of law. However, state legislation must not contravene federal law (NABU 2022: 5).

Bern Convention

The Convention on the Conservation of European Wildlife and Natural Habitats (Bern Convention) came into force in 1982. In the following years, all member states of the Council of Europe, including Germany, as well as four African riparian states, Belarus, and the EU signed the Bern Convention. The goal of the convention, according to Article 1, is 'to conserve wild flora and fauna and their natural habitats, especially those species and habitats whose conservation requires the co-operation of several States, and to promote such co-operation' (Council of Europe 2022). Emphasis is given to endangered and vulnerable species, including endangered and vulnerable migratory species.

The Bern Convention resembles CITES insofar as it organizes species according to their degree of endangerment. The EU has transposed the Bern Convention primarily through two directives: the Birds Directive and the Habitats Directive. As directives, and unlike EU regulations, they are not applicable directly in EU member states. Member states are, however, required to pass national legislation that achieves the goals outlined in these directives. Furthermore, EU member states are requested to designate certain areas in their territories, both on land and at sea, to form 'a network of core breeding and resting sites for rare and threatened species, and some rare natural habitat types which are protected in their own right' (*Natura 2000*, European Commission 2022). Species protected under the EU Birds and Habitats Directives are also grouped into annexes depending on their endangerment. These annexes largely overlap with the annexes of the Bern Convention (Sina et al 2016: 25–7).

Germany designates all species listed in Annex IV of the Habitats Directive, and some birds listed in the Birds Directive, as strictly protected. They must not be killed or harmed in any way, for example, by altering their natural habitat. All other European birds and the remaining species of the Habitats Directive are designated as specially protected. The killing and capturing of these species are largely banned. Exceptions are granted in various other German laws that, for instance, regulate logging, hunting and fishing. Here, the clash between anthropocentric versus non-human species' interests manifests itself. Under certain circumstances, the killing of animals is permitted if human interests are served. For instance, more than a million deer and more than half a million boars and almost half a million foxes are killed during licensed hunts (Huth 2021). In addition to Annex IV, another key measure to protect the species listed in the two directives is the designation of nature reserves (Klaas et al 2016: 16f).

Enforcement of CITES and the Bern Convention

With prison sentences of up to five years and administrative fines that offset any potential gains made from violating the BNatSchG, German law sets tougher penalties than most EU member states (Sina et al 2016: 74–86). Yet Germany's problem is not inadequate wildlife protection legislation. Instead, it lacks a robust enforcement structure. As Sollund observes, governments sign the same conventions. Yet, implementation and enforcement vary widely because of states' 'different law-making processes and different interpretations of what the legal implications of the treaties entail' (Sollund 2021: 11). What must be added is that states' enforcement capacity also differs, partially due to varying resources (for example, public administrations in the Global South are often underfunded due to the lack of state revenues). However, hamstringing enforcement agencies is also an inconspicuous method to undermine legislation without provoking too much political backlash.

At border crossings where passengers and freight directly enter Germany from outside EU territory – mainly, the country's major air- and seaports – two federal agencies monitor international wildlife trade: German Customs and the BfN. Although the Federal Ministry for the Environment (BMU) is the official management authority of CITES in Germany, the BfN serves as the lead agency for CITES enforcement. The BfN is an agency under the authority of the BMU. It is responsible for issuing all CITES-related import and export certificates. It provides training as well as scientific and technical expertise. Furthermore, if Customs detects a violation of wildlife law that relates to specially, but not strictly, protected species (an administrative violation), the BfN initiates proceedings to impose administrative fines. It can also request Customs to initiate criminal proceedings when it suspects criminal behaviour. Customs, occasionally in cooperation with the BKA, prosecutes all cases related to strictly protected species (BfN 2010: 19–21).

Once endangered species have crossed Germany's borders, either captured, as products, or as free animals, the 16 federal states are charged with the enforcement of wildlife legislation. We can roughly divide between wildlife trafficking (covered by CITES) and crimes against wildlife at home (covered by the Bern Convention). In the latter case, public authorities monitor, for instance, that protected birds are not captured, large carnivores are not killed, and endangered species are not disturbed in their natural habitats by construction projects. In the case of CITES, public authorities issue documentations that prove legal possession of endangered species and licences to market them domestically. Furthermore, they register endangered species. Finally, they conduct inspections and confiscate endangered species in illegal possession (BfN 2010: 19–21).

Public authorities issue fines for all violations concerning specially protected species and their products. If they and other witnesses suspect that strictly protected species have been endangered, public authorities must inform law enforcement agencies (police or public prosecutor) so that a criminal investigation is initiated (Klaas et al 2016: 20).

Most environmental laws in Germany are federal laws, but with few exceptions law enforcement falls under the authority of the states. In fact, federal laws are mostly executed by the 16 states (Scharpf 2008). While smaller states, such as Saarland, keep the authority over wildlife protection at the state level, other states have further delegated authority to the regional level, and sometimes even further down to the municipal level, such as

Hesse and North Rhine-Westphalia (NRW), respectively (BfN 2020). In general, we can distinguish between three ideal types of varying degrees of centralization.

- In four *centralized states*, all authority related to the protection of endangered species rests with public authorities at the state level, usually the State Ministries for the Environment or related state agencies (Brandenburg, Hamburg, Mecklenburg-West Pomerania and Saarland). These four states together account for less than 10 per cent of Germany's population.
- In six *decentralized states*, the authority is delegated to the municipal level where Lower Nature Protection Agencies (*Untere Naturschutzbehörde*, UNB) in cities and rural districts are responsible for issuing licences, conducting inspections, monitoring construction projects, and so on (Baden-Württemberg, Bavaria, NRW, Rhineland-Palatinate, Saxony and Thuringia). Baden-Württemberg is a special case. Here, public authorities in four regional districts as well as dozens of municipal administrations jointly share authority. Yet cooperation between these entities is wanting. Almost two-thirds of Germany's population resides in these six federal states.
- In six *cooperative, mixed-centralized states*, authority either rests exclusively with Higher Nature Protection Agencies (*Obere Naturschutzbehörde*, ONB) that are situated at an intermediate level between the state and municipal level, comparable to British regional councils, and which closely cooperate (Hesse); or the burden is shared between municipal and state authorities, whereby the municipal authorities, UNBs, are merely responsible for inspections and confiscations (Berlin, Bremen, Lower Saxony, Saxony-Anhalt and Schleswig-Holstein). In the latter five cases, state authorities closely cooperate with the UNBs, providing guidance and expertise. The six federal states are home to about a quarter of Germany's human population.

Given this patchwork of enforcement agencies, Germany has an unusually high number of local CITES management authorities (238, of which close to 100 UNBs are in Bavaria and almost 60 in NRW). In the six decentralized states, the performance of SLBs accordingly makes the biggest difference, leading to variation of policy implementation even within a single federal state.

In Germany's federal system, the police force falls under the authority of the states, and severe crimes such as organized and political crimes are prosecuted by the State Crime Agencies (LKAs). However, wildlife crime cases are rarely handled by LKAs. The justice system is hierarchically organized from the local to the federal level. Most proceedings involving wildlife crime do not involve law enforcement at higher levels of the state

Figure 8.2: Wildlife protection enforcement

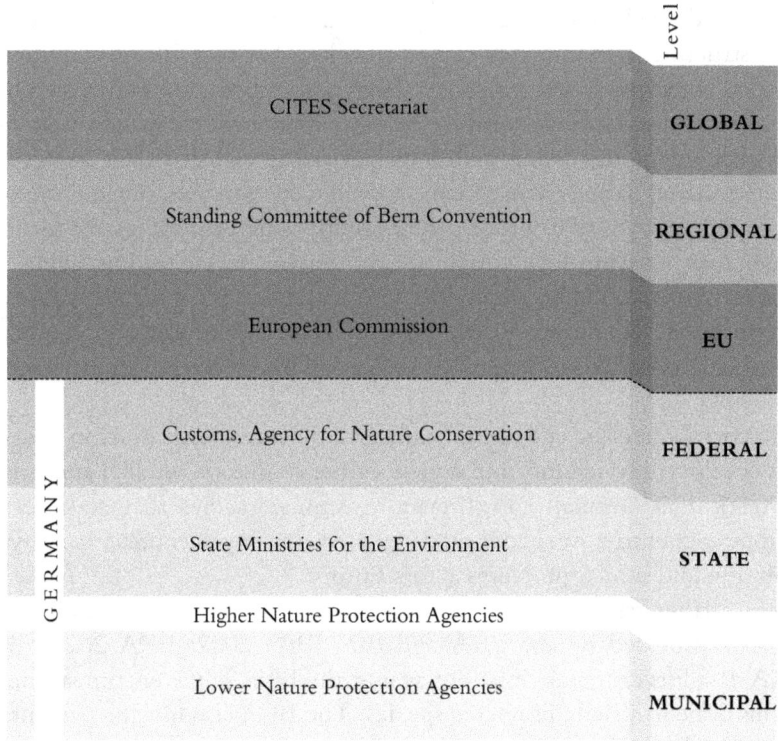

hierarchy, even in Germany's centralized states. If criminal cases are tried, which they rarely are, they usually end up in district courts.

In short, as Figure 8.2 summarizes, Germany's wildlife law is enforced through a bewildering number of different agencies at the local, state and federal levels, and enforcement is further divided between those law enforcement agencies that initiate criminal proceedings and public authorities that sanction administrative violations through fines.

Methodology

To assess how well Germany fulfils its obligations under the Bern Convention and CITES, both qualitative and quantitative methods and data are employed. Between 2020 and 2022, I interviewed 31 public officials, politicians and representatives of non-governmental organizations (NGOs) at various levels of Germany's federal system and in different positions. Almost all interviewees were in senior positions with ten or more years of experience. Due to the

COVID-19 pandemic, almost all interviews were conducted via Zoom, four interviews took place in person, and in four other cases, the interviews were conducted in writing through email exchanges. The open-ended, semi-structured oral interviews lasted anywhere between 23 and 87 minutes. All oral interviews were recorded, later transcribed, and coded in QDA (qualitative data analysis) software Atlas.ti. The email exchanges were also uploaded and coded. Almost all interviewees agreed that their names and professional affiliations would be made public. In two cases, the interviewees requested anonymity to protect their identity due to their involvement in undercover investigations conducted by the German Customs Office. In another case, two public employees who worked in the same UNB, as well as two public employees of the State of Baden-Württemberg, requested anonymity to speak more openly. A list of all interviewees can be found in Appendix A.

To corroborate and add to the findings of the interviews, desktop research was conducted to identify and review earlier studies on wildlife and nature protection in Germany. Furthermore, similar studies that cover other European countries were consulted to place Germany in context, identifying common and similar problems across Europe.[3]

For further triangulation, quantitative analysis was conducted, relying on data provided by the BKA and BfN (BfN 2022; BKA 2022). The BKA data lists criminal violations against the BNatSchG, encompassing all harms done to strictly protected species. The BKA also lists the percentage of cases solved. The BKA does so for the 16 federal states and for all 400 municipalities. For this research, the last five years for which data were available were chosen (2016–20). The BfN dataset is more limited. It only encompasses the 16 states and only two years (2018–19). The BfN data provide information about the number of inspections conducted and the number of administrative fine procedures initiated in the 16 states. There is a catch though. Municipalities are not required to submit their statistics to the BfN, and many have chosen not to do so. Since the number of unreported cases is likely very high (interviewees estimated that only around 10 per cent of all cases are detected), the BKA and BfN data give us only a rough idea about the extent of criminal violations and administrative violations that take place. The data tell us more about the efforts that public authorities and law enforcement agencies are willing and/or able to put into the fight against wildlife crime. For this research, these efforts constitute the critical variable to assess Germany's ability and willingness to meet its obligations under CITES and the Bern Convention. Analysis of these data was conducted via multivariate panel regression models using Stata.

---

[3] For easily accessible case studies, see EFFACE, 2022.

Tough laws, wanting enforcement and lenient sentencing

When asked whether German laws included penalties that were severe enough, two-thirds of the interviewees responded in the affirmative. When asked whether these laws had a sufficiently deterrent effect, the unanimous response was that this effect was marginal, because: (a) the probability of being caught was low; and (b) actual sentences imposed were lenient (see also, Klaas et al 2016: 20). An analysis of the interviews reveals two distinct chains of causation to explain why detection rates are low and sentencing is lenient.

Low detection rates. Several interviewees stated that societal awareness of wildlife exploitation has increased, especially for species that are prominently featured in the media, such as elephants and rhinos (Ints 4+, 10, 13; EM1; see also: Klaas et al 2016: 20). However, interviewees also stated that species protection was an abstract idea for many citizens. While the suffering of an individual animal was palpable, the extinction of an entire species was not, except for the extinction of bees (Ints 4+, 10+). Wildlife protection is not a rallying point in German politics (Int 4+). Even the Green Party, which is a strong actor in Germany's political system, has not paid particular attention to this issue. Climate change, renewable energy and animal farming regularly appear on the political agenda; the fate of endangered species, however, much less so. As a parliamentarian of the Green Party in the state parliament of NRW frankly admitted, 'I have always so many issues on my agenda. And the whole question of species protection I have not addressed at all in a long time' (Int 24).

Given the lack of public pressure and political support for the protection of endangered species in Germany, it is unsurprising that federal and state governments have failed to allocate sufficient resources to put teeth into the enforcement of related laws. In fact, several interviewees noted that resources have been diverted towards other tasks, causing budget cuts, layoffs, personnel relocations to other agencies, and fewer opportunities for professional development (Ints 2, 4+, 14; see also: Klaas et al 2016: 21). For instance, as customs officials noted, today's focus is on illegal employment and money laundering. Wildlife protection no longer plays the role that it did some 20–30 years ago (Ints 2, 3). The lack of personnel is mentioned by almost every interviewee, irrespective of position and level of governance (for example, Ints 7, 9+, 11, 13, 19, 21; EM2). In the same breath, interviewees frequently note the lack of training and expertise among public officials who have limited or no biological expertise (for example, Ints 2, 4+, 10+, 15, 16, 20). Moreover, the lack of standardized software that would connect the data collected by more than 200 CITES management authorities is considered a serious obstacle towards stricter enforcement, easily allowing perpetrators to evade inspections and prosecution by relocating to other jurisdictions (Ints 4+, 19). Finally, wildlife crime gets increasingly more sophisticated and organized with an increasing reliance on online forums. Global and national authorities barely keep up with these developments (Ints 2, 3, 4+, 12; see also, Marshall et al 2020).

At the same time, understaffed public authorities, often lacking specialized knowledge, face formidable opponents. Owners, breeders and traders of rare species are often experts who easily intimidate public officials when they conduct inspections (Int 4+). Moreover, they are well organized. For instance, the German Association for Herpetology and Study of Terrariums (*Deutsche Gesellschaft für Herpetologie und Terrarienkunde e. V.*) and the Federal Association for Professional Nature and Species Protection (*Bundesverband für fachgerechten Natur- und Artenschutz*) serve as influential lobby organizations for the owners, breeders and traders of wildlife. The associations are well connected to decision makers in Berlin and Brussels (Ints 2, 7, 13). In contrast, as representatives of an environmental NGO frankly admitted, NGOs who advocate for tougher wildlife protection are not influential enough to counter the political power of these associations (Int 9+).

Lenient sentencing. While the maximum penalties for violations against the BNatSchG are considered sufficient, interviewees also point out that for several reasons, these maximum penalties are rarely exhausted. For instance, in a case where 1.2 tons of ivory were smuggled into Germany, the offenders merely received deferred jail sentences of less than two years (Süddeutsche Zeitung 2020). One reason is that the law is tortuous and often imprecise. This is because the law refers to other legislation, both German and EU, which refers to additional legislation, and so on. This kind of 'chain referencing' is a challenge even for seasoned jurists, especially when the laws are not regularly updated (keep in mind, for instance, that CITES appendices are updated every two to three years). Moreover, it is difficult to prove intent, given the complexity of the law, which would lead to tougher sentencing than negligence (Fachtagung Artenschutzrecht 2021: 7f). Finally, the subject is complex. Biological knowledge of rare and endangered species is hard to come by (Klaas et al 2016: 15). 'Simple' crimes such as theft and assault do not require this knowledge (Ints 15, 23).

The complexity and ambiguity of wildlife legislation requires trained, experienced and well-resourced law enforcement and courts, which are in short supply. Police officers, prosecutors and judges have little to no training in this subject, and they do not encounter these forms of violations often enough to develop expertise over time. Exceptions to the rule are courts and law enforcement agencies in the vicinity of large airports where wildlife crime occurs regularly (Ints 2, 15, 17, 19, 23). In addition to wanting expertise and resources, officials often do not consider wildlife crime a serious crime. Prosecutors and judges are, therefore, eager to close a case as soon

Table 8.1: Co-occurrence of general enforcement problems and disadvantages of decentralization

	5.2.1 Advantages Gr=10		5.2.2 Disadvantages Gr=147	
	Count	Coefficient	Count	Coefficient
4.2 (Lack of) expertise Gr=85	0	0.00	33	0.17
4.3 (Lack of) resources Gr=72	0	0.00	27	0.14

as possible, cutting deals with defendants who get away with the payment of a small fine or, more rarely, deferred jail sentences. Prosecutors thereby frequently rely on Art 153a of Germany's criminal code that allows them to close a case before going to trial, citing a lack of public interest and the absence of a severe crime (Ints 2, 7, 10+, 17, 19, 23). Knowing full well that criminal prosecutions often lead to mild sentences, public officials in the UNBs and other agencies prefer to hand out administrative fines instead of referring cases to law enforcement even if they suspect that a crime has taken place (Ints 1+, 19, 23).

In short, lack of political and public support, strong push-back from organized interest, lack of resources and expertise, and lenient sentencing are the obstacles that interviewees frequently mentioned to explain why Germany's wildlife legislation does not deter potential offenders. These shortcomings are not unique to Germany but appear to be widespread in other countries as well (Wyatt 2013: 108; Nurse 2015: 113–77; Maher and Sollund 2017: 119; Fachtagung Artenschutzrecht 2021: 3). Yet Germany's federal system further compounds these obstacles (Klaas et al 2016: 15f). An analysis of the coded interviews clearly demonstrates this finding. The co-occurrence of codes attached to general problems of enforcement with codes attached to disadvantages of decentralized governance is significant, as Table 8.1 shows.

Aggravating problems: Germany's federal system

As mentioned earlier, the implementation of the BNatSchG is left to the municipalities in six federal states, comprising almost two-thirds of German's population. The UNBs of these municipalities are often understaffed and regularly manned with administrative staff with little to no knowledge of wildlife, instead of biologists. Moreover, the enforcement of the BNatSchG occupies only a small percentage (5–10 per cent) of their duties, which is unsurprising considering the low frequency of related cases at the lowest level of governance. Officials, therefore, have no opportunity to develop expertise over time, and what is learned during rare training sessions is quickly forgotten. Another problem is the frequent turnover in these positions. Working for the UNB is neither lucrative nor career-boosting, and to move up the ladder requires assuming new responsibilities. The same holds true for local judges and prosecutors who do not encounter wildlife cases enough during their short stints to develop knowledge and expertise, and for whom these cases are not career-enhancing (Ints 1+, 4+, 10+, 11, 18, 23).

Under these circumstances, SLBs rarely leave their office to conduct any time-consuming inspections and further investigations that require expertise, which they often do not have. Because there is plenty of other work to do, they prioritize easy cases at the expense of more complex cases that are time-intensive. This is a coping strategy that is quite common for SLBs (Cinque et al 2021: 19). Supervisors usually nod this economization through, and since there is no pressure from citizens either to enforce wildlife legislation carefully, there is little motivation to put in extra effort and hours. The same holds true for local police officers who equally lack resources, expertise and motivation. Moreover, economic interests sometimes oppose stricter enforcement. Developers, owners of pet shops and zoo directors, to name a few, consider the laws and regulations that stem from the Bern Convention and CITES time-intensive to follow, and smuggling rare species into the country is often cheaper than breeding them within the country legally. And as powerful actors in local politics, they are formidable opponents (Ints 2, 10+, 24).

In cooperative states, these problems are less severe. A good example is Lower Saxony. Here, a state division focuses on wildlife protection, employing officials who have developed expertise through their training and years of experience. They take over the labour-intensive work of registering species and issuing licences, leaving inspections and confiscation to the municipal level. Moreover, they provide SLBs at the municipal level with advice and expertise, and occasionally take part in raids. Moreover, being isolated from local politics, these higher-level officials serve as lightning rods for the SLBs who refer angry citizens who are well connected to local politicians to their colleagues at the state level. Finally, their influence on law enforcement and weight in courts are considerably stronger than the voice of local officials (Ints 21, 22). The experience in other collaborative states is similar (Int 14, EM3).

The cooperative model thereby holds an advantage over centralized governance. While the latter can also develop expertise and professionalism due to specialization and a higher caseload, it does not allow its state agencies to have their eyes and ears on the ground through SLBs in the UNBs. Local knowledge thereby gets lost (Ints 19, 21, 23). At the same time, in decentralized states, motivated SLBs try to emulate the cooperative structure to increase their discretion through various ways. Formal and informal cooperation thereby plays a key role. In general, almost all interviewees considered cooperation through formal channels helpful and effective (public prosecutors were, however, often considered less approachable). In decentralized states, the BfN thereby appears to serve as a surrogate for state agencies in the cooperative states. In NRW, a special unit for environmental crime (*Stabsstelle Umweltkriminalität*), housed in the Ministry for the Environment, assisted local UNBs and law enforcement agents in complex criminal investigations. The unit was dissolved after the Social Democrat–Green coalition lost its majority in 2017 state elections to a right-wing coalition. Furthermore, in three decentralized states (Bavaria, NRW and Rhineland-Palatia) SLBs in the UNBs can solicit expert advice through the *Naturschutzbeirat*, advisory councils of NGO volunteers with specialized environmental knowledge (Ints 10+, 15, 18, 20).

In addition to formal channels and organizations, informal cooperation assumes an important role in decentralized states. SLBs often get to know each other through training sessions and contact information is exchanged. When problems arise, a quick phone call sometimes helps in complex cases. Informal meetings and trainings are also organized, which sometimes take place twice or more a year and might or might not involve higher-level officials (Ints 1+, 10+, 18). However, it all comes down to the willingness of individuals to exert themselves. Formal and informal channels of cooperation exist, but local officials do not face disciplinary action if they do not use them. Numerous reasons such as career advancement, wanting support from superiors, and local push-back could thwart an official's motivation to seek help and advice. The performance in decentralized states should therefore be more uneven, varying from municipality to municipality. Quantitative analysis supports this assumption.

Quantitative analyses and findings

Graph 8.1 shows the likely impact that Germany's federal system has on states' capacity to prosecute violations that stem from the Bern Convention and CITES.

The graph shows 80 observations (16 states × five years) of criminal violations of the BNatSchG that the BKA compiled for the years 2016–20. In this graph, the states are divided into three groups depending on the degree of centralization (see section 'Legal framework and patchwork enforcement'). What catches the eye is the wide variety of performances across the states in the decentralized group. This spread stands in stark contrast to the states in the cooperative group that perform more evenly, especially when the only outlier is excluded (on the top, Berlin 2016). Based on the insights generated from the qualitative analysis, this divide is unsurprising. Less expected, and deserving further research, is the spread among states in the centralized group.

Graph 8.1: Degree of centralization and criminal violations of BNatSchG reported

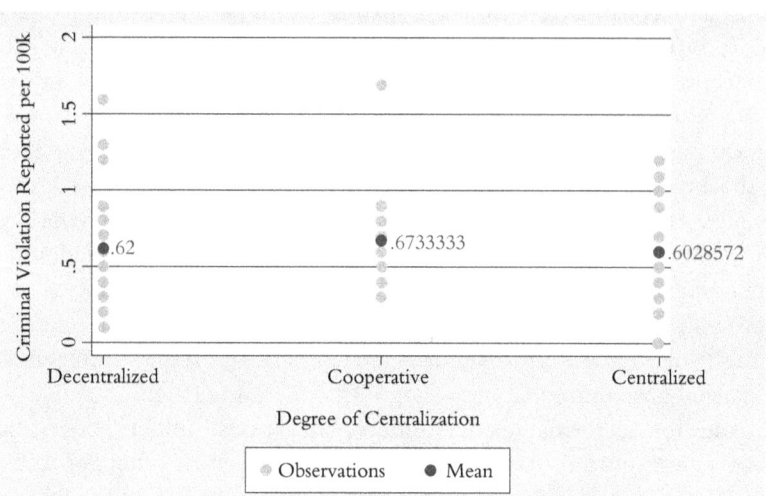

Based on the qualitative research, the cooperative states arguably perform better than the decentralized states. The calculated mean supports this assumption. We also see that the percentage of criminal cases solved, and number of administrative controls performed are strongly and positively correlated with cooperative states (see Appendix B). Yet, the decentralized states do not perform as badly as expected. For instance, they perform better than the centralized states. To solve this puzzle, the BKA data on the municipalities were included in several panel regression models (Appendix B). It turns out that municipalities that perform better than the average are significantly and positively correlated with overall state performance. In other words, over-performing SLBs can significantly boost a state's performance. As previously discussed, even though decentralized states make it harder for SLBs to do their job, motivated bureaucrats find ways to overcome these hurdles through formal and informal ways of cooperation with officials in other agencies and NGO representatives. However, this also means that discretion is an important factor in the decentralized states. Even in countries with centralized states, discretion can play a considerable role (Runhovde 2017; Sollund 2021). With their eyes and ears on the ground, they are closer to the 'sites of crime'. In fact, the number of administrative controls performed (2018–19) and average criminal cases reported (2016–20) are significantly and positively correlated with decentralized states (Appendix B).

A final finding from the panel regression models is that the participation of the Green Party in state government coalitions is strongly correlated with the number of criminal cases reported and the number of administrative fine proceedings initiated – but negatively! This finding contradicts a study conducted by Göhrs, Hubo and Krott (2022), which concludes that the Green Party generally supports nature conservation interests and pushes for the implementation of the biodiversity goal of Natura 2000 included in the Habitats Directive. However, as some interviewees hinted, wildlife protection does not top the political agenda of the Green Party and political goals vary from municipality to municipality (Int 11). Moreover, fulfilling Germany's obligations under the Bern Convention and CITES likely requires stronger and better-funded bureaucracies. Yet the Green Party does not necessarily embrace state expansion (Int 10+). Therefore, the findings of these two studies might not contradict each other but address different research questions.

In short, the quantitative findings of this study bolster the findings from its qualitative analysis. Cooperative states generally perform better and more coherently than decentralized states. Nevertheless, despite all odds, the latter do not perform as badly as expected, due to the efforts of some local officials to overcome the institutional obstacles created by decentralized governance structures, making their municipalities over-perform. The poor and scattered performance of centralized states is unexpected and deserves further research. Finally, wildlife crime is not politicized in Germany. In the political platform of the only party that should be especially inclined to address this problem, the Green Party, wildlife protection does not feature prominently.

Conclusion

Germany supports the old saying that laws are only as good as their enforcement and adjudication. While Germany has dutifully transposed international treaties and European legislation aimed at regulating wildlife trade (CITES) and protecting European endangered species (Bern Convention) into federal law, it has failed to put sufficient resources behind law enforcement. Moreover, courts and prosecutors rarely exhaust the range of penalties that the law offers, with sentencing mostly falling well below the maximum penalties enshrined in the BNatSchG. This is a shortcoming that is observed across Europe (Gelinsky 2022). Lax enforcement and lenient sentencing undermine one of the central functions of the law – that is, deterring illicit behaviour. Leaving the implementation of the law to its 16 federal states further compounds the problem, as it spreads the already insufficient resources thin in those states in which enforcement is transferred down to the municipal level. Here, SLBs' resources and experience are so limited, that effective enforcement is the exception rather than the rule. Due solely to the motivation and ingenuity of some SLBs, often with a degree in Biology, the six decentralized states, covering almost two-thirds of Germany's population, do not perform as badly as one would expect.

Germany's lawmakers can learn a lot from the comparison of decentralized and cooperative states. First, centralizing authority without eliminating municipal agencies appears to be the happy medium, fostering expertise and maintaining local knowledge. Second, states and the federal government should empower SLBs, by offering more opportunities for cooperation between municipalities and training. Third, the creation of police units, public prosecutor offices and court departments that focus on environmental and wildlife crime will reduce the turnover rate among SLBs, as it offers officials a rewarding career path. Moreover, specialization increases the case rate for these officials, allowing them to accumulate experience and expertise. Fourth, in addition, I strongly advise the creation of special offices in the 16 ministries for the environment, tasked with supporting SLBs in their attempts to build solid cases against offenders. Every interviewee who had heard about the work of the *Stabsstelle Umweltkriminalität* in NRW praised the office and bemoaned its dissolution (for example, Ints 1+, 10+, 11, 12, 19, 21). Finally, Germany urgently needs a central database for endangered species to facilitate interagency collaboration. These suggestions are in line with proposals made for other countries (Nurse 2015: chapter 11). In the end, introducing these measures would be neither inordinately expensive nor politically contested, but it would help Germany to bring its domestic performance in line with its international commitments and engagement. They would add teeth to a paper tiger.

References

Altheer, S. and Lameter, K. (2020). 'The rush for the rare: reptiles and amphibians in the European pet trade'. *Animals* 10: 1–14.

Behnke, N. and Kropp, S. (2021). 'Administrative Federalism'. In: S. Kuhlmann, I. Proeller, D. Schimanke and J. Ziekow (eds) *Public Administration in Germany*. Basingstoke, UK: Palgrave Macmillan: 35–51.

Brodkin, E. Z. and Marston, G. (2013). *Work and the Welfare State: Street-Level Organizations and Workfare Politics*. Washington, DC: Georgetown University Press.

BfN (Bundesamt für Naturschutz) (2010). *Vollzugshinweise zum Artenschutzrecht*. Available at: www.bfn.de/sites/default/files/BfN/cites/Dokumente/vollzugshinweise.pdf

BfN (2020). *Zuständigkeiten in den Bundesländern*. Available at: www.bfn.de/sites/default/files/BfN/cites/Dokumente/zustaendigkeit_in_den_bundeslaendern.pdf

BfN (2021). *Bundesrecht*. Available at: www.bfn.de/bundesrecht

BfN (2022). *Verstöße und Ahndungen Landesbehörden* (2018–2019). Available at: www.bfn.de/verstoesse-und-ahndungen-landesbehoerden#anchor-6319

BKA (Bundeskriminalamt) (2022). *Polizeiliche Kriminalstatistik (2016–2020).* Available at: www.bka.de/DE/AktuelleInformationen/StatistikenLagebilder/PolizeilicheKriminalstatistik/pks_node.html

Cinque, S., Sjölander-Lindqvist, A. and Sandström, C. (2021). 'Frontline bureaucrats in wildlife management: caught in the dilemma between effectiveness and responsiveness'. *Environmental Policy and Governance* 32(1): 17–28.

CITES (Convention on International Trade in Endangered Species of Wild Fauna and Flora) (2022a). *The CITES Species.* Available at: https://cites.org/eng/disc/species.php

CITES (2022b). *What Is CITES?* Available at: https://cites.org/eng/disc/what.php

Council of Europe (2022). *Convention on the Conservation of European Wildlife and Natural Habitats.* Available at: www.coe.int/en/web/conventions/full-list/-/conventions/treaty/104

EFFACE (European Action to Fight Environmental Crime) (2022). *EFFACE – A Research Project on Environmental Crime.* Available at: https://efface.eu/index/index.html

European Commission (2022). *Natura 2000.* Available at: https://ec.europa.eu/environment/nature/natura2000/index_en.htm

Fachtagung Artenschutzrecht (2021). *Tagungsbericht, 17. December 2021.* Unpublished.

Gabehart, K. M. (2022) 'Rural society, democratic exclusion, and the cultural divide: moving towards a research agenda of the study of ruralness'. *Public Integrity* [online first], DOI: 10.1080/10999922.2022.2061132

Gelinsky, K. (2022). 'Umweltkriminalität wirksamer bekämpfen'. *Frankfurter Allgemeine Zeitung,* 1 November. Available at: www.faz.net/aktuell/wirtschaft/umweltkriminalitaet-wirksamer-bekaempfen-18429576.html

Glaser, A. (2011). *German Environmental Law in a Nutshell. Annual Report-2011-Germany.* IUS Publicum Network Review. Available at: www.iuspublicum.com/repository/uploads/04_04_2011_9_47_Glaser.pdf

Göhrs, M., Krott, M. and Hubo, C. (2022). 'Political parties as allies for the forestry sector: a case study from Germany'. *Forest Policy and Economics* 138: 102–11.

Hardin, G. (1968). 'The tragedy of the commons'. *Science* 162(3859): 1243–8.

Hupe, P., Hill, M. and Buffat, A. (eds) (2015). *Understanding Street-level Bureaucracy.* Bristol, UK: Bristol University Press.

Huth, F. (2021). *Jagdsaison: Diese Tiere werden am meisten von Jägern getötet.* Peta Deutschland. Available at: www.peta.de/themen/jagdsaison/

Klaas, K., Sina, S. and Gerstetter, C. (2016). *Wildlife Crime in Germany. In-depth Analysis for the ENVI Committee.* Available at: www.europarl.europa.eu/RegData/etudes/IDAN/2016/578958/IPOL_IDA%282016%29578958_EN.pdf

Lipsky, M. (1980). *Street-level Bureaucracy*. New York: Russell Sage Foundation.

Lipsky, M. (2010). *Street-level Bureaucracy: Dilemmas of the Individual in Public Service*. New York: Russell Sage Foundation.

Maher, J. and Sollund R. (2017). 'Wildlife Trafficking: Harms and Victimization'. In: R. Sollund, C. Stefes and A. R. Germani (eds) *Fighting Environmental Crime in Europe and Beyond*. Basingstoke, UK: Palgrave Macmillan: 99–128.

Marshall, B. M., Strine, C. and Hughes, A. C. (2020). 'Thousands of reptile species threatened by under-regulated global trade'. *Nature Communication* 11. Available at: https://doi.org/10.1038/s41467-020-18523-4

May, P. J. and Winter, S. (2000). 'Reconsidering styles of regulatory enforcement: patterns in Danish agro-environmental inspection'. *Law and Policy* 22(2): 143–73.

NABU (Naturschutzbund) (2022). *Das Artenschutzrecht*. Available at: www.nabu.de/imperia/md/content/nabude/artenschutz/201207_broschuere_artenschutzrecht.pdf

Nurse, A. (2015). *Policing Wildlife: Perspectives on the Enforcement of Wildlife Legislation*. Basingstoke, UK: Palgrave Macmillan.

Rinfret, S. R. and Pautz, M. C. (2013). 'Attitudes and perspectives of frontline workers in environmental policy: a case study of Ohio's Environmental Protection Agency and Wisconsin's Department of Natural Resources'. *Journal of Public Affairs* (13): 111–22.

Rozell, M. J. and Wilcox, C. (2019). *Federalism: A Very Short Introduction*, Introductions. New York: Oxford University Press.

Runhovde, S. R. (2017). 'Taking the path of least resistance? Decision-making in police investigations of illegal wildlife trade'. *Policing: A Journal of Policy and Practice* 11(1): 87–102.

Scharpf, F. W. (2008). 'Community, diversity and autonomy: the challenges of reforming German federalism'. *German Politics* 17(4): 509–21.

Sevä, M. and Jagers, S. C. (2013). 'Inspecting environmental management from within: the role of street-level bureaucrats in environmental policy implementation'. *Journal of Environmental Management* 128: 1060–70.

Sina, S., Gerstetter, C., Porsch, L., Roberts, E., Smith, O., Klaas, K., et al (2016). *Wildlife Crime*. Study for the ENVI Committee, Brussels. Available at: www.europarl.europa.eu/RegData/etudes/STUD/2016/570008/IPOL_STU%282016%29570008_EN.pdf

Sollund, R. (2016). 'The Animal Other'. In: M. Hall, J. Maher, A. Nurse, G. Potter, N. South and T. Wyatt (eds) *Greening Criminology in the 21st Century: Contemporary Debates and Future Directions in the Study of Environmental Harm*. London: Routledge: 79–99.

Sollund, R. (2021). 'Green criminology: its foundation in critical criminology and its way forward'. *The Howard Journal* 60(3): 304–22.

Stefes, C. (2021). 'Wildlife protection in Germany: sound legislation and deficient implementation'. *Revista Catalana De Dret Ambiental* 12(1): 1–24.
Süddeutsche Zeitung (2020). *Bewährung für Elfenbein-Schmuggler: Tierschützer enttäuscht.* 12 November. Available at: www.sueddeutsche.de/panorama/ kriminalitaet-cottbus-bewaehrung-fuer-elfenbein-schmuggler-tierschuetzer-enttaeuscht-dpa.urn-newsml-dpa-com-20090101-201111-99-299169
Wouter, K. (2020). 'Principle of subsidiarity'. Available at: www.coastalwiki.org/wiki/Principle_of_subsidiarity
Wyatt, T. (2013). *Wildlife Trafficking. A Deconstruction of the Crime, the Victims, and the Offenders.* Basingstoke, UK: Palgrave Macmillan.
Zacka, B. (2017). *When the State Meets the Street: Public Service and Moral Agency.* Boston, MA: The Belknap Press of Harvard University Press.

Appendix A: List of Interviewees

Abbreviation	Name	Organization	Location, Date
Int.1+	Anonymous	UNB, NRW	Zoom, n.d.
Int.2	Anonymous	German Customs	Zoom, n.d.
Int.3	Anonymous	German Customs	Zoom, n.d.
EM.1	Anonymous	Regional Council, BW	Email, n.d.
EM.2	Anonymous	District Office, BW	Email, n.d.
Int.4+	Balzer, Sandra Böhmer, Franz	BfN	Zoom, 5 Jan 2021
Int.6	Blaufuß, Kathrin	German Federal Parliament	Zoom, 6 Jan 2021
Int.7	Brücher, Helmut	CITES Expert	Zoom, 21 Dec 2020
Int.8	Casselmann, Andrea	ONB, Regional Council Kassel, Hesse	Zoom, 12 Dec 2021
Int.9+	Cyriacks, Peer Stöcker, Ulrich	Environmental Action Germany	Zoom, 5 Jan 2021
Int.10+	Distelrath, Florian von Maravić, Irina	UNB Cologne, NRW	Cologne, 24 Nov 2021
EM.3	Dornbusch, Petra	CITES-Office, State Office for the Environment, Sax-Anh	Email, 23 Nov 2021
Int.11	Esser, Georg	UNB, Mönchengladbach, NRW	Zoom, 3 Dec 2021
Int.12	Fiedler, Sebastian	German Federal Parliament	Berlin, 14 Dec 2021
Int.13	Freyer, Daniela	ProWildlife	Zoom, 7 Jan 2021
Int.14	Gall, Thomas	Ministry for the Environment, Sch-Hol	Zoom, 29 Dec 2020
Int.15	Hinzmann, Jürgen	Ministry for the Environment, NRW	Zoom, 22 Feb 2021; Düsseldorf, 14 Apr 2021

Abbreviation	Name	Organization	Location, Date
EM.4	Hirschfeld, Axel	Committee Against Bird Slaughter	Email, 13 Jan 2021
Int.16	Hügel, Kornelia	UNB, Speyer, RP	Zoom, 5 Jan 2022
Int.17	Köhncke, Arnulf	World Wildlife Fund	Zoom, 10 Mar 2021
Int.18	Kraft, Stefanie	UNB, Speyer, RP	Zoom, 6 Jan 2022
Int.19	Kricke, Randolph Dr	UNB, Duisburg, NRW	Zoom, 12 Jan 2021
Int.20	Kruscha, Sonja	UNB, Bottrop, NRW	Zoom, 26 Nov 2021
Int.21	Leferink, Jens	State Office for Water Policy, Coastal- and Nature Protection, Low Sax	Zoom, 22 Apr 2021
Int.22	Mocek, Moritz	UNB, Salzgitter, Low Sax	Zoom, 6 Dec 2021
Int.23	Pfohl, Michael	Public Prosecutor, BW, ret.; Prof, Univ. Tübingen	Gomaringen, 11 Dec 2021
Int.24	Rüße, Norwich	State Parliament, NRW	Zoom, 26 Nov 2021

Note: + indicates that two individuals were interviewed at the same time

Appendix B: Panel Regression Models

Panel Regression Models

	Dependent Variables							
	Average criminal cases reported per 100k (2016-2020)		Percent solved of criminal cases reported		Number of administrative controls per 100k (2018-2019)		Number of administrative fine proceedings per 100k (2018-2019)	
	coefficient	p-value	coefficient	p-value	coefficient	p-value	coefficient	p-value
Independent Variables & Controls								
Degree of Centralization								
0=dencentralized	0.127	0.048*	9.547	0.066	10.31	<0.001***		
1=cooperative	0.256	0.001***	13.907	0.028*	5.691	0.025*	0.664	0.194
2=centralized							1.377	0.011*
Percent years Green Party in government	−0.964	0.001***	13.084	0.588	17.183	0.075	−7.384	0.001***
Population density (per sq. km.)	0.0001	0.064	−0.002	0.335	−0.001	0.127	0.0002	0.322
GDP per capita	−1.980E−06	0.635	0.001	0.008**				
Average income					−0.178	<0.001***	0.002	0.871
Educational attainment					−0.014	0.003**	0.002	0.052

Panel Regression Models

	Model 1 coef	Model 1 p	Model 2 coef	Model 2 p	Model 3 coef	Model 3 p	Model 4 coef	Model 4 p
Percent of underperforming municipalities in a Länder Percent of underperforming municipalities in a Länder	-0.154	0.516	-36.321	0.058	-14.782	0.022*	2.829	0.047*
Percent of overperforming municipalities in a Länder Percent of overperforming municipalities in a Länder	2.617	<0.001***	31.58	0.364	-6.23	0.712	3.677	0.329
Criminal cases recorder per 100K (2018-2019)					-3.364	0.35	0.444	0.577
R-squared			**R-squared**		**R-squared**		**R-squared**	
Within	0.0000		Within	0.0000	Within	0.5896	Within	0.4680
Between	0.0000		Between	0.0000	Between	1	Between	1.0000
Overall	0.5101		Overall	0.1820	Overall	0.5903	Overall	0.4687
Wald chi2	81.780		**Wald chi2**	17.29	**Wald chi2**	31.7	**Wald chi2**	19.41
Prob > chi2	0.0000		**Prob > chi2**	0.0156	**Prob > chi2**	0.0002	**Prob > chi2**	0.0219

*significant at p=0.05 alpha level; **significant at p=0.001 alpha level; ***significant at p=0.001 alpha level Note: Panel regressions utilize random effects model to account for any unmeasured variables that may be correlated with one or more of the x variables. A Hausman test also indicated a random effects model to be a better fit.

9

The Norwegian Chain of Wildlife Treaty Effectiveness

David R. Goyes

Introduction

In the past seven decades, more than 2,000 treaties that pertain to wildlife have been ratified (Brandi et al 2019). Treaties are written agreements of two or more states, regulated by international law – the international community entrust them with the task of preserving wildlife. Yet this plethora of international wildlife treaties cannot automatically be equated with increased preservation of wildlife. From 1970 to 2016, 'between 17,000 and 100,000 species' have become extinct (van Uhm 2016: 19), and there has been 'an average 69% decline in the relative abundance of monitored wildlife populations around the world between 1970 and 2018' (WWF 2022: 5). Beyond being ratified, wildlife treaties need to be implemented to have an effect.

Treaties impact reality through a chain of effectiveness that extends from the international to the national to the local (Liljeblad 2004). The links of the chain are: international proposition, state ratification, domestic implementation through legal action, domestic resource allocation, and local behavioural change (Underdal 1992; Jackson and Bührs 2015). A whole field of research – *regime effectiveness studies* – exists to analyse each of the links in the chain and evaluate the conditions under which a treaty will be effective (Underdal 1992).

Scholars investigating regime effectiveness face a major challenge: The further away the phenomenon being investigated is from the treaty, the more difficult it is to arrive at decisive conclusions about effectiveness. It is, for instance, risky – to say the least – to claim that the text of a treaty *caused* the change of behaviour of a society. Too many complex elements are at play to claim causality. This difficulty notwithstanding, scholars can gather data to identify the *correlation* of treaties with changes in the international, national and local levels. Trends provide insights into how treaties work and the conditions under which they thrive.

We know, for example, that treaties that are broad and with few binding obligations attract more signatory parties than those that are focused and contain compulsory duties (Bodansky et al 2017); preferential trade agreements elicit more domestic legislative action than international environmental agreements (Brandi et al 2019); states with a federal political structure are more likely to allocate resources than unitary states (Mauerhofer et al 2015; see also Stefes, this volume); and, behaviour is more likely to change in states where stakeholders participated in the adoption of the treaty than in those from which stakeholders were excluded (Atisa 2020). Few scholars have undertaken the task of evaluating the full chain of implementation of wildlife treaties. Jonathan Liljeblad (2004) attempted to cover the full effectiveness chain of the Convention on International Trade in Endangered Species of Wild Fauna and Flora (CITES), and unsurprisingly argued that countries struggle to create global to national and national to local linkages to implement the convention.

In this chapter, I contribute to regime effectiveness studies by investigating the chains of implementation of two wildlife treaties: CITES (1973) and the Bern Convention on the Conservation of European Wildlife and Natural Habitats (1979). I do so through a case study focused on Norway, part of the CRIMEANTHROP project.[1] The effectiveness of wildlife treaties in Norway is polemic. Commentators argue that the state engages in state crime through its constant breaches of the treaties and that the states intentionally go against its commitments by euthanizing species (regarding the Bern Convention, see Sollund and Goyes 2021; Trouwborst et al 2017; regarding CITES, see Sollund 2021).

As I show in this chapter, Norway is threatening the species it promised to protect. Where does the failure in the chain of implementation lie? I endeavour to respond to this question in this chapter, which is divided into four sections after this introduction. In 'Link one: the conventions', I present the background information of CITES and the Bern Convention and evaluate the stage of treaty proposition. 'Link two: domestic legislation' contains the evaluation of the legislative action Norway undertook to implement the treaties. In 'Link three: behavioural change', I detail how much the conventions affect the practice of wildlife policy practitioners.

---

[1] Criminal Justice, Wildlife Conservation and Animal Rights in the Anthropocene. Funded by the Research Council Norway, project number 289285 (FRIPRO) directed by Ragnhild A. Sollund.

In the 'Conclusion' I compare the findings of this case study with the general literature.

Link one: the conventions

Wildlife treaties are part of international environmental law (IEL). The protection of wildlife is one of the primary concerns of IEL, and treaties are an important instrument to this end. Yet, several caveats frame the ways in which IEL endeavours to protect wildlife. First, national sovereignty is the cornerstone of IEL (Dupuy and Viñuales 2019). Principle 21 of the Declaration of the United Nations Conference on the Human Environment (1972, the Stockholm Declaration) reads: 'States have ... the sovereign right to exploit their own resources pursuant to their own environmental policies, and the responsibility to ensure that activities within their jurisdiction or control do not cause damage to the environment of other States or of areas beyond the limits of national jurisdiction' (United Nations 1972).

Commentators disagree on their evaluations of the sovereignty principle. Some praise it for being a tool against colonialism (Schrijver 2009); others criticize it for clashing against ideals of global justice (Armstrong 2015).

The second caveat is that while the manifest function of treaties in IEL is to achieve a reciprocal adjustment of interests by the states, in practice international environmental treaties are characterized by asymmetrical obligations to the parties. Environmental treaties – of which wildlife treaties are a variety – are not dependent on reciprocity but are based primarily on geopolitical divisions. During negotiations, states use their political and economic strength to frame the treaties in ways that favour their interests rather than create stipulations for the 'global good' (Goyes 2017).

Third, IEL has had different interests throughout history: it began as a tool to protect nature as an economic asset. Later, it was also tasked with resolving conflicts related to the sovereignty of states over wildlife (Bodansky et al 2017). And lately, some argue that IEL has moved from protecting wildlife as a resource, to a combination of safeguarding economic interests while simultaneously conserving wildlife for its ecological and aesthetic value (Dupuy and Viñuales 2019). Into that context appeared CITES and the Bern Convention.

CITES came into existence because, from the 1960s, various organizations, mainly the International Union for Conservation of Nature, made efforts to urge governments to take action to prevent illegal wildlife trade (Huxley 2000). The original goal was 'to set up a system through which the trade controls in importing countries could be matched with those in the exporting countries', as a way to advance conservation (Huxley 2000: 11). A decade after the implementation of CITES, various NGOs began discussing issues of animal rights and animal welfare (Huxley 2000: 11). This initiated a conflict between NGOs and the initial proponents of the convention. The latter responded with concerns that NGO intervention would 'derail or divert the convention from its original direction' (Huxley 2000: 10). Despite debates, CITES still conserves a spirit of trade regulation (Goyes and Sollund 2016).

The overarching goal of CITES is to 'save wild species from extinction' by regulating wildlife trade (Hutton and Dickson 2000; Wyatt 2021; Sollund and Lie's introduction, this volume), and it commits to sustainability in order to maintain trade (Sollund 2019). Its main mechanisms are 'regulation and restriction of the international trade in wildlife' (Hutton and Dickson 2000: 15). CITES (n.d.) uses a system of three lists of endangered species:

- Appendix I 'lists species that are the most endangered among CITES-listed animals and plants. ... They are threatened with extinction and CITES prohibits international trade in specimens of these species except when the purpose of the import is not commercial'. Yet, there are exceptions – with a commercial reasoning – for travelling exhibitions and circuses.
- Appendix II 'lists species that are not necessarily now threatened with extinction but that may become so unless trade is closely controlled'.
- Appendix III 'is a list of species included at the request of a Party that already regulates trade in the species and that needs the cooperation of other countries to prevent unsustainable or illegal exploitation'.

CITES currently has 184 parties to the convention worldwide.

Meanwhile, The Bern Convention is a regional treaty (see Sollund and Lie's introduction, this volume). It originated in 'a request made by the Parliamentary Assembly of the Council of Europe in 1973 requesting European regulations for the protection of wildlife' (Diaz 2010: 186). Its purpose is to protect European wild plants and animals – particularly those endangered – and their habitats, as well as advancing cooperation among countries to this end. (The treaty also endeavours to protect the wildlife and habitats of some North African countries). One of the obligations that the Bern Convention imposes on states is to take suitable administrative and legal measures to maintain adequate population levels of species to secure their survival (Council of Europe Portal n.d.). The Bern Convention also functions as a basis for 'ample collaboration between the countries', for instance, through collective decisions that express the 'common view' of the partners, and through the Emerald Network that creates natural protection areas in Europe (Bugge 2019: 297).

The Bern Convention also works with a system of lists: Appendix I lists 'strictly protected flora species', Appendix II includes 'strictly protected fauna species', Appendix III registers 'protected fauna species' and Appendix IV records 'prohibited means and methods of killing, capture and other forms of exploitation' (Council of Europe Portal n.d.).

Both treaties came to existence thanks to the action of lobbying organizations with the stated goal to conserve wildlife. But, what are the latent goals of the ratified treaties? Which messages do they send? Are those messages coherent with the stated goals? I (Goyes 2021) applied discourse analysis methodology to: (1) the bulk of documents that shape the treaties; (2) 100 Resolutions of the Meetings of the Parties to the Convention of CITES (1979–2019); (3) nine Resolutions of the Standing Committee of the Bern Convention (1989–2019); and (4) 208 Recommendations of the Standing Committee of the Bern Convention (1982–2019).

My main finding is that both treaties allow the use of wildlife for profit-making. They are *econocentric*: concerned with economic health at the expense of environmental and human health, wellbeing and protection (McClanahan et al 2015; Brisman et al 2018; Brisman and South 2018; Goyes and South 2019). This coincides with what other researchers have argued (see for example, Sollund 2019) – and is a problematic basis for treaties that allegedly intend to protect wildlife.

The treaties also contain a decision-making monopoly. They rely on quantitative science and on instrumental political knowledge. These knowledge systems are mechanisms used to impose social organization: they allocate exclusive power to some actors to regulate behaviour in relation to wildlife, while denying the possibility for more open, democratic and argument-based ruling. For instance, scientific quantitative language is a *monopolized* social language because it silences everyone beyond the inner circle (Christie 2009). This produces a context in which very few actors are able to participate in determining the distribution of social goods, such as respect for one's life and habitat, in the arena of wildlife management. While, for example, NGOs are 'welcome to observe' the Standing Committee meetings of the Bern Convention, in practice their complaints usually lack power to affect the contents and implementation of the treaty. Thus, treaties exclude many stakeholders (such as NGOs and other civil society groups), something that the specialized literature has shown generates problems of implementation due to the lack of engagement, understanding and agreement with the instrument.

Despite those similarities, I found that the Bern Convention and CITES have various opposing pillars. The Bern Convention relies on regional governance while CITES underpins nationalism. CITES aims for species conservation while the Bern Convention hopes for ecosystem conservation. The Bern Convention privileges political instrumental views, while CITES argues for 'objective' quantitative science. Those dissimilarities also generate problems of effectiveness. States are supposed to implement wildlife treaties via *public policies*: '*a coordinated action plan* established by an official authority, in which resources are assigned' (Goyes 2015: 146, emphasis added). A public policy that implements CITES and the Bern Convention should be able to apply both simultaneously. Yet, they point in different directions, at times contradicting each other. Those tensions are mainly reflected in that policy makers will have to choose whether to (a) be focused either on a national or a pan-European identity, (b) prioritize either species or ecosystems as a whole or (c) be either reliant on objective scientific knowledge or based on diplomatic considerations. Norway has focused on national economic interests, deploying diplomatic power to justify its decisions. The contradictions also give policy makers discretional powers. They can cherry pick the logics they want to embrace from the conventions, as long as they stick to econocentrism. The ambivalence of the treaties combined with the permanent sovereignty doctrine removes from the conventions the ambitious commitment that inspired them to protect wildlife.

The evaluation of *the treaty* part of the chain predicts problems with the effectiveness of CITES and the Bern Convention. Based on such problematic basis, how does domestic implementation work?

Link two: domestic legislation

The Norwegian state uses a *dualistic principle* regarding treaties and national law. The dualistic principle means that 'international law first becomes national when the relevant Norwegian authorities have decided on the measures that transform international rules into Norwegian law' (Bugge 2019: 84). In other words, international law is relevant in a Norwegian territory only once national authorities create laws on the topic (Aarli and Mæhle 2018). In case of conflict, authorities should prioritize national law over international mandates (Bugge 2019). Norway has two methods of converting international law into national law: *transformation*, in which parliament issues laws that 'fulfil the commitments derived from the treaty' (Aarli and Mæhle 2018), and *incorporation*, in which the international rules are made national as they are.

To understand how Norway transformed the two treaties into domestic legislation, I studied the *critical legislative events* of the process (Goyes 2023b). Critical legislative events are 'the points at which laws are produced that provide a new approach to a problem' (Chambliss 1993: 3). Regulation 1276 of 2002 marked a new way of incorporating CITES' obligations in the country, and the Nature Diversity Act of 2009 supposedly embraces the commitments derived from the Bern Convention. For both regulatory instruments, which are the relevant critical legislative events, I studied the texts of the laws, parliamentary initiatives and pre-legislative research. Most of those documents are available on Lovdata (https://lovdata.no) except for the pre-legislative research of Regulation 1276 of 2002, which I accessed through a right of petition to the Ministry of Foreign Affairs. The Bern Convention and CITES have generated much legislative activity in Norway. Lovdata, the foundation that publishes Norwegian judicial information, lists 98 documents associated with laws connected with CITES and 246 from the Bern Convention (laws, parliamentary initiatives, pre-legislative research, public propositions, reforms, registries, regulations and speeches).

Then, to understand the broad social dynamics that dictated the way in which Norway implemented the treaties, I connected the critical legislative events with *socio-environmental critical events*, the most important conflicts in Norway about human interaction with nature. All the material I used to map socio-environmental conflicts was archival and included communications from the parliament about the environment, court rulings and historical material.

The trajectory along which Norway internalized the mandates of CITES and the Bern Convention is short and straightforward, but it internalized each of the conventions differently. When Norway ratified CITES in 1976, the government deemed that the existing legal framework contained all the necessary tools and mechanisms to fulfil the mandates of the convention (Arntzen de Besche Advokatfirma As 2017). The country's authorities used existing general regulation for imports and exports and a regulation under the Animal Welfare Act on import of exotic species, with the only twist being that it was the Ministry of Environment that oversaw issuing trade authorization for listed species. The adoption of CITES occurred through *hard incorporation*, that is, using the exact text of the convention. In 1983, the government revised Article 1a of the *Regulation on the Completion of Imports* (*Forskrift om gjennomføring av innførselsreguleringen*), to ensure practitioners would use the text of the convention itself. In 1989, the Directorate of Environmental Protection reconsidered hard incorporation and began drafting a CITES-specific regulation. The main failure, in the Directorate's eyes, was that existing regulation was 'completely generic', thereby failing to meet the demands of 'the rule of law', 'public information' and 'penal prosecution of illegal trade with endangered species' (Utenriksdepartementet 2002: 566). Those failures were identified by two other actors: the Norwegian Tax Administration, which sought to clarify the terms and procedures, and environmental NGOs, which sought to strengthen the protection of nature (Bugge 2019).

While the discussions of Norway's integration into the European Union delayed the initiative to create a specific CITES regulation for over a decade, on 12 November 2002, the Norwegian Ministry of International Affairs (Utenriksdepartementet) put forward a Royal Resolution – a decision the king approves upon the initiative of the government – to 'formalise the CITES framework, which has been implemented in Norway since the Convention was ratified on July 27, 1976' (Utenriksdepartementet 2002: 564). The outcome was Regulation 1276 of 15 November 2002 known as the Regulation of Implementation of the Convention of 3 March 1973, on International Trade of Endangered Species of Wild Flora and Fauna. Regulation 1276 of 2002 uses the technique of *soft incorporation*, that is, using the convention as a template but with minor changes, copying most of the convention in an internal regulation (thereby using it as a framework law) but making some changes in accord with national regulations and internal interests. In the words of the Ministry of Foreign Affairs, Regulation 1276

> mainly follows the mandates of the Convention but when it comes to the regulation for the species on list I, the suggestion is formulated as a prohibition but with possibility for dispensation. In practice, the outcome is the same as in the Convention because the requirements for authorisation of these species in the Convention are so strict that in reality it means prohibition. (Utenriksdepartementet 2002: 566)

In comparison, the Bern Convention is incorporated into Norwegian law through *transformation*. The Arntzen de Besche law firm neatly expressed this: 'the [Bern] Convention is not directly incorporated into Norwegian law, but the Convention's commitments are fulfilled particularly through the *Nature Diversity Act and the Wildlife Law* [NDL]' (Arntzen de Besche Advokatfirma As 2017). The Norwegian government confirmed twice that it transformed its commitments derived from the Bern Convention into the NDL. First, when proposing the NDL, the Ministry of Climate and Environment wrote, 'the Bern Convention is an important premise for most of this law's decisions' (Miljøverndepartement [Norwegian Environment Agency] 2008–09: 48). Second, in the biennial report that Norway sent to the Bern Convention's Standing Committee for the 2009–10 period, in which the government noted the issuing of a 'new act on nature diversity', which sought to 'protect biological, geological and landscape diversity and ecological processes through conservation and sustainable use' (Norway to the Standing Committee of the Bern Convention 2015: 3).

The NDL is the overarching Norwegian law for the protection of the biological, geological and ecological diversity of the country's natural environment. NDL focuses on the protection and sustainable use of nature, particularly on preserving diversity for the present and the future. The law also intends to protect ecosystems based on their role in the survival of endangered species and for their cultural, aesthetic and scientific value. In addition to deterring negative interventions in nature, NDL also includes positive actions in support of the law's goals (Bugge 2019). NDL's Article 5 centrally establishes that 'species and their genetic diversity must be protected in the long term, and that species' populations are able to survive in their natural environments'. In practice, however, the law is informed by the desire to balance the protection of the species and their ecosystems, the freedom to exploit wildlife economically and the protection of interests that are threatened by the presence of wild carnivores (Bugge 2019: 262).

For instance, Article 18 allows for the killing of wild, critically endangered predators to prevent damage to livestock.

When incorporating CITES' mandates, Norwegian legislators copied the text of the convention. In contrast, when internalizing Norway's obligations derived from the Bern Convention, Norwegian lawmakers rephrased the text. Why? The Norwegian Ministry of Climate and Environment hinted at the answer in its proposition of the NDL: 'international trade regulations set some limits on the means to advance the protection and sustainable use of natural diversity. The Ministry has responded to those limits in its legislative work' (Miljøverndepartement 2008–09: 21). The ministry was concerned that the Bern Convention would stand in the way of economic growth. CITES, because it promoted trade, could be incorporated into Norwegian law, whereas it was necessary to rephrase the Bern Convention, that is, transform it, because it had the potential to interfere with economic profit. Norwegian lawmakers' respect for economic concerns is not coincidental: a century of environmental conflicts in Norway engrained deference to economics in the government.

Therefore, the second link (domestic legislation) was pretty much defined by economic factors and internal political affairs, more than by the stated rationale of the treaties (first link) of protecting wildlife. As I described above, both treaties are econocentric. The latent spirit of the treaties thus informed the domestic action.

How do the contents of the treaties and of the domestic legislation affect the behaviour of those in charge of implementing them?

Link three: behavioural change

The *narrative turn* in the social sciences came about most strongly in the early 1980s, when scholars began to explore in depth the centrality of stories in processes of individual cognition, building images of the self, and community identity and behaviour (Maines 1993). Sociological interest in stories and storytelling was present before the advent of the narrative turn, mainly in the work of symbolic interactionists with an interest in 'how people gave accounts to avert threats to their self-image and status' and of ethnographers documenting 'how people used stories in conversation to maintain interactional order' (Polletta et al 2011: 112). The narrative turn, however, paid serious attention to stories not as 'things people told' but as 'things that people lived' (Polletta et al 2011: 112). Discourse analysts and their interest in uncovering how society, through language, builds the linguistic contexts in which people live (Gee 2014) significantly affected the narrative turn by suggesting that the discourses circulating in society become the fabric for the stories that individuals use for interpreting reality and inspiring their future behaviour.

Narrative analysis, as a valuable methodological and analytical perspective, has burgeoned in the social sciences during the last three decades and is also gaining traction in the physical sciences. In this context, the interdisciplinary sector of ecological management and restoration is increasingly embracing a narrative approach. Contemporary analyses include explorations of how stories are fundamental for co-producing networks of environmental governance and to inspire collaborative behaviour (Ingram et al 2014), research on the value of stories in facilitating participatory environmental governance by bringing together dispersed informal networks (Ingram et al 2019), and studies of how community and political narratives about environmental resources can result in ineffective policies despite evidence that better options exist (Warner 2019).

In wildlife conservation and restoration sectors, storytelling has not yet been recognized as an important and effective technique for engaging behaviour-changing pathways. Yet, Redford and colleagues (2012: 757) remind academics of the importance of stories in studying those sectors:

> The stories conservation practitioners have told to gain public support may be chosen for analysis rather than the science underlying them. Our reliance on storytelling is understandable because storytelling is an ancient human behaviour and a very effective way to engage an audience. We tell compelling stories about the impending loss of a species and the speed of ecosystem destruction. We tell success stories to inspire people to replicate success. These stories, originally told by conservation practitioners, are written down and widely shared by public affairs, development, and communication scribes. As with court scribes of old, these scribes make the stories more engaging, more inspiring, and scarier—with the aim of engaging more donors and reaching a broader public.

The overall knowledge about the power of stories contrasted to the latent awareness of their importance in the conservation and restoration sectors inspired me to study the stories offered by wildlife management stakeholders (activists, civil servants and parliamentarians) to evaluate if – and eventually to what extent – wildlife treaties and their derived domestic legislation affect behaviour.

Between February and October 2021, I interviewed 15 core stakeholders in the management of Norwegian wildlife (Goyes 2022),[2] five from each of three groups. First, members of the Standing Committee on Energy and the Environment of Stortinget, the Norwegian parliament. Arguably, Stortinget

---

[2] Approved by the Norwegian Centre for Research data.

is the most important institution in Norway for wildlife management. These interviewed parliamentarians represent four of the nine political parties represented in Stortinget when I conducted the interviews: Arbeiderpartiet (The Labour Party), Miljøpartiet De Grønne (The Green Party), Rødt (The Red Party), and Venstre (The Liberal Party). Arbeiderpartiet is the largest party in Norway, with the most representatives in Stortinget and a long history of being in government. The three others are among the parties that are considered most animal friendly by animal protection NGOs.[3] Second, civil servants of the Ministry of Climate and Environment, Norwegian Environment Agency, Norwegian Scientific Committee for Food and Environment, and Norwegian National Authority for Investigation and Prosecution of Economic and Environmental Crime (Økokrim). These are all government or government-funded organizations. Third, representatives of some of the principal NGOs championing wildlife protection in Norway: Foreningen Våre Rovdyr (Union for our Predators), Greenpeace Norway, NOAH (For Animal Rights), and World Wildlife Fund Norway.

How can stories be useful for understanding human action? A story is a constructed work that 'creates a connection and has a meaning, gives the unmanageable a manageable form' (Andersen 2008: 125). Four elements underlie the structure of all stories: an *opening* that introduces what the story is about and who the characters are, a *challenge* that describes what the characters need to accomplish, an *action* that addresses the challenge, and a *resolution* that presents how the characters and their world have changed as a result of the action (Schimel 2012).

Interviewing five individuals per group allowed me to collect narratives from central stakeholders in the design and implementation of wildlife management. In choosing the interviewees, I considered their proximity to *and* interest in environmental matters. My expectation was that they were in the best position to have relevant knowledge of the application of wildlife treaties in their spheres. The interviews were *narrative*, centred on 'the stories the subjects tell, on the plots and structures of their accounts' (Brinkmann and Kvale 2015: 178) and usually revolved around a 'generative narrative question' that invited interviewees to talk freely and tell stories (Flick 2005: 97). In the interviews, I requested participants' *stories* around the axes of personal identity, personal beliefs, professional practice (including anecdotes), interaction with international wildlife treaties, and their views on the best way to manage wildlife.

NGOs, civil servants, and parliamentarians alike do not include international environmental conventions in their repertoire of stories. Charlotte (a pseudonym), who works at an NGO did not mention *wildlife*

---

[3] See for example, https://dyrevern.no/landbruksdyr/stor-valgguide-pa-dyrevelferd-hvilket-parti-er-best/ and www.dyrsrettigheter.no/noah/ditt-valg-deres-fremtid-2/

treaties when talking about her life and work. So I asked directly, and she replied bluntly: "I rarely refer to them in my communications or in meetings or in advocacy work. I think we talk more from an ethical level."

Oliver, a civil servant, only made indirect reference to the treaties in his narrative: "I do not have them [treaties] very high on my mind at all. ... I use my scientific principles to produce reports rather than applying the principles of the treaty to my scientific activity."

Amelia, a parliamentarian, said: "They [the treaties] are not arguments I use in my daily work because it is our ideology more than laws and rules that I use ... so, yes, it is a strategic use of them, as an argument."

The only exception was William, another parliamentarian who said:

'Wildlife treaties are important. Even when politics are not shaped by them, I know that we have ratified them and the bureaucracy must work to create the basis to include them in the decisions ahead, to comply with these conventions and treaties ... even when one is not clear about them in the daily work when we define policies.'

Yet, while William is knowledgeable about the contents and particularities of wildlife treaties, he recognizes their minimal impact in daily political practices.

Research in the field of conservation and restoration shows that programmes need coordinated cooperation to be effective (Hames et al 2014) and that narratives are crucial in determining whether stakeholder networks in environmental management cooperate or not (Ingram et al 2014, 2019), yet the stories held by representatives of the three main groups of management stakeholders I interviewed lead them to mistrust each other. NGOs blame parliamentarians for not caring about wildlife, and civil servants accuse NGOs of being too emotionally involved and parliamentarians for being too driven by economics (Goyes 2023a). Parliamentarians think NGOs and civil servants fail to see the entire picture. Conservation and restoration scholars have also demonstrated that the success of conservation and restoration programmes lies in proper top-down management in addition to bottom-up initiatives (McDonald 2003). Yet, NGOs, civil servants and parliamentarians like Amelia do not include international environmental conventions in their repertoire of stories. A result may be that the highest order of instruction for wildlife management remains unused because international conventions seemingly fail to penetrate the repertoire of stories of those in charge of applying them.

Conclusion

The effectiveness of wildlife treaties depends on a chain that extends from the international to the local. One can divide the chain into many links depending on the level of detail one wants to include, but a basic structure contains three links: the contents of the treaty, the national legislative action derived from the treaty, and the local implementation of the treaty by stakeholders. Regarding those three links the scientific literature has established that the treaties that are vague and impose fewer obligations tend to be more ratified by states (link one). States deploy more resources to faithfully legislate the treaties that deal with trade than with conservation (link two). Local stakeholders are more prone to change their behaviour if they participated in the process of integrating the treaties into domestic legislation (link three) – their inclusion in the process makes them more engaged with the policy and more willing to transform their views and practices following the guidelines. Wildlife treaties struggle to make the chain of implementation work (links one to three).

Comparing the general knowledge with my findings about the Norwegian chains of implementation of CITES and the Bern Convention, shows that:

Link one: The treaties should work in tandem to shape the public policy of the signatories. Yet, the many contradictions between them provide broad discretionary powers to the parties – something that translates into ambiguous obligations. As the general literature correctly predicts, many states have ratified both treaties, presumably due to their vagueness (that is, both a lack of direct commitments and a lack of 'teeth' to enforce the few specific obligations).

Link two: The Norwegian state has strictly implemented CITES mandates in the country, while taking many liberties when legislating the obligations derived from the Bern Convention. The explanation for that phenomenon is that while CITES is a trade treaty, the Bern Convention might hinder broader and more significant trade interests, particularly those related to animal husbandry and hunting. Once again, the general literature correctly predicted that trade agreements are prioritized over conservation ones.

Link three: Out of the 15 interviewees, only one incorporated the treaties into their narratives. That person was an experienced parliamentarian who participated in the debates about whether to ratify them. The treaties were absent from the stories most stakeholders told, which suggests that the treaties failed to affect their behaviour. Again, the literature correctly predicts that failures in incorporating stakeholders into the national debates about the treaties results in absence of changed behaviour.

In conclusion, CITES and the Bern Convention are effective in the two first links of the chain of effectiveness. At their core, they advance the econocentric view. They are less effective, however, on the third link, as they fail to influence the behaviour of the practitioners in charge of implementing them.

References

Aarli, R., and Mæhle, S. S. (2018). *Juridisk metode i et nøtteskall [Legal method in a nutshell]*. Gyldendal.

Andersen, M. M. (2008). *Skriveboka [Writing Book]*. Aschehoug.

Armstrong, C. (2015). Against 'permanent sovereignty' over natural resources. *Politics, Philosophy & Economics, 14*(2), 129–51. https://doi.org/10.1177/1470594x14523080

Arntzen de Besche Advokatfirma As (2017). *Vurderinger av naturmangfoldloven og Bernkonvensjonen i tilknytning til forvaltningen av ulv – Høringsuttalelse*. Retrieved 19 September 2023 from www.regjeringen.no/contentassets/8390e25a83fb40e0a51fb7ad376fff7f/wwf.pdf

Atisa, G. (2020). Policy adoption, legislative developments, and implementation: the resulting global differences among countries in the management of biological resources. *International Environmental Agreements, 20*, 141–59.

Bodansky, D., Brunnee, J., and Rajamani, L. (2017). *International Climate Change Law*. Oxford University Press.

Brandi, C., Blümer, D., and Morin, J.-F. (2019). When do international treaties matter for domestic environmental legislation? *Global Environmental Politics, 19*(4), 14–44.

Brinkmann, S., and Kvale, S. (2015). *InterViews: Learning the Craft of Qualitative Research Interviewing*. SAGE.

Brisman, A., and South, N. (2018). Autosarcophagy in the Anthropocene and the Obscenity of an Epoch. In C. Holley and C. Shearing (eds), *Criminology and the Anthropocene* (pp 25–49). Routledge.

Brisman, A., McClanahan, B., South, N., and Walters, R. (2018). *Water, Crime and Security in the Twenty-First Century*. Palgrave.

Bugge, H. C. (2019). *Lærebok i miljøforvaltningsrett [Textbook for environmental protection law]*. Universitetsforlaget.

Chambliss, W. (1993). On Lawmaking. In W. Chambliss and M. Zatz (eds), *Making Law: The State, the Law, and Structural Contradictions* (pp 3–35). Indiana University Press.

Christie, N. (2009). *Små ord for store spørsmål [Small words for big questions]*. Universitetsforlaget.

CITES (n.d.). *The CITES Appendices*. Retrieved 14 March from www.cites.org/eng/app/index.php

Council of Europe Portal (n.d.). *Details of Treaty No. 104*. Council of Europe. Retrieved 14 March from www.coe.int/en/web/conventions/full-list/-/conventions/treaty/104

Diaz, C. L. (2010). The Bern Convention: 30 years of nature conservation in Europe. *RECIEL. Review of European Community & International Environmental Law, 19*(2), 185–96.

Dupuy, P.-M., and Viñuales, J. (2019). *International Environmental Law*. Cambridge University Press.

Flick, U. (2005). *An Introduction to Qualitative Research* (2 edn). SAGE Publications.

Gee, J. P. (2014) *An Introduction to Discourse Analysis: Theory and Method*. Routledge.

Goyes, D. R. (2015). La Necesidad de Una Política Preventiva Verde en Colombia [The Need of a Green Preventive Public Policy in Colombia]. In M. Gutiérrez Quevedo (ed), *Política Criminal y Prevención* (pp 129–84). Universidad Externado de Colombia.

Goyes, D. R. (2017). Corporate lobbying and criminalization. *Crime, Law & Social Change*, 69(2), 1–19.

Goyes, D. R. (2021). Contending philosophical foundations in international wildlife law: a discourse analysis of CITES and the Bern Convention. *Revista Catalana de Dret Ambiental*, 12(1), 1–35.

Goyes, D. R. (2023a). The importance of stories in wildlife management. *Ecological Management & Restoration*, 23(3), 237–43. https://doi.org/https://doi.org/10.1111/emr.12567

Goyes, D. R. (2023b) National legislative adoption of international wildlife law after treaty ratification. *Crime Law and Social Change*. https://doi.org/10.1007/s10611-023-10117-7

Goyes, D. R., and Sollund, R. (2016). Contesting and contextualising CITES: Wildlife trafficking in Colombia and Brazil. *International Journal for Crime, Justice and Social Democracy*, 5(4), 87–102.

Goyes, D. R., and South, N. (2019). Between 'conservation' and 'development'. The construction of 'protected nature' and the environmental disenfranchisement of indigenous communities. *International Journal for Crime, Justice and Social Democracy*, 8(3), 89–104.

Hames, F., Townsend, A., Ringwood, G., Clunie, P., and McPhail, J. (2014). Effective engagement of the Native Fish Strategy is delivered by coordinated and contextual effort. *Ecological Management & Restoration*, 15(s1), 13–27. https://doi.org/https://doi.org/10.1111/emr.12099

Hutton, J., and Dickson, B. (2000). Introduction. In J. Hutton and B. Dickson (eds), *Endangered Species Threatened Convention: The Past, Present and Future of CITES* (pp xv–xx). Routledge.

Huxley, C. (2000). CITES: The vision. In J. Hutton and B. Dickson (eds), *Endangered Species Threatened Convention: The Past, Present and Future of CITES* (pp 3–12). Routledge.

Ingram, M., Ingram, H., and Lejano, R. (2014). What's the story? Creating and sustaining environmental networks. *Environmental Politics*, 23(6), 984–1002. https://doi.org/10.1080/09644016.2014.919717

Ingram, M., Ingram, H., and Lejano, R. (2019). Environmental action in the Anthropocene: the power of narrative-networks. *Journal of Environmental Policy and Planning*, *21*(5), 492–503. https://doi.org/10.1080/1523908X.2015.1113513

Jackson, W., and Bührs, T. (2015). International environmental regimes: understanding institutional and ecological effectiveness. *Journal of International Wildlife Law & Policy*, *18*(1), 63–83. https://doi.org/10.1080/13880292.2014.957030

Liljeblad, J. (2004). *The Convention on International Trade of Endangered Species: Local Authority and International Policy*. Quid Pro Books.

Maines, D. R. (1993). Narrative's moment and sociology's phenomena: toward a narrative sociology. *Sociological Quarterly*, *34*(1), 17–38.

Mauerhofer, V., Kim, R. E., and Stevens, C. (2015). When implementation works: a comparison of Ramsar Convention implementation in different continents. *Environmental Science & Policy*, *51*, 95–105. https://doi.org/https://doi.org/10.1016/j.envsci.2015.03.016

McClanahan, B., Brisman, A., and South, N. (2015). Privatization, Pollution and Power: A green criminological analysis of present and future global water crises. In G. Barakk (ed), *The Routledge International Handbook of the Crimes of the Powerful* (pp 243–54). Routledge.

McDonald, B. T. (2003). Persistence and cooperation: undervalued keys to restoration? *Ecological Management & Restoration*, *4*(2), 82–82. https://doi.org/https://doi.org/10.1046/j.1442-8903.2003.00139.x

Miljøverndepartement (2008–09). *Om lov om forvaltning av naturens mangfold (naturmangfoldloven) [On the law of the protection on nature's diversity (Nature Diversity Law)]*. Oslo. Retrieved 19 September 2023 from www.regjeringen.no/contentassets/a821d3fd355e4440bac64fa6e7e59642/no/pdfs/otp200820090052000dddpdfs.pdf

Norway to the Standing Committee of the Bern Convention (2015). *Biennial Report (2009–2010)*. Retrieved 19 September 2023 from https://rm.coe.int/biennial-report-2015-2016-norway/1680a03d0b

Polletta, F., Chen, P. C. B., Gardner, B. G., and Motes, A. (2011). The sociology of storytelling. *Annual Review of Sociology*, *37*(1), 109–30. https://doi.org/10.1146/annurev-soc-081309-150106

Redford, K., Groves, C., Medellin, R., and Robinson, J. (2012). Conservation stories, conservation science, and the role of the Intergovernmental Platform on Biodiversity and Ecosystem Services. *Conservation Biology*, *26*(5), 757–59.

Schimel, J. (2012). *Writing Science: How to Write Papers that Get Cited and Proposals that Get Funded*. Oxford University Press.

Schrijver, N. (2009). *Sovereignty over Natural Resources*. Cambridge University Press.

Sollund, R. (2019). *The Crimes of Wildlife Trafficking: Issues of Justice, Legality and Morality*. Routledge.

Sollund, R. (2021). The development of the enforcement of CITES in Norway: discretionary omissions and theriocides. *Revista Catalana de Dret Ambiental*, *12*(1), 1–34.

Sollund, R., and Goyes, D. R. (2021). State-organized crime and the killing of wolves in Norway. *Trends in Organized Crime*, *24*, 467–84. https://doi.org/10.1007/s12117-021-09420-3

Trouwborst, A., Fleurke, F. M., and Linnell, J. D. C. (2017). Norway's wolf policy and the Bern Convention on European Wildlife: avoiding the 'manifestly absurd'. *Journal of International Wildlife Law & Policy*, *20*(2), 155–67. https://doi.org/10.1080/13880292.2017.1346357

Underdal, A. (1992). The concept of regime 'effectiveness'. *Cooperation and Conflict*, *27*(3), 227–40. www.jstor.org.ezproxy.uio.no/stable/45083884

United Nations (1972). *Declaration of the United Nations Conference on the Human Environment*. In: Audio Visual Library of International Law. Retrieved 19 September 2023 from https://rm.coe.int/biennial-report-2015-2016-norway/1680a03d0b

Utenriksdepartementet (2002). *Forskrift til gjennomføring av Konevensjon av 3.mars 1973 om internasjonal handel med truede arter av vill flora og fauna (CITES) [Regulation on the completion of the Convention of 3 March 1973 on International Trade with Endangered Species of Wild Fauna and Flora (CITES)]*. Oslo.

van Uhm, D. (2016). *The Illegal Wildlife Trade*. Springer.

Warner, B. P. (2019). Explaining political polarization in environmental governance using narrative analysis. *Ecology and Society*, *24*(3), Article 4. https://doi.org/10.5751/ES-10999-240304

WWF (2022). *Living Planet Report 2022 – Building a Nature-positive Society*. Retrieved 19 September 2023 from https://wwfint.awsassets.panda.org/downloads/embargo_13_10_2022_lpr_2022_full_report_single_page_1.pdf

Wyatt, T. (2021). *Is CITES Protecting Wildlife? Assessing Implementation and Compliance*. Routledge.

10

Rewilding in the UK: Harm or Justice?

Tanya Wyatt

Introduction

One feature of the Anthropocene – the proposed name of the current geological epoch because of the noticeable, significant and damaging effects humans have had and are having on the planet (Crutzen 2002) – is the significant loss of biodiversity and increased rate of extinctions. One million species face extinction due in part to overexploitation and illegal trade of wildlife (IPBES 2019) and the rate of extinctions (largely the result of human actions) is 100 to 1,000 times higher than at other points in history (Wilson 2016). Whereas debates and efforts regarding biodiversity loss and extinction are often centred on Africa, Asia and the Americas, Europe too, including the UK, is facing a biodiversity crisis. According to Sir David Attenborough, 'It's tempting to assume loss of wildlife is a problem happening on the other side of the world. The truth is the UK is one of the most nature-depleted countries on the planet and the situation is getting worse' (*The Guardian* 2021). Recognition of the poor state of nature in the UK is increasing and is contributing to a rewilding movement to restore the environment. As the Chief Executive of the UK Wildlife Trusts, Craig Bennett, has said, 'Just protecting the nature we have left is not enough; we need to put nature into recovery, and to do so at scale and with urgency' (*The Guardian* 2021).

This chapter is a side exploration emerging from a larger study (Criminal Justice, Wildlife Conservation and Animal Rights in the Anthropocene – CRIMEANTHROP – see the introduction to this collection). The study unpacked whether species justice (both at the individual and systemic level) and ecological justice (at the level of biodiversity) (White 2013) can be achieved by adapting the Convention on International Trade in

Endangered Species of Wild Fauna and Flora (CITES) and the Convention on the Conservation of European Wildlife and Natural Habitats (Bern Convention), or whether justice can only be achieved when individual non-human animals are granted rights (Nussbaum 2006; Sollund 2013). (See the Special Edition of the *Catalan Journal of Environmental Law* for findings of CRIMEANTHROP.[1])

Norway, Germany and Spain currently have large mammalian carnivores/ predators (that is, wolves, lynx, bears) either from surviving populations or from reintroductions. In contrast, in the UK there are no current populations of large land predators (there are birds of prey, which are not the focus of this chapter). Yet, as mentioned, there is a growing movement to return extinct species, or to 'rewild' them to Great Britain.[2] In the context of CRIMEANTHROP's exploration of wildlife conservation and law enforcement as well as analysing how species justice can be achieved, rewilding raises a number of issues. From a green criminological lens, this chapter investigates, first, the narratives of opposition and support for return of the lynx to Great Britain, focusing on the non-human animal and environmental harms and benefits that are predicted. Second, the chapter analyses how CITES and the Bern Convention as they are transposed in UK legislation can account for rewilding. Before analysing these two aspects of rewilding in the UK, I provide some background on green criminology as the lens of investigation, CITES and the Bern Convention, and rewilding of the lynx. I also give a brief description of the methodology used before the analysis and final discussion.

Green criminology

As mentioned in the introduction, the now firmly established subdiscipline of green criminology is known for challenging the boundaries of orthodox criminology. Its expanded gaze to activities that are harmful as well as criminal is critical to exposing suffering and injury, particularly regarding the environment (see Hall (2015), Lynch and Stretesky (2016), Gladkova et al (2020) and South and Brisman (2020) for more complete discussions of the harm versus crime debate in green criminology) and is relevant to debates around rewilding as rewilding may pose harms that have yet to be considered. For instance, Brisman and South (2019), in their discussion of de-extinction through cloning, speculate as to the consequences of reintroducing species to a landscape that has changed since the species

---

[1] *Revista Catalana de Dret Ambiental* 12(1), 2021.
[2] Great Britain is the island containing England, Scotland and Wales. The United Kingdom is the larger political entity including Northern Ireland, the crown dependencies and the overseas territories.

became extinct. They note that reintroduction of extinct species may disrupt ecosystems, which could lead to re-extinction of the reintroduced species – a form of harm. Furthermore, in their exploration of de-extinction, they note that these reintroduction efforts appear to ignore the origins of species endangerment and extinction, thus not addressing the harms that have led to the need for reintroduction. They ask in the words of Zimmer (2013: 41) if such efforts are really a 'salvation' or are they a 'distraction' that decreases the motivation to uncover the causes and underlying problems leading to endangerment of species. Furthermore, what about 'the narcissism and vanity of human belief that science can reverse the mistakes of the past. Extinction—the death of species—is not to be feared' (Brisman and South 2019: 926).

White (2018), in discussing environmental victimization, raises important points that are relevant to the possible harms and speciesism of rewilding. He argues that 'context (both social and ecological) is vital to understanding and responding to specific instances of environmental victimisation. That is, particular circumstances must be taken into account in the conceptualisations of victimisation and in the moral weighing up of interests and harms in any given situation' (White 2018: 240). I suggest the same approach is warranted for assessing the harms of rewilding – it is critical to understand the social and ecological contexts relevant to balancing the moral interests in these proposed sites of rewilding.

White (2018) suggests that actual harms can be assessed through historical analysis, legal precedent and empirical research. He proposes that possible harms be assessed by evaluating the uncertainty and estimating the probability of harm. Thus, there is need for the relevant authorities to undertake a cost-benefit analysis grounded in evaluating whether the harm that is purposefully being caused results in a greater good (White 2018). At the heart of such a cost-benefit analysis are the conflicts of interests between people, non-human animals and the environment. For Bennison (2010), these conflicts of interest ought to be evaluated in terms of ecological criteria taking into account the whole environment and moral criteria considering non-human animal rights and welfare. In addition to assessing the type and degree of harm to people, non-human animals and the environment, the type and degree of harm to the particular place and its temporal impact on people, non-human animals, and the environment should also be taken into consideration (White 2013).

In green criminology, non-human animals, but also plants and the environment itself, are seen as victims of harm and crime (see Beirne 1999; Sollund 2019; Nurse and Wyatt 2020, among others). Many green criminologists then approach investigations of human activity via species justice. White (2008, 2013), in developing frameworks for green criminological exploration, proposed that there are three approaches to achieving justice: environmental, ecological and species. Environmental justice uncovers the disparities between and among human communities with respect to their access to a healthy environment. Ecological justice recognizes that the planet is an interconnected system that has value beyond the value given to it by people. This approach tries to reach a balance between people and planet. Species justice interrogates the two levels of injustice that are perpetrated against non-humans. The two levels are the individual level (individual non-human animals and plants are subjected to suffering, injury and death) and the systemic level (species as a whole are targets of violence). For instance, in industrial farming of non-human animals, the non-human animals individually suffer from the cruel conditions and slaughter, but there is also systemic injustice in that the whole group of non-human animals is continually exploited.

Inextricable from species justice is speciesism. Speciesism is the discriminatory or prejudicial treatment of a being based upon their species (Ryder 1971; Singer 2015 [1975]). It appears to occur on two levels. First, humans tend to be speciesist in that they prioritize humans over all other species. Second, humans tend to be speciesist by favouring some non-human species more than others (Sollund 2012; Wyatt 2021b; Hutchinson et al 2022). The human-assigned value to other species has been proposed to be a complex mix of the commercial value of the species, their charisma and their survival status (Hutchinson et al 2022). Rewilding not only pits human interests (for example, farming, logging, hunting) against non-human animal interests, but it also pits non-human animal interests against that of other non-human animal interests (that is, livestock, endangered species, companion animals, and wildlife). The different species have different statuses, and these are important in relation to their legal protection (White 2018). Flynn and Hall (2017) call this 'hierarchical speciesism' – some non-human animals (and plants) are less protected or not protected at all in policy and law and thus more exposed to harm.

As will be discussed shortly, the rewilding of lynx to the UK is worthy of green criminological exploration through a species justice approach because of the historic injustice to the lynx, the underpinning speciesism in the rewilding debates of the lynx and other species, and the urgent need to tackle individual and systemic species injustice to restore and repair the environment. The proposal to rewild the lynx and the effort to achieve species justice sits with a legal framework – CITES and the Bern Convention – that is outlined next.

CITES and the Bern Convention

CITES is the international convention governing trade in certain wildlife, which came into force in 1975. The species covered by CITES are 38,000+

wildlife whose populations are threatened by international trade. A vast majority of those species are listed on Appendix II, which allows trade within certain parameters that will not threaten the species' survival. All big cat species, including the lynx, are listed on CITES. The four species of lynx are Appendix II species (CITES n.d.), which means, as mentioned, that some trade is allowed with the required export permit.

In 1982, the Convention on the Conservation of European Wildlife and Natural Habitats (Bern Convention) (1979: no page) came into force; it aims to 'conserve wild flora and fauna and their natural habitats, especially those species and habitats whose conservation requires the co-operation of several States, and to promote such co-operation'. Like CITES, the Bern Convention employs a listing system with appendices specifying which species need protection by the parties. Appendix II lists strictly protected fauna species, and Appendix III names protected fauna species. The UK has 379 species of the more than 1,500 plant and non-human animal species listed (JNCC 2019).

As mentioned, in the world, there are four lynx species – the bobcat and Canadian lynx in North America, the Eurasian lynx in Europe and parts of Asia, and the Iberian lynx in Europe. There are also several subspecies of the Eurasian lynx, of which the Balkan lynx subspecies is relevant here because it is listed on the Bern Convention. Both the Balkan and Iberian lynx – *Lynx lynx balcanicus* and *Lynx pardinus* – are listed on Appendix II, meaning they are strictly protected (Council of Europe 2018). The Eurasian lynx – *Lynx lynx* – is listed on Appendix III, protected fauna (Council of Europe 1998). The killing and capturing of lynx, as well as destruction of their habitat and dwellings, are closely monitored and only supposed to be permitted in extreme cases. The protection of individual wildlife falls to the party to the Bern Convention in which the wildlife lives. As documented in the UK case study of CRIMEANTHROP, not all parties provide protection to wildlife listed in the Bern Convention. The UK, for instance, allows badgers – an Appendix III species – to be culled in the tens of thousands in a controversial effort to control bovine tuberculosis (Wyatt 2021a).

When listed species are killed, the Bern Convention sets out how this is permitted. In the case of mammals, Table 10.1 shows the 'Prohibited means and methods of killing, capture and other forms of exploitation' listed in Appendix IV.

Some exceptions to Table 10.1 are that explosives can be used for whales and nets and traps can be used, but not for large numbers of wildlife at once. The relevance of Appendix IV will become apparent when I discuss the opposition and support for rewilding the lynx in the UK. First, some context as to why the lynx is being proposed for rewilding and where in the UK this is proposed.

Table 10.1: Prohibited means and methods of killing, capturing and exploiting mammals

Snares	Explosives
Live animals used as decoys which are blind or mutilated	Sighting devices for night shooting comprising an electronic image magnifier or image converter
Tape recorders	Traps
Nets	Poison and poisoned or anaesthetic bait
Electrical devices capable of killing and stunning	Semi-automatic or automatic weapons with a magazine capable of holding more than two rounds of ammunition
Artificial light sources	Gassing or smoking out
Mirrors and other dazzling devices	Aircraft
Devices for illuminating targets	Motor vehicles in motion

Adapted from Council of Europe 1995: 1.

Rewilding and the lynx in the UK

As the United Nations Environment Programme and United Nations Food and Agricultural Organization (2021) are advocating for, there is an urgent need to prevent, halt and restore degradation to the environment. Rewilding is part of how damaged ecosystems might be restored. As mentioned, the UK's ecosystems have been greatly damaged. The Dasgupta Review[3] (Dasgupta 2021) notes that the UK has failed to engage with nature sustainably and this is endangering the nature-based goods and services people are reliant on, as well as the prosperity of current and future generations. The Review calls for, among other things, conserving and restoring nature's 'assets'. The Review is clearly anthropocentric; nature should be restored to support human life and because restoration is more cost effective. It does, however, highlight that in the UK, food production and consumption are the leading drivers of ecosystem degradation.

Food production and consumption are the likely drivers of extinction of the Eurasian lynx in the UK. Approximately 1,300 years ago, a combination of deforestation of the lynx's habitat for grazing land and crops, and the killing of the lynx for their fur led to their extinction (Lynx UK Trust 2021). The Lynx UK Trust is one organization initiating the rewilding of what they argue is a native species for environmental and moral reasons. The organization regards the lynx as a native species because if it were

---

[3] This review was commissioned by the UK Government to provide evidence of the economic value of biodiversity.

not for humans, the lynx would still be on the British Isles. Lynx are apex predators, who are critical in maintaining the balance in ecosystems. In the UK, apex predators (apart from humans and some birds of prey) are extinct. A return of lynx would help forest and biodiversity regeneration in part by controlling the overabundance of deer. The millions of roe deer in England, Wales and Scotland have no natural predators; with so many of them, they overgraze areas and prevent natural forest regeneration, which also impedes the restoration of the biodiversity of the woodlands (that is, plants and small non-human animals). Lynx are specialist roe deer hunters, although lynx will eat other types of deer, small mammals and birds. One plan for reintroduction is a five-year trial in Kielder Forest in Northumberland in north-east England and Queen Elizabeth Forest in Scotland. The Lynx UK Trust (2021: no page) indicates these sites were chosen 'after extensive research into the potential ecology and social/cultural impacts'. Both areas have high density of roe deer populations, have limited roads and railways, and lower density of farmland. A second initiative in Scotland being undertaken by Scotland: The Big Picture, Trees for Life, and the Vincent Wildlife Trust is scouting the feasibility of rewilding lynx to the Cairngorms and Argyll (BBC News 2021; Cockburn 2021).

The latter criteria for rewilding – farmland – seems to be the biggest concern for opponents to rewilding the lynx. Much of the Lynx UK Trust (2021) communication is assuring the public that lynx rarely prey upon domestic livestock, such as sheep. To a lesser degree, the organization also provides information that lynx rarely eat companion animals such as dogs and cats. The evidence that sheep and other domesticated non-humans are infrequent meals for lynx, stems from successful rewilding efforts in France, Germany and Switzerland, as well as ongoing scientific studies of lynx behaviour throughout their ranges in Europe and beyond. Lynx are solitary and secretive, are rarely seen by people, and there are no recorded instances of them attacking a person. The Lynx UK Trust (2021) also is trying to assure people that the small number of lynx, who will form the pilot project, will be closely monitored with constant GPS tracking to gauge their impact on people, livestock and the environment. In addition to the restoration of the environment, the Lynx UK Trust (2021) suggests that the tourism to see the lynx may provide economic benefits to nearby communities, as has happened in the Harz mountains in Germany where lynx were rewilded.

Of interest from a green criminological and species justice lens is the organization's statement that: 'As well as a moral obligation to right the wrong of exterminating lynx in the first place, the return of this big cat will breathe life into the UK's damaged ecosystems, and will help with climate change mitigation by promoting forest regeneration' (Lynx UK Trust 2021: no page). Thus, the Lynx UK Trust supports rewilding not only for the benefits to the environment as well as to people, but also because such rewilding has justice implications for the lynx.

Methods

The UK case study, like all of the CRIMEANTHROP case studies, employed a mixed-methods qualitative approach. I received ethical approval through Northumbria University in August of 2019 (#17569) and data collection took place between September 2019 and March 2020. The mixed methods involved a literature review, collecting and analysing documents, and eight semi-structured interviews with relevant experts in the UK. While not relevant to a discussion of rewilding, the original document collection and analysis included a Freedom of Information request to the Crown Prosecution Service for court cases related to CITES, the biennial reports from the UK government to the CITES Secretariat (seven reports available from 2003 through 2017), the legal complaint by the Born Free Foundation, Badger Trust, and Eurogroup for Animals claiming that the UK has violated the Bern Convention by culling badgers, and the UK government's biennial reports to the Bern Convention Secretariat (only 2009–10 and 2015–16 were available). For this chapter, further information about the consultations conducted regarding lynx rewilding and the initial proposal for that rewilding were analysed along with news media coverage of the proposed reintroduction. The information shared from the news media coverage is the opinions of the people interviewed and of the public who commented on the article, and may or may not be grounded in evidence.

The eight interviews (six men and two women) included staff from wildlife civil society organizations (4), law enforcement (3) and the government (1). Only two of these, as I will share shortly, spoke about rewilding. The identity of the interviewees is anonymous and confidential, thus is cited through a coding system (that is, CS1, LE2, G1, and so forth). I asked the interviewees about CITES and the Bern Convention as well as rewilding. The sample of participants was purposive based on people's expertise and experience with wildlife in the UK. Other relevant government experts were unavailable to participate due to restructuring of departments in preparation for, and in the aftermath of, the UK leaving the European Union. The narratives surrounding lynx rewilding in the UK analysed under a green criminological lens highlight the tension between humans and nature.

Harm or justice?

Humans drove the lynx to extinction in the UK over 1,000 years ago. Rewilding provides the opportunity to, at least in part, undo this. But rewilding of the lynx is met with resistance because some people believe that the lynx will cause harm, as I outline later, drawing on media coverage of interviews conducted with people in the proposed reintroduction areas. In this section, I unpack rewilding as its own form of harm as well as it being an element of justice in trying to restore ecosystems within which humans have caused extinctions. First, I look at the opposition to rewilding of the lynx and then at the support.

The opposition

For the most part, it appears that opposition to the lynx stems from the fear that lynx will not eat deer, or at least not only eat deer, but will also eat livestock, (endangered) wildlife, companion animals and human children. As mentioned, these are people's opinions. As reported by Feehan (2021), the Head of the National Sheep Association is opposed to rewilding lynx because there are 1,000 sheep farmers within 30 miles of Kielder Forest, one of the proposed rewilding locations. The National Farmers Union Scotland (NFUS) is also opposed (BBC News 2021). They say rewilding of the lynx is 'wholly unacceptable' based upon a 2017 trip to Norway. On this trip, the NFUS were told that approximately 20,000 sheep were lost to predators of which 21 per cent were caused by lynx (BBC News 2021). These figures correspond to the Norwegian official figures as to who was paid compensation for their lost livestock. The reported numbers of predated sheep in 2021 was 16,864 with 4,087 taken by lynx, slightly up from 2020 (Miljodirektoratet 2021). It should be noted that this is a compensation scheme and there is the possibility that some farmers are taking advantage of claims of predation to receive money when livestock have not been lost or were lost in other ways. Supposedly, fewer farmers in some parts of Norway are keeping sheep because of the predation. One of the British farmers who visited Norway reported, 'The Norwegians told us that to reintroduce predators into our country would be an absolute catastrophe' (BBC News 2021: no page).

Dozens of public comments to Feehan's news article in the *Daily Mail* agreed that sheep will be targeted by the lynx, which again is their opinion. For instance, 'Wild animals will always eat sheep, and pets'; 'Probably will kill sheep because they are easier to catch'; and 'Deer are fairly fast, they [lynx] will find it easier to attack sheep, and maybe children'. The death of others besides sheep was a frequent theme of the opposing comments. 'Anyone thought this through before the family pets get eaten?'; 'The Lynx would kill off the already endangered Pine Marten. It's just got a foothold again in Kielder from being nearly extinct and these fools want to introduce something from 1300 years ago that eats them'; 'Could do with less domestic cats; they will attack people and cats'.

Another theme of opposing comments was that people should be eating the deer and can control the deer population numbers: 'What a waste of good venison'; 'There are enough rifles to control the deer. Get rid of overpaid quangos'; 'What idiots come up with this stuff? If they need deer culled they just ask for a cull and then they can go in the food chain instead of being ripped to pieces by a cat'; 'Can't humans just eat them instead?'; 'So instead of a clean kill by a bullet, deer will now be chased and ripped to pieces by a lynx. Good thinking that'. One person even suggested developing a deadly virus to kill the deer. A few people commented that the lynx have no natural predators either, so what would stop their population numbers from becoming out of control. Several of these comments raise an interesting aspect that death by a lynx is cruel, so better for a quick death by a human bullet. Similarly, those in opposition have expressed welfare concerns of releasing wild animals into a 'busy, industrial forest' (BBC News 2021: no page). There was also sentiment throughout the comments like: 'They were eradicated for a reason, they were not hunted to death for food!' – implying perhaps that lynx are destructive and/or interfere with human activity. In contrast, one person noted that: 'This kind of interference never goes well – the interference was the lynx being wiped out in the first place. When will the meddling stop?' So, they acknowledge people were the cause of the extinction, but do not support trying to correct that action through rewilding.

Others were not only sceptical of rewilding as having any benefits, but also mistrusted the motivations of the charity:

> The majority of these so-called 'trusts' are simply set up as vehicles for paying the salaries of their directors. Why should a couple of people, for that's all the Lynx 'trust' is, be able to drive an unpopular agenda such as this, an agenda that could affect the livelihoods of numerous farmers for absolutely no benefit to the environment. (Feehan 2021: comments)

The government did not approve the first application by the Lynx UK Trust to rewild the lynx. Interestingly, the rejection by then Secretary of State Michael Gove, based upon Natural England recommendations, said the proposal 'did not demonstrate sufficient local support ... and the socio-economic benefits of the trial were unclear' (BBC News 2021: no page).

The support

People who support rewilding seem to base their opinions on evidence of the environmental benefits of adding predators back into ecosystems. A financial backer of the rewilding said:

> They [lynx] are widely considered to be perfect reintroduction candidates because they are no risk to humans, pose very little threat to

livestock and are charismatic and beautiful animals, which are drivers of ecotourism in rural communities which can generate millions of pounds each year. (Feehan 2021: no page)

Furthermore, a robust compensation scheme for farmers has already been put in place (Feehan 2021; Lynx UK Trust 2021). The Lynx UK Trust (2021: no page) note:

> For any individual sheep that is taken by a lynx in the UK, we have arranged compensation which outweighs market value. Claims for compensation will be evidenced by GPS data collected from the lynx radio collars, so there is no concern regarding not being able to prove that lynx predation is the sheep's cause of death.

Others have noted that 'fears that lynx might kill sheep have been proven to be largely unfounded; indeed, one study showed that because lynx also predate on foxes, the number of lambs killed would actually reduce' (Moss 2020: no page). Furthermore, the Lynx UK Trust challenge that the situation in Norway is applicable to the Scottish and UK context. According to the Chief Veterinarian at the Lynx UK Trust (2021: no page):

> In Norway, sheep often graze unattended in forests, with little to no protection, leaving them more vulnerable to lynx attacks. Sheep are also more abundant than deer. Again, this is not the normal in the UK. In Scotland, the vast majority of forested areas contain no sheep, with most being grazed in open habitats instead.

In the current financial circumstances, some argue rewilding is the sound economic move. Managed conservation is thought to have failed (the state of nature attests to this) and culling of deer is expensive (Moss 2020). Furthermore, farmers face economic uncertainty because of the instability created when the UK left the European Union market as well as from the end of EU farm subsidies. Lynx would bring economic benefits such as higher rural employment associated with the increase of wildlife tourism (Moss 2020).

The Lynx UK Trust also notes that the concern for sheep is more than simply economic and having predators in the area is a cause of stress for livestock. However, they are wanting to work with local communities and farmers to address these concerns (Feehan 2021; Lynx UK Trust 2021). The Lynx UK Trust have spent 18 months talking to residents and communities (Feehan 2021) and during their public consultations, they received over 9,500 responses, with a 92.8 per cent public approval rating for the reintroduction of lynx (Lynx UK Trust 2021).

Support stems from how good for the environment returning the lynx would be (Feehan 2021; Moss 2020) and, as many people commented, because lynx are beautiful (Feehan 2021). One of my interviewees who mentioned rewilding thought it was a positive development and we should be working more towards restoration, but it would probably not be supported and that there would be political obstacles (LE1). That brings me to the legal practicalities of rewilding.

CITES, the Bern Convention and rewilding

As mentioned, the Eurasian lynx is already listed on CITES. Since parties to CITES are required to transpose the convention, including the species' lists, into their national legislation, the lynx is already covered under the Wildlife and Countryside Act 1981 in the UK as well as the Control of Trade in Endangered Species Regulations 2018. Thus, in terms of CITES, there are no obstacles to the lynx being protected. It is worth noting that CITES is only concerned with *international trade*, so domestic persecution or wildlife crimes against the lynx are not the remit of CITES. However, the legislation just mentioned addresses wildlife crime.

In terms of the Bern Convention, one interviewee remarked:

'So rewilding depends on what you mean by rewilding. In this case you want to talk about potential species reintroductions. So, there is an obligation of sorts within the Bern Convention. It's, I'm trying to remember the exact words but it's around exploring the potential I think of restoring lost species or something along those lines. It may even be in an annex, but it is there, there's something there. Within the UK there are challenges around what the definition of a native species is, so currently for example the wild boar, which no one would argue is a species that should really be or at least was part of the system here in the UK. But the wild boar that we have here are not listed as native, they are feral. So they have all sorts of issues around no status and so on. So there are things that to enable rewilding do need to be catered for in the laws, but it's all doable within the framework. So if you look at what has happened with the beaver for example they are going through the UK process and it can work. I mean lynx is a wee bit potentially more complicated [referring to the lynx being a predator].' (CS4)

The Lynx UK Trust (2021) makes the same argument. They note that 'Annex IV of Article 22 of the EU Habitats and Species Directive requires Member States to assess the potential and desirability of reintroducing species which have been lost, and to look at other Member States' experiences to support such assessments' (Lynx UK Trust: no page). Thus, under the Bern

Convention, rewilding appears to be supported and expected, although as noted earlier, the status of species as native or feral may cause debates.

Of concern in the UK context is the current depleted state of nature and the perception of some people's attitudes towards wildlife. For instance, one person commented on the *Daily Mail* article:

> Natural England spend much of its time killing our wildlife (currently badgers), while hunts and gamekeepers wipe out the rest. Won't be long before any released lynx disappear – as farmers and landowners only want bleak landscapes devoid of any wildlife that doesn't make them a profit or that they can't (legally) kill for fun. (Feehan 2021: comments)

Others have made similar observation that the UK's remaining larger predators – birds of prey – are frequent victims of persecution from farmers and the gamebird industry (RSPB 2021). This ties into Brisman and South's (2019) observation that de-extinction does not address the root causes of the historical persecution. In recognition that the lynx may be the victim of wildlife crimes if rewilded, the Lynx UK Trust (2021) are asking as part of their application that the appropriate legal protections be given to the lynx and that any poaching would result in severe sanctions. They also intend to engage the public and provide education to schools and local communities as a strategy to prevent poaching.

Discussion and conclusion

For the lynx, 'returning the shy and elusive animal is less about science and more about people's willingness to live alongside a species that's become forgotten on these shores' (Cockburn 2021: no page). But there is sound science supporting rewilding – the success of the lynx in continental Europe as well as rewilding of other predators such as wolves in Yellowstone National Park (White 2018) among others. In these instances, the harm done by rewilding, such as the loss of life of livestock, companion animals and other wildlife, appears to have been minimal compared to the benefits of rewilding. The benefits evidenced are improved ecosystem health, increased revenue from wildlife tourism, and higher rural employment. The financial loss to the farmers is addressed and the loss of livestock and other life is very small. In contrast, other species prosper with the improvement of the ecosystem, financial gains are made in local communities supporting the ecotourism, and more people are employed. Thus, I suggest the potential harm to the farmers and the sheep is outweighed by the positive outcomes for the lynx, the communities and the ecosystems.

Other important benefits are intangible. By returning species to spaces where humans have caused their extinction is the righting of an historic wrong. As noted by the Lynx UK Trust (2021) and others supporting these efforts (Moss 2020; Feehan 2021), we have a moral duty to restore ecosystems. Furthermore, rewilding the lynx contributes to the breaking down of speciesist barriers within our societies. Livestock and people should not be prioritized over wildlife. When governments permit rewilding of predators, speciesism can be challenged and possibly reduced. This can perhaps take place through people's positive experiences with predators, which disrupts negative stereotypes and expectations of the harm that the predator would cause. Rewilding also helps to tackle both individual and systemic species injustice. On the individual level, each lynx will have a habitat and will be, as Regan (1983 [2004]) proposed, a subject-of-a-life. On the systemic level, species justice is achieved by restoring a predator to the ecosystem. Predators, not just lynx, have been persecuted throughout human history and rewilding predators, at least in part, addresses this historic systemic violence and injustice. Furthermore, predators' role in restoring damaged ecosystems also contributes to achieving species justice by repairing the systemic damage humans have inflicted on the environment.

Rewilding should not replace preservation of habitats and wildlife. These initiatives must continue. In addition, as noted for de-extinction, rewilding efforts should not be a distraction to the underlying motivations causing extinction and biodiversity loss. Thus, alongside rewilding, we must ensure that the drivers of the lynx extinction 1,300 years ago have been addressed as well as understanding and addressing current pressures on lynx populations. This is true of all species. The legal provisions are there within CITES, and explicitly within the Bern Convention, to support rewilding of lynx and other species. As the UN has noted, our conservation efforts are not doing nearly enough to save the planet (Greenfield 2021). We must rewild on a massive scale and 'the revival of ecosystems must be met with all the ambition of the space race' (Greenfield 2021: no page). The proposal to rewild the lynx in the UK is a small part of this critical project to restore the wildlife of a damaged planet.

References

BBC News. 2021. Into the wild: Could lynx be reintroduced to Scotland? Available at: www.bbc.co.uk/news/uk-scotland-highlands-islands-55857 070. Accessed 14 June 2021.

Beirne, P. 1999. For a nonspeciesist criminology: Animal abuse as an object of study. *Criminology*, 37(1), 117–48.

Bennison, R. 2010. Ecological inclusion: Unity among animals. In: M. Bekoff (ed) *Encyclopedia of Animal Rights and Animal Welfare*. Vol. 1. Santa Barbara, CA: Greenwood Press: 194–8.

Brisman, A. and South, N. 2019. A criminology of extinction. Biodiversity, extreme consumption and the vanity of species resurrection. *European Journal of Criminology*, 17(6): 918–35.

Cockburn, H. 2021. Lynx study seeks views on reintroducing wild population of cats to Scotland. *The Independent.* Available at: www.independent.co.uk/climate-change/news/lynx-scotland-rewilding-reintroduction-b1789404.html. Accessed 14 June 2021.

CITES (Convention on International Trade of Endangered Species of Wild Fauna and Flora). No Date. Lynx. Available at: https://cites.org/eng/taxonomy/term/485. Accessed 7 June 2021.

Convention on the Conservation of European Wildlife and Natural Habitats. 1979. Bern, Article 1.

Council of Europe. 1995. Appendix IV Prohibited Means and Methods of Killing, Capture and Other Forms of Exploitation. Available at: https://rm.coe.int/168097eb58. Accessed 7 June 2021.

Council of Europe. 1998. Appendix III Protected Fauna. Available at: https://rm.coe.int/168097eb57. Accessed 7 June 2021.

Council of Europe. 2018. Appendix II Strictly Protected Fauna. Available at: https://rm.coe.int/168078e2ff. Accessed 7 June 2021.

Crutzen, P. 2002. The Anthropocene. *Journal de Physique,* 12: 1–5.

Dasgupta, P. 2021. *The Economics of Biodiversity: The Dasgupta Review – Headline Messages.* Available at: https://assets.publishing.service.gov.uk/government/uploads/system/uploads/attachment_data/file/957629/Dasgupta_Review_-_Headline_Messages.pdf. Accessed 14 June 2021.

Feehan, K. 2021. Wild lynx is set to be reintroduced to Britain to cut soaring deer population despite farmers' fears they will attack sheep instead. *The Daily Mail.* Available at: www.dailymail.co.uk/news/article-9183759/Wild-lynx-set-reintroduced-Britain-cut-soaring-deer-population.html. Accessed 14 June 2021.

Flynn, M. and Hall, M. 2017. The case for a victimology of nonhuman animal harms. *Contemporary Justice Review,* 20(3): 299–318.

Gladkova, E., Hutchinson, A. and Wyatt, T. 2020. Green Criminology in an International Context. *Oxford Encyclopaedia of International Criminology* [online]. https://doi.org/10.1093/acrefore/9780190264079.013.665

Greenfield, P. 2021. World must rewild on massive scale to heal nature and climate, says UN. *The Guardian.* Available at: www.theguardian.com/environment/2021/jun/03/rewild-on-massive-scale-to-heal-nature-and-climate-says-un-decade-on-ecosystem-restoration-aoe?fbclid=IwAR2gWPBJAEi5KU0jAB-wd67bpfrXt5Wg_KaRmKEV_6fuMcxI8U0trv4PPtc. Accessed 25 June 2021.

The Guardian. 2021. Wildlife charities raise £8m to boost nature schemes across England and Wales. Available at: www.theguardian.com/environment/2021/apr/07/wildlife-charities-launch-10-schemes-to-boost-nature-across-england-and-wales. Accessed 7 June 2021.

Hall, M. 2015. *Exploring Green Crime: Introducing the legal, social and criminological contexts of environmental harm.* London: Macmillan.

Hutchinson, A., Stephens-Griffin, N. and Wyatt, T. 2022. Speciesism and the wildlife trade: who gets listed, downlisted, and uplisted. *International Journal of Crime, Law and Social Democracy*, 11(2): 191–209. https://doi.org/10.5204/ijcjsd.1945

IPBES (Intergovernmental Science-Policy Platform on Biodiversity and Ecosystem Services). 2019. IPBES Global Assessment Summary for Policymakers. www.ipbes.net/sites/default/files/downloads/summary_for_policymakers_ipbes_global_assessment.pdf. Accessed 7 May 2019.

JNCC (Joint Nature Conservation Committee). 2019. Bern Convention. Available at: https://jncc.gov.uk/our-work/bern-convention/. Accessed 28 January 2021.

Lynch, M. J. and Stretesky, P. B. 2016. *Exploring Green Criminology: Toward a green criminological revolution*. Abingdon: Routledge.

Lynx UK Trust. 2021. Available at: https://lynxuk.org/. Accessed 14 June 2021.

Miljodirektoratet. 2021. Small increase in sheep lost to wild game in 2021. Available at: www.miljodirektoratet.no/aktuelt/nyheter/2022/januar-2022/liten-okning-i-tapte-sau-til-rovvilt-i-2021/. Accessed 10 August 2022.

Moss, S. 2020. Missing lynx: how rewilding Britain could restore its natural balance. *The Guardian*. Available at: www.theguardian.com/environment/2020/jul/12/missing-lynx-how-rewilding-britain-could-restore-its-natural-balance. Accessed 14 June 2021.

Nurse, A. and Wyatt, T. 2020. *Wildlife Criminology*. Bristol: Bristol University Press.

Nussbaum, M. 2006. *Frontiers of Justice: Disability, nationality, species membership*. Boston, MA: Harvard University Press.

Regan, T. 1983 [2004]. *The Case for Animal Rights*. Los Angeles: University of California Press.

Royal Society for the Protection of Birds. 2021. Birdcrime: fighting raptor persecution. Available at: www.rspb.org.uk/globalassets/downloads/documents/birds-and-wildlife/crime/2021/bc2021_report.pdf. Accessed 23 September 2023.

Ryder, R. 1971. Experiments on Animals. In S. Godlovitch, R. Godlovitch and J. Harris (eds) *Animals, Men and Morals*. London: Victor Gollanz: 41–82.

Singer, P. 2015 [1975]. *Animal Liberation: The definitive classic of the animal movement [Fortieth Anniversary Edition]*. New York: Open Road.

Sollund, R. 2012. Speciesism as Doxic Practice, or Valuing Plurality and Difference. In: R. Ellefsen, R. Sollund and G. Larsen (eds) *Eco-global Crimes: Contemporary problems and future challenges*. Aldershot: Ashgate: 91–115.

Sollund, R. 2013. Animal abuse, animal rights and species justice. In: American Society of Criminology 69th Annual Meeting, Atlanta. *Animal Abuse, Animal Rights and Species Justice*. 1–35.

Sollund, R. 2019. *The Crimes of Wildlife Trafficking: Issues of justice, legality and morality*. London: Routledge.

South, N. and Brisman, A. (eds). 2020. *Routledge International Handbook of Green Criminology* (2nd edn). London: Routledge.

United Nations Environment Programme and United Nations Food and Agricultural Organization. 2021. United Nations Decade on Restoration 2021–2030. Available at: www.decadeonrestoration.org/. Accessed 14 June 2021.

White, R. 2008. *Crimes Against Nature: Environmental criminology and ecological justice*. New York: Willan.

White, R. 2013. *Environmental Harm: An eco-justice perspective*. Bristol: Policy Press.

White, R. 2018. Green victimology and non-human victims. *International Review of Victimology*, 24(2): 239–55. https://doi.org/10.1177/0269758017745615

Wilson, E. O. 2016. *Half Earth: Our planet's fight for life*. New York: Liveright Publishing.

Wyatt, T. 2021a. The non-human animal in CITES and Bern Conventions implementation in the UK. *Revista Catalana de Dret Ambiental*, 12(1): 1–34.

Wyatt, T. 2021b. *Wildlife Trafficking: A deconstruction of the crime, victim and offender* (2nd edn). London: Palgrave Macmillan.

Zimmer, C. 2013. Back to life. *National Geographic* [online]. Available at: https://www.nationalgeographic.com/magazine/article/species-revival-bringing-back-extinct-animals. Accessed 23 September 2023.

11

We Only See What We Know: Animal Conservation and Human Preservation

Mark T. Palermo

Introduction

In pre-religious and shamanistic cultures, the relationship with the natural world was strong, reality based and pragmatic. In an age of trans-humanist urges and struggles for non-human animal conservation and representation, the relationship with nature has become a matter of policy.

Notwithstanding animistic revivals, urbanization and a recreational, consumeristic and medicalized relationship with the natural world further distance us from nature from an ontological perspective.

Furthermore, the progressive commodification of life has translated, when it comes to non-humans, into the gradual acceptance of behaviours which ordinarily would qualify as moral impossibilities. Exploitation and trafficking are, de facto, regulated by international trade agreements. The latter furthers the acceptance of the concept of *nature* as merchandise.

The objective of this chapter is to underscore the unavoidable all-encompassing nature of green criminology as it relates to animal conservation with a cross-disciplinary theoretical engagement approach, and to outline some of current animal conservation shortcomings.

> Beasts of every land and time
> Hearken to my joyful tidings
> Of the Golden future time
>
> George Orwell, 2021 [1945]

Philosophical framework

In *The Gay Science*, Friedrich Nietzsche in 1882 writes that one of man's four errors has been to place himself above animals and nature in a fallacious hierarchical order (Nietzsche 1977: 156). In the third book of the *The Gay Science*, he further comments: 'I fear animals regard man as a creature of their own kind which has in a highly dangerous fashion lost its healthy animal reason – in other words they see him as the mad animal, as the laughing animal, as the weeping animal, as the unhappy animal' (Nietzsche 1977: 190).

It is beyond the scope of this writing to elaborate on the pertinent and extensive philosophical literature relevant to human–animal relations. The current predominant, and perhaps inevitable, hierarchical anthropocentric stance is long standing in western thought. It has developed inflexibly from Greek philosophy onward, through Christian-Aristotelian cosmological orthodoxy, to the more animal-friendly Rousseauian attribution of ideas and sense to non-human animals (Rousseau 1987: 45).

When exploring the realm of animal rights and related ethics it is nearly impossible to subvert the subject-object framework, not because non-human animals are not conscious and sentient beings, quite the contrary in fact, but simply in light of the fact that humans – also in the context of ethics and rights – are the ones doing the observing and recording – as well as the deciding.

Notwithstanding, if one hopes to truly be able to allow for non-human animal representation, there is a need to move beyond a dualistic separation towards an *anthropology beyond the human* (Kohn 2013: 7), adopting a monistic approach in which 'how humans represent jaguars and how jaguars represent humans can be understood as integral, though not interchangeable, parts of a single, open-ended story' (Kohn 2013: 9). Understanding how animals – both free and 'domesticated' – perceive humans may help minimize intrusions and habitat disruptions, improving conservation approaches (Goumas et al 2020).

This is a chapter situated within an extra-disciplinary theoretical engagement approach (Brisman 2014). It is an attempt to avoid the all-too-common compartmentalization characterizing so much of contemporary social science. The latter, in fact, runs the risk of becoming rigid, losing touch with the necessarily all-encompassing nature of the field of criminology and of green criminology in particular. Rather, there is a need to develop a theoretical laboratory for thinking about environmental issues (Natali 2016: 2). To look beyond/outside criminology's borders (Brisman 2014) is an essential approach when tackling complex issues which are multifactorial in nature and culturally diverse (Sollund 2015).

Of mice and men

For ages, non-human animals have been caught by humans. They were – and are – caught in nets, in traps, in holes, with little capacity to free themselves. In recent years they are asymmetrically caught between advocacy, activism and academia, not necessarily in that order, and have become the ideological foundation of politics, inspiring movements from both left and right (Bertuzzi 2018) and the creation of new and compassionate parties (Lucardie 2020). While they by far outnumber humans, non-human animals have been equated with minorities and the disabled (Regan 2004; Lucardie 2020) even though they lack any characteristic that could even remotely allow for such a comparison, particularly as it pertains to animals in the wild, quite capable of fending for themselves within the limits of life and destiny. Sadly, though, they share with minorities and the disabled the unfortunate fate of having been – and being – experimented upon in totalitarian regimes and democracies alike (Brandt 1978; Weindling et al 2016). It is surprising, therefore, yet perhaps not so much, that in spite of their de facto state of subjection, they do not qualify as vulnerable subjects when it comes to clinical trials, as is the case of pregnant women, foetuses, prisoners and children (Wendler 2020). There seems to be no peace for them and, while the subject of much debating, they remain the object of much experimentation (Ormandy et al 2019), and the victims of research and development trials at times in violation of multilateral treatises aimed at animal protection, for example CITES (Convention on International Trade in Endangered Species of Wild Fauna and Flora). One example for all is the 'harvesting' of thousands of *Epipedobates* frogs from Ecuador for the development of analgesic substances (Goyes and Sollund 2018). Grievously, the saga of epibatidine, the toxic alkaloid isolated from *Epipedobates* frogs, now almost 50 years into its writing, has not yet translated into a clinically applicable success story. As of today, something common to many compounds studied in experimental pharmacology, epibatidine remains a 'promising' molecule and a 'potential' therapeutic tool (Salehi et al 2018). Unfortunately, its dangerous broad spectrum of activity, which induces off-target effects in a number of systems, precludes any realistic therapeutic development (Lloyd and Williams 2000). Indeed, 96 per cent of drugs that pass preclinical tests (including animal testing) fail to proceed to the 'market'. In other words, they never reach a single patient (Akhtar 2015).

The epibatidine example alone should alert us when reading of promising and potential tools in pharmacotherapy, which so often (mis)lead us into the nebulous realm of eternal possibilities. In the present context it is even more disconcerting given the enormous number of living beings abducted and sacrificed during the process, in defiance of any international agreement meant to safeguard them. Finally, it seriously questions the continued and obstinate use of animal lives in experimentation despite evidence for the discordance between human disease and animal models of disease (Akhtar 2015).

Irrespective of any debating relevant to the use, misuse and actual efficacy of animal experimentation, it is safe to say, agreeing with John Pippin, that even in the most compassionate hands, animal research is cruel, sad and deadly for animals (Pippin 2012).

Past to present

Some 10,000–40,000 years ago, during the last Ice Age, someone bothered to depict animals on cave walls. The reason for the paintings is truly unknown, yet it is thought to be related to (pre)religious shamanic practices (Winkelman 2010: 74).

In pre-religious and shamanistic cultures, the relationship with the natural world was strong, reality based and pragmatic. Animals have been invested in time with symbolic qualities and apotropaic powers, in both folk parlance as well as shamanistic practices (Harner 1980: 57–72).

The elements, the landscape and animals alike, were invested with spiritual significance, which went beyond magical thinking and a desire for controlling one's circumstances and governing one's fears.

Therianthropes (chimeric combinations of human and animal features) are widely represented even beyond pre-religious cultures. Anubis, the Egyptian guardian of burial sites, was represented some 3,000 years ago by the combination of a human body and the head of an African wolf. The wolf itself is widely represented in symbolic iconography. It is a totemic animal for National Socialism (Mohnhaupt 2021: 31), a wet nurse for ancient Rome founders Romulus and Remus and an allegorical symbol warning against the dangers of life in Charles Perrault's *Little Red Riding Hood*.

Observation of natural phenomena, including pathological ones, contributed to the development of myths. Cyclopia, for example, a rare congenital malformation in which during embryonic development the two orbits fuse into a single cavity, has most certainly inspired mythological man-eating creatures in epic poems in ancient Greece and Turkey, but also Old England, respectively Polyphemus, Tepegöz and Grendel (Turgut et al 2019).

In premodern cultures, by necessity in tune with *nature*, seasonal rhythms and animal life, symbolism while being allegorical was also bound to practical knowledge of natural surroundings and of animal behaviour, and considered substantial in its quality.

As examples of nature symbolism, irrespective of the verifiability of the origin, is the embodiment of the corn-spirit in animals, present across folk customs in northern European countries. Be these wolves or dogs, among others, the phenomenon is strongly connected to propitiatory rituals surrounding the harvest (Frazer 1998); or the 'Carnival of the Man-Deer' in southern Italy in which, prior to the onset of spring, a man disguised as a deer falls to a sacrificial ritual to ensure fertility of the land (Testa 2017). Human–animal transformations are common also in so-called hunting animism (Willerslev 2015a: 151) and both western and eastern traditions have knowledge of animal-like hominids such as the North American Sasquatch, the Italian Uomo Selvatico (Centini 1989: 10) or the Himalayan Yeti. The latter has been anecdotally associated with regional Tibetan bears and genetic studies have been carried out to explain the nature of the myth (Sykes et al 2014) in yet another attempt to *demystify* – within the framework of scientism – the unexplainable.

Notwithstanding animistic revivals (Willerslev 2015b: 275), presently such strong relationship with the symbolism of environment is probably found only in non-urban communities experiencing nature from day to day, beyond ethnographic folklore, and living with *wildlife*, and animals in general, as cohabitants or competitors, and not only as companions. In areas of the world where secularization has yet to openly predominate, the relationship with the natural world is more mutualistic and maintains a strong spiritual approach, while being also highly pragmatic (Goyes et al 2021). There is no doubt that traditional knowledge, experience and understanding of nature must be valued and should contribute to conservation efforts (Aigo and Ladio 2016). This can be said not only of the south or the far east of the world but also of European rural communities with strong ties to tradition in terms of land management and relationship with local fauna (Bignal and McCracken 2000).

Notwithstanding, traditional approaches to *wildlife* and natural resources collide with current existing rules and laws governing its utilization. As a result, common practices, such as fishing and hunting, become equivalent to poaching (Pohja-Mykrä 2016) in a manner not dissimilar to firewood collecting and even mushroom picking, requiring paid permits and subject to legal limits. That said, while this may be the result of legislation and societal changes, some traditional approaches to hunting, while not yet considered illegal (surprisingly, in view of their cruelty), are promisingly under legitimate scrutiny in light of obvious harmful and inhumane elements implicit in the practices. One example for all is the use of leghold traps for the capture of furbearing animals regulated, theoretically, by the oxymoronic Agreement on International Humane Trapping Standards (AIHTS). Indeed, given the fate of the trapped animal it seems contradictory to speak of 'humane' standards. Notwithstanding, far from being humane, AIHTS is fraught with inconsistencies, resulting in loopholes and translating into needless suffering for animals, (Proulx et al 2020). Logically, killing a living being should be unlawful, irrespective of traditional 'age-old' approaches, and a similar paradox, in the case of human animals, is evident in the case of war waging, the death penalty and, for many, assisted suicide, abortion and euthanasia. And yet, 'ethics' seems to enjoy a significant amount of moral flexibility allowing for 'case by case' relativism, with the understanding that a 'Kantian' moral *categorical imperative* can be easily overcome, for a number of different 'human' (certainly not humane) necessities, and be substituted by a – still 'Kantian' – moral *hypothetical imperative*, translating into a more convenient ethics '*du jour*' (Palermo 2020a).

Identity and cultural issues may be at the heart of a polarized confrontation between local livestock farmers and conservation law enforcement, such as that seen, for instance, in Italian South Tyrol (Stauder et al 2020 in the case of large carnivore protection). As evidence of the age-old and ubiquitous difficulty with change, be it social, economic or environmental, tensions resulting from the clash between longstanding customs and current environmental awareness and legislation take place in other countries as well (Sollund and Goyes 2021). However, what may be interpreted as backwardness, may indeed represent a struggle for autonomy and could be thought of as a form of civil disobedience and cultural resistance against change (Krange and Skogen 2011). Such issues may remain relatively remote and easily brushed off as collateral damage for the majority of people given that over half of humanity lives in urban contexts. In fact, the progressive rural and mountain area abandonment compounds an ongoing current dissociation from the true day-to-day experience of natural settings, which rarely goes beyond a time-limited recreational one. Paradoxically, in a 'well-armed' country such as the United States of America where bearing arms is a constitutional right and the National Rifle Association advertises itself as 'America's longest-standing civil rights organization' (home.nra.org 2022), the number of hunters has been progressively declining, raising concerns relevant to funding for conservation, given that some of the revenue from hunting licences is diverted to wildlife agencies (Manfredo et al 2020).

Urbanization has been intriguingly connected not only to a distancing from the natural world, as would appear to be logical, but also vis-à-vis a reduction of the capacity for appreciating the human–nature interdependence, to diminished cognitive flexibility (Aminpour 2022). Interestingly this is the opposite of what is seen relevant to the impact of a full immersion in natural settings as far as executive skills and creativity are concerned (Atchley et al 2012) which are instead enhanced.

CITES, and the commodification of life

Life has become a matter of policy and *wildlife* is no exception. Agreements have been stipulated transnationally aimed at its safeguarding. For example, the 1979 Bern Convention (Convention on the Conservation of European Wildlife and Natural Habitats) came into effect in 1982, and CITES

(Convention on International Trade in Endangered Species of Wild Fauna and Flora), signed in 1973, was enforced in 1975.

There are profound axiological differences (Goyes 2021) between the two, which reflect cultural attitudes relevant to value and the acceptable commercialization of the natural world, despite the logical and indisputable relevance of their implicit principles and goals. But there is also evidence of an ineffective translation into explicit action (MacDonald et al 2021; Sollund 2022; Goyes, this volume; Stefes, this volume), if not actual conflict between what the conventions declare and the end results of a faulty implementation (Sollund 2022). Among other causes, ineffective translation and faulty implementation may reflect an all-too-common disjunction between arbitrary policy and the evidence-based need of an ecosystem (Svancara et al 2005) or, more worrisome, may be further evidence that large multilateral treaties may not be as effective as one would hope for (Hoffman et al 2022). It is noteworthy that, in contrast to considerable evidence in support of trade and finance treaties' effectiveness, human rights and environmental agreements have not been shown to consistently improve state practices (Hoffman et al 2022; Goyes, this volume). The latter perhaps reflects the intrinsic difficulties in the transnationalization of law (Orangias 2021) or the logically inhomogeneous evolution of public trust thinking when applied to ecosystems, across countries and cultures (Hare and Blossey 2014). Public trust thinking (PTT) is a philosophical approach to natural resources, including wildlife, characterized by commitments to public control, broad public interests and conservation for future generations (Giacomelli et al 2019). The 'public trust doctrine' (PTD) implies that certain 'natural resources' – including wildlife – are defined as part of an 'inalienable public trust' and certain authorities are designated as 'public trustees' to guard those resources. Furthermore, every citizen, as 'beneficiary of the trust', may – in principle – invoke its terms to hold the trustees accountable and to obtain judicial protection against encroachments or impairments (Sand 2014). At present, PTD aims primarily at safeguarding nature and wildlife as resources, yet there is clearly the need to extend any fiduciary obligations to non-human species as well (Hare and Blossey 2014).

Additionally, relevant to the complexities surrounding international agreements, the pervasive and growing lack of trust in environmental organizations, bordering on frank denial of anthropogenically caused climate change (Krange et al 2021), thrives on a culture of conspiracy theories (Sternisko et al 2020), questioning the credibility of environmental science, and perhaps that of science in general. In addition, the complexity of the 'free-for-all' global environmental movement, which includes groups and organizations from both the far left and the radical right, the substantial differences between urban vs rural attitudes and agendas toward nature, and the aforementioned difficulties with social changes affecting culture and identity, further the lack of trust in public institutions. Indeed, it is upon the 'small' problems of the 'local' person that conspiracy theories and a culture of suspicion prey. On the other hand, the very concept of conspiracy theory has become one way to silence dissenting views and to minimize the concerns of those affected by ongoing social erosion and rapid cultural change. While all the above unravels, CITES, at present, is the world's *wildlife* trade 'regulator'.

There is something fundamentally wrong, however, with the concept of *wildlife trade* (Goyes and Sollund 2016). Wild, in fact, implies, as per a standard definition 'living in a state of nature; not tamed or domesticated' (Websters 1989), in essence, free. A definition of *trade* is 'an act or process of buying, selling or exchanging commodities, at either wholesale or retail prices, within a country or between countries'. So, indeed, wildlife trade should be an impossibility. In point of fact, CITES governs a sort of 'defilement of life' in which 'all areas of life are subject to production' (Han 2021: 61). In truth, once anything is seen as having a price, society itself becomes one big market (Sayer 2002: 47). Also of note is that given the wild nature of the hunted individual, in the case of freeborn non-human animals, or collected specimens in the case of flora, the sustainability of the behaviour is unfeasible in light of the finite essence of the traded 'commodity'. It is therefore completely disengaged from any purported conservation resolution.

The dismal truth is that life, nature and its inhabitants have become a consumer issue (Brisman and South 2020). Land is a commodity (Floysand and Jokobsen, 2007) disengaged from local social structures and essential cultural value systems. The latter are the aspects providing for true social and cultural meaning and interpersonal contact. The disengagement, inevitably, spills over into the relationship with fauna and flora, which are no longer part of human *myths* but instead have become not only basic goods to be traded and owned, or medicinal antidotes for a stressful and unhappy life, but also the focus of catastrophic – yet reality-based – apocalyptic eco-anxiety relevant to the end of the world, climate change, global warming, loss of biodiversity, extinction, and so on. In other words, to *Anthropocene*, the proposed geological epoch of humanity (Crutzen and Stoermer 2000).

Indeed, we are embedded in a culture of social emergency as evidenced by the chronic, unrelenting and daily bombardment with primarily negative and catastrophic information and prognostications. The omnipresent images of ecological deterioration may have after-effects ranging from fear to apathy, with social activism somewhere in between (Palermo 2020b). The pervasiveness of technology and virtual communities, too, often gives a sense of personal responsibility for global events and change (see Greenpeace campaigns as an example). This, particularly as it concerns younger consumers, compounds the above-mentioned anxiety.

Commodification surreptitiously leads to the promotion of *sustainable consumer behaviours*, one of the contemporary oxymorons in political and economic discourse. In fact, it promotes and underlies, logically and necessarily, a new form of consumerism characteristic of the so-called *green economy*. Engaging in sustainable consuming becomes also a facile – yet unrealistic – countermeasure to the aforementioned apocalyptic anxiety and guilt (Culiberg et al 2022) which caters to the citizen as consumer (Ricci et al 2016). Similarly, commercial captive breeding and so-called *wildlife farms* represent other linguistic contradictions with an appeasing quality for consciences and with a still questionable positive impact on conservation outcomes (MacDonald et al 2021).

So-called Social Ecological Thought (SET) marketing seeks to reconcile financial growth with ecological wellbeing (Dyck and Manchanda 2021) in the context of a virtue ethics framework. This in hopes of avoiding a more cynical greenwashing (Siano et al 2017). Green finance has been present since the late 1990s, in the wake of the Exxon Valdez oil spill, to promote social and environmental financial policies (Chen 2022). Its purported aim is to provide financial resources for environment-friendly schemes, with ecological security as the primary motivation (Mngumi et al 2022). Within this context the CITES framework, while being environment and natural resource friendly, may not be as socially informed as local communities would wish for (Abensperg-Traun 2009). Indeed, given that the livelihood of many may rely on the very trade or utilization of protected species, a conflict may easily arise similar to that seen in the context of European large carnivore protection. Nonetheless, beyond CITES regulations, sometimes the answer to the most basic question – what is legal and what is illegal – is not straightforward (MacDonald et al 2021).

Conclusions and future directions

Human attitudes, behaviours and feelings cannot seem to avoid polarization with the unavoidable consequence of ideological extremism and antipodean perspectives. No area of life escapes this Manichean disposition where one's *rights* are another's *wrongs*. A logical and dangerous side-effect of dualistic rigidity is the loss of knowledge-based common sense (and experience) and the inevitable onset of *Holy Wars* between *isms*. From resource-oriented conservation ethics, through holistic biotic and abiotic interdependence, to a more radical libertarian extension approach (Peppoloni and Di Capua 2021: 167–8) there is an ongoing struggle as far as our relationship with nature is concerned.

There is an inescapable need to organize, categorize and measure. Every human trait, state and emotion has been studied. Wisdom, happiness and grief (Sato et al 2019; Kakarala et al 2020; Meeks and Jeste 2009) have undergone analysis with a functional MRI, seemingly seeking neuroscientific approval for feeling and being in the world (Palermo 2022). Similarly, 'connectedness to nature' is measured as a marker of environmental concern (Nisbet et al 2009) another example of an omnipresent, omnipotent and perhaps overwhelming scientism we are fed on a daily basis. In spite of the world allegedly *going green*, becoming *eco-friendly* and *sustainable*, our progressive disengagement from our natural surroundings, and ignorance thereof, would seem to contradict the purported epidemic of environmental virtuosity. Just as it is difficult to teach virtue *ex cathedra*, academically as well as religiously (Hawking et al 2020) something better learned through observable examples, so it is unlikely that a communion with nature will be stimulated via 'a clear and compelling message about the importance of biodiversity and what we risk in depleting it' (Novacek 2008).

Humans share over 98 per cent of their genotype with other non-human primates and claims are made on popular science websites that 50 per cent of human DNA is common to plants and trees (Dessimoz Lab 2020; thednatests.com). Undoubtedly plants and animals have a common evolutionary history which eventually diverged and, for all intents and purposes, they can be considered evolutionary sisters (Bouteau et al 2021) sharing a so-called Last Universal Common Ancestor (LUCA). The presence of orthologs, genes which evolved from a common ancestral gene by speciation and that usually retain similar functions in different species, including humans and plants (Wada et al 2017) is further evidence of this longstanding biological relationship. One example is that of Arabidopsis thaliana, a small flowering plant related to cabbage. Strikingly, the majority of human genes have conserved orthologs in Arabidopsis (Xu and Møller 2011).

Perhaps the *archetypal tree* described by the founder of Analytic Psychology Carl Jung as a source of transformation and renewal (Jung 2012: 40–2) and as a symbol of the *totality of the self* may go beyond a symbolic interpretation and may well be connected to a partially shared nature that many, for the most part, choose to ignore. While this will surprise some and amuse others, it may reconcile with a contemporary confutation of materialistic absolutism (Tart 2009: 19–32) and with a renewed interest in animism, which has been belittled and brushed aside in the best-case scenario as unverifiable, and in the worst relegated to the heterogeneous cauldron of New Age fancies. This is quite perplexing given the ubiquitous nature of institutionalized ritualistic beliefs and behaviours also known as 'religions'.

Peter Handke, the 2019 winner of the Nobel Prize for Literature, in his *Essay on the Mushroom Hunter* (Handke 2015: 170) concludes his book claiming that to the four elements of air, water, earth and fire, a fifth element is to be added: that of the fairy-tale. Indeed, stories come to our rescue in times like these, as in Singer's *Zlateh the Goat* when Aaron, the young protagonist, says to his goat Zlateh, who saved his life during a snowstorm: 'You cannot speak, but I know you understand. I need you and you need me. Isn't that so?' (Singer 2021: 98).

Sadly, scientism and scientific imperialism narrowed epistemology (Mazur 2021) by emphasizing in public and academic discourse the cultural boundaries of knowledge, including social science. Or worse, they contributed to create them.

Focusing, from a speciesism perspective, on the 2 per cent difference which separates us from our fellow primates, compounds a lordly yet spurious distance from the natural world we belong to and, de facto, robs us of a powerful explanatory and interpretative framework relative to our own *being* in the world.

The very concept of evolution, not as theory but as fact and simply defined as a generic gradual growth and development, or more 'biologically' as a continuous genetic adaptation of organisms or species to the environment, has gotten us in trouble. In fact, it inevitably – by habit and choice – leads us to comparative attitudes using humans as a hierarchical reference point of a pyramidal approach to life.

Furthermore, comparative anatomical homologies and vestigial organs, as well as our own sensitivity to natural surroundings, the weather and the lunar cycles (Raible et al 2017) as far as our physiology is concerned, is further evidence of our own – obvious yet minimized – animal nature. The latter beyond contemporary philosophical pondering (Agamben 2002; Derrida 2006) which counterintuitively has come to further compound the distance between human and non-human animals and, paradoxically, runs the risk of perpetuating the very anthropocentric stance much current commentary wishes to circumvent.

To further remind us of our essence, it is worth remembering the use, until recently, of porcine insulin for the treatment of human insulin-dependent diabetes mellitus.

We are arrogant parvenues compared to non-human animals. According to Foucault, 'we are so blinded by the recent manifestation of man that we can no longer remember a time – and it is not so long ago – when the world, its order, and human beings existed but man did not' (Foucault 1970: 322).

Anthropocentrism is a human-made representation grounded in a longstanding cultural tradition. It is a reductionistic account stemming from a relativistic stance based on human criteria. This is inevitable, being humans who write, ponder and fret over life. Similarly to ethnocentrism, anthropocentrism is related to the chronic *us* vs *them* or *it* vs *the other* position: human vs animal or matter vs spirit. If one were to compare the human–animal relationship with one of a transcultural nature or look through an ethno-psychiatric lens (Nathan 2013), it would be easy to see that non-human animals represent our contemporary *other* (Sollund 2016; Antić 2021). In truth we are exposed to *otherness* many times a day: neighbours, passers-by, colleagues, even our loved ones are *others*. Yet we do not identify them as such. From a social categorization perspective (Liberman et al 2017) we belong to the same group: we are human.

On the other hand, ecocentrism and biocentrism are also human-made representations bound to an ongoing paradigm change in cultural attitudes towards nature. All three frameworks, irrespective of language manipulations, cannot change our incapacity to experience another's subjectivity. How can one adopt the perspective of the non-human animal? Has moving from *animal* to *non-human animal* made a difference in their status? Or only in our status? Philosopher Mark Rowlands asked: 'Who speaks for Wolf?' (Rowlands 1998), but how do we know what wolves want? Biologist Uexküll encouraged us to think like a bee, to understand the bee's *Umwelt* (Buchanan 2008), but how do bees think? A difficult question, akin to a Rinzai Zen koan and meant to help us doubt if we are heading in the right direction.

Species justice and animal rights, similarly to human justice and relevant rights, should be a given, and neither are. The attribution or negation of moral agentic capacity to non-human animals as a prerequisite or basis for their right to not be harmed (Regan 2004) furthers an anthropocentric magnanimous attitude which can only distance us from the crux of the problem: our relationship with otherness. Is it actually necessary to attribute moral qualities to a non-human animal to justify protection? And, for that matter, is it necessary to attribute moral qualities to a human to justify protection? Furthermore, while the complex relationship between moral status, sentience and consciousness in human animals, despite a large knowledge base, is still unravelling from a neurocognitive perspective, in the case of non-human animals we are still in the infancy of any objective understanding (Paul et al 2020) given the implicit difficulties in exploring non-human animal consciousness. Indeed, while understanding is crucial in the context of ethically charged situations in the case of human animals, such as end of life decisions, persistent vegetative states and legislation relevant to pregnancy termination, in the case of non-human animals a similar solid comparative grasp may prove essential in the context of animal advocacy.

Notwithstanding, legal technicalities such as correlativity and reciprocity of rights and duties, and will theory (Stucki 2020), for example, abound even in the world of animal rights, and when applied to non-human animals can easily mislead one into the temptation of denying them any possibility of protection beyond paternalism. The problem, as is often the case in dealing with alterity, is the erroneous use of human standards for non-human entities. The mechanism is similar to what occurs in cross-cultural contexts.

This is why, while important and interesting, from a comparative or evolutionary perspective, ongoing scientific inquiry into the cognitive, language and symbolic capacities of non-human animals, although challenging and still in its infancy (Stevens 2010), cannot be the basis for species justice. In the meantime, it might help to remind ourselves, every so often, that we *descend* from them. Not vice versa.

Only when we internalize the fact that *we are such stuff as – animals – are made* on,[1] and, with all due respect for current trans-humanist disparate aspirations (McNamee and Edwards 2006) our vestigial tail as well as our own chronobiology should be further confirmation of this, only then animal ethics, geo-ethics and human ethics will coalesce into one world view.

Policy alone, including international agreements such as CITES and the Bern Convention, will change nothing until they are grounded in emotional (as in non-cognitive, not as in *romantic*) understanding (Goralnick et al 2012). Political propaganda and its rhetoric, as well as advertising, are evidence of this. Cognitive approaches, including moral whys and decalogues will not go far, as in any other area of human life where change is sought and necessary. No amount of information will change attitudes in a permanent manner. This may lie behind CITES/Bern or similar agreements' shortcomings. They fail to move us. They are as remote and alien to most as the beneficiaries of their 'protection'. The organizational issues – undeniable and predictable – perhaps are only rationalizations, but they allow for justificatory irresponsibility on the part of citizens and policy makers alike.

References

Abensperg-Traun, M. (2009) 'CITES, sustainable use of wild species and incentive-driven conservation in developing countries, with an emphasis on southern Africa'. *Biological Conservation*, 142(5): 948–63. https://doi.org/10.1016/j.biocon.2008.12.034

Agamben, G. (2002) *L'aperto: L'uomo e l'animale*. Turin: Bollati Boringhieri.

Aigo, J. and Ladio, A. (2016). 'Traditional Mapuche ecological knowledge in Patagonia, Argentina: fishes and other living beings inhabiting continental waters, as a reflection of processes of change'. *Journal of Ethnobiology and Ethnomedicine*, 12(1): 56. https://doi.org/10.1186/s13002-016-0130-y

Akhtar, A. (2015) 'The flaws and human harms of animal experimentation'. *Cambridge Quarterly of Healthcare Ethics*, 24(4): 407–19.

Aminpour, P., Gray, S. A., Beck, M. W., Furman, K. L., Tsakiri, I., Gittman, R. K. et al (2022) 'Urbanized knowledge syndrome—erosion of diversity and systems thinking in urbanites' mental models'. *npj Urban Sustainability*, 2(11). https://doi.org/10.1038/s42949-022-00054-0

Antić, A. (2021) 'Transcultural psychiatry: cultural difference, universalism and social psychiatry in the age of decolonisation'. *Culture, Medicine, and Psychiatry*, 45: 359–84. https://doi.org/10.1007/s11013-021-09719-4

---

[1] Paraphrasing Prospero in William Shakespeare's *The Tempest,* Act IV, Scene 1, 'We are such stuff as dreams are made on'.

Atchley, R. A., Strayer, D. L. and Atchley, P. (2012) 'Creativity in the wild: improving creative reasoning through immersion in natural settings'. *PLoS One*, 7(12): e51474.

Bertuzzi, N. (2018) 'The Italian animal advocacy archipelago and the four animalisms'. *Partecipazione e Conflitto*, 11(3): 865–90. DOI: 10.1285/i20356609v11i3p865

Bignal, E. M. and McCracken, D. I. (2000) 'The nature conservation value of European traditional farming systems'. *Environmental Reviews*, 8(3): 149–71.

Bouteau, F., Grésillon, E., Chartier, D., Arbelet-Bonnin, D., Kawano, T., Baluška, F. et al (2021) 'Our sisters the plants? Notes from phylogenetics and botany on plant kinship blindness'. *Plant Signaling and Behavior*, 16(12): 2004769. DOI: 10.1080/15592324.2021.2004769.

Brandt, A. M. (1978) 'Racism and research: the case of the Tuskegee syphilis study'. *The Hastings Center Report*, 8(6): 21–9.

Brisman, A. (2014) 'On theory and meaning in green criminology'. *International Journal for Crime, Justice and Social Democracy*, 3(2): 21–34.

Brisman, A. and South, N. (2020) 'A criminology of extinction: biodiversity, extreme consumption and the vanity of species resurrection'. *European Journal of Criminology*, 17(6): 918–35.

Buchanan, B. (2008) *Onto-ethologies: The Animal Environments of Uexküll, Heidegger, Merleau-Ponty and Deleuze*. Albany: State University of New York Press.

Centini, M. (1989) *Il sapiente del bosco: il mito dell'Uomo Selvatico nelle Alpi*. Milan: Xenia.

Chen, J. (2022) 'Green Fund: what it is, how it works, FAQs'. Retrieved 19 September 2022 from www.investopedia.com/terms/g/green_fund.asp

Crutzen, P. J. and Stoermer, E. F. (2000) 'The Anthropocene'. *IGBP Newsletter*, 41: 17–18.

Culiberg, B., Cho, H., Kos Koklic, M. and Zabkar, V. (2022) 'The role of moral foundations, anticipated guilt and personal responsibility in predicting anti-consumption for environmental reasons'. *Journal of Business Ethics*, 182: 465–81. https://doi.org/10.1007/s10551-021-05016-7

Derrida, J. (2006) *L'animale che dunque sono*. Milan: Jaca Book.

Dessimoz Lab (2020) 'The banana conjecture'. Retrieved 24 November from https://lab.dessimoz.org/blog/2020/12/08/human-banana-orthologs

Dyck, B. and Manchanda, R. V. (2021) 'Sustainable marketing based on virtue ethics: addressing socio-ecological challenges facing humankind'. *AMS Review*, 11(1–2): 115–32. https://doi.org/10.1007/s13162-020-00184-7

Floysand, A. and Jakobsen, S. E. (2007) 'Commodification of rural places: a narrative of social fields, rural development and football'. *Journal of Rural Studies*, 23(2): 206–21.

Foucault, M. (1970) *The Order of Things*. New York: Pantheon.

Frazer, J. G. (1998) *Il ramo d'oro. Studio sulla magia e sulla religione*. Turin: Bollati Boringhieri.

Giacomelli, S., Hare, D., Gibbert, M. and Blossey, B. (2019) 'Public trust thinking and public ownership of wildlife in Italy and the United States'. *Environmetal Policy and Governance*, 29: 209–19. https://doi.org/10.1002/eet.1848

Goralnik, L., Millenbah, K. F., Nelson, M. P. and Thorp, L. (2012) 'An environmental pedagogy of care: emotion, relationships, and experience in higher education ethics learning'. *Journal of Experiential Education*, 35(3): 412–28. https://doi.org/10.1177/105382591203500303

Goumas, M., Lee, V. E., Boogert, N. J., Kelley, L. A. and Thornton, A. (2020) 'The role of animal cognition in human-wildlife interactions'. *Frontiers in Psychology*, (11): 589978. DOI:10.3389/fpsyg.2020.589978

Goyes, D. R. (2021) 'Contending philosophical foundation in international wildlife law: a discourse analysis of CITES and the Bern Convention'. *Revista Catalana de Dret Ambiental*, 12(1): 1–35.

Goyes, D. and Sollund, R. (2016) 'Contesting and contextualising CITES: wildlife trafficking in Colombia and Brazil'. *International Journal for Crime, Justice and Social Democracy*, 5(4): 87.

Goyes, D. R. and Sollund, R. (2018) 'Animal abuse, biotechnology and species justice'. *Theoretical Criminology*, 22(3): 363–83.

Goyes, D. R., Abaibira, M. A., Baicué, P., Cuchimba, A., Ñeñetofe, D. T. R., Sollund, R. and Wyatt, T. (2021) 'Southern green cultural criminology and environmental crime prevention: representations of nature within four Colombian Indigenous communities'. *Critical Criminology*, 29(3): 469–85.

Han, B. C. (2021) *La scomparsa dei riti: Una topografia del presente*. Milan: Nottetempo Edizioni.

Handke, P. (2015) *Saggio sul Cercatore di Funghi*. Milan: Guanda.

Hare, D. and Blossey, B. (2014) 'Principles of Public Trust Thinking'. *Human Dimensions of Wildlife*, 19(5): 397–406. DOI:10.1080/10871209.2014.942759

Harner, M. (1980) *The Way of the Shaman: A Guide to Power and Healing*. San Francisco, CA: Harper & Row.

Hawking, M., Kim, J., Jih, M., Hu, C. and Yoon, J. D. (2020) 'Can virtue be taught? A content analysis of medical students' opinions of the professional and ethical challenges to their professional identity formation'. *BMC Medical Education*, 20(1): 380. https://doi.org/10.1186/s12909-020-02313

Hoffman, S. J., Baral, P., Rogers Van Katwyk, S., Sritharan, L., Hughsman, M., Randhawa, H. et al (2022) 'International treaties have mostly failed to produce their intended effects'. *Proceedings of the National Academy of Science USA*, 119(32): e2122854119.

Jung, C. G. (2012) *L'albero filosofico: Edizione integrale di riferimento*. Turin: Bollati Boringhieri.

Kakarala, S. E., Roberts, K. E., Rogers, M., Coats, T., Falzarano, F., Gang, J. et al (2020) 'The neurobiological reward system in Prolonged Grief Disorder (PGD): a systematic review'. *Psychiatry Research: Neuroimaging*, 303: 111135. https://doi.org/10.1016/j.pscychresns.2020.111135

Kohn, E. (2013) *How Forests Think*. Berkley, Los Angeles, London: University of California Press.

Krange, O. and Skogen, K. (2011) 'When the lads go hunting: the "Hammertown mechanism" and the conflict over wolves in Norway'. *Ethnography*, 12(4): 466–89.

Krange, O., Kaltenborn, B. P. and Hultman, M. (2021) 'Don't confuse me with facts': how right wing populism affects trust in agencies advocating anthropogenic climate change as a reality'. *Humanities and Social Sciences Communications*, 8: 255.

Liberman, Z., Woodward, A. L. and Kinzler, K. D. (2017) 'The origins of social categorization'. *Trends in Cognitive Sciences*, 21(7): 556–8. https://doi.org/10.1016/j.tics.2017.04.004

Lloyd, G. K. and Williams, M. (2000) 'Neuronal nicotinic acetylcholine receptors as novel drug targets'. *Journal of Pharmacology and Experimental Therapeutics*, 292(2): 461–7.

Lucardie, P. (2020) 'Animalism: a nascent ideology? Exploring the ideas of animal advocacy parties'. *Journal of Political Ideologies*, 25(2): 212–27.

MacDonald, D. W., Harrington, L. A., Moorhouse, T.P. and D'Cruze, N. (2021) 'Trading animal lives: ten tricky issues on the road to protecting commodified wild animals'. *Bioscience*, 71(8): 846–60.

Manfredo, M. J., Teel, T. L., Don Carlos, A. W., Sullivan, L. et al (2020) 'The changing sociocultural context of wildlife conservation'. *Conservation Biology*, 34(6): 1549–59.

Mazur, L. B. (2020) 'The epistemic imperialism of science: reinvigorating early critiques of scientism'. *Frontiers in Psychology*, 11: 609823. https://doi.org/10.3389/fpsyg.2020.60982

McNamee, M. J. and Edwards, S. D. (2006) 'Transhumanism, medical technology and slippery slopes'. *Journal of Medical Ethics*, 32(9): 513–18. https://doi.org/10.1136/jme.2005.013789

Meeks, T. W. and Jeste, D. V. (2009) 'Neurobiology of wisdom: a literature overview'. *Archives of General Psychiatry*, 66(4): 355–65. https://doi.org/10.1001/archgenpsychiatry.2009.8

Mngumi, F., Shaorong, S., Shair, F. and Waqas, M. (2022) 'Does green finance mitigate the effects of climate variability: role of renewable energy investment and infrastructure'. *Environmental Science and Pollution Research International*, 29(39): 59287–99. https://doi.org/10.1007/s11356-022-19839-y

Mohnhaupt, J. (2021) *Bestiario Nazista*. Turin: Bollati Boringhieri.

Natali, L. (2016) *A Visual Approach for Green Criminology*. London: Palgrave Macmillan.

Nathan, T. (2013) *La Folie des Autres: Traité d'Ethnopsychiatrie Clinique*. Paris: Dunod.

Nietzsche, F. (1977) *La Gaia Scienza*. Milan: Adelphi.

Nisbet, E. K., Zelenski, J. M. and Murphy, S. A. (2009) 'The nature relatedness scale: linking individuals' connection with nature to environmental concern and behavior'. *Environment and Behavior*, 41(5): 715–40. https://doi.org/10.1177/0013916508318748

Novacek, M. J. (2008) 'Colloquium paper: engaging the public in biodiversity issues'. *Proceedings of the National Academy of Sciences of the United States of America*, 105(Suppl 1): 11571–8. https://doi.org/10.1073/pnas.0802599105

Orangias, J. (2021) 'Towards global public trust doctrines: an analysis of the transnationalisation of state stewardship duties'. *Transnational Legal Theory*, 12(4): 550–86. DOI: 10.1080/20414005.2021.2006030

Ormandy, E. H., Weary, D. M., Cvek, K., Fisher, M., Herrmann, K., Hobson-West, P. et al (2019) 'Animal research, accountability, openness and public engagement: report from an international expert forum'. *Animals*, 9: 622. https://doi.org/10.3390/ani9090622

Orwell, G. (2021 [1945]) *Animal Farm*. Milan: Mondadori.

Palermo, M. T. (2020a) 'Moral reason and academic integrity: memory impairment, corrigenda and the pursuit of knowledge'. *International Journal of Offender Therapy and Comparative Criminology*, 64(4): 295–8. https://doi.org/10.1177/0306624X20902301

Palermo, M. T. (2020b) 'From social deviance to art: vandalism, illicit dumping, and the transformation of matter and form'. *Social Sciences*, 9(6): 106. https://doi.org/10.3390/socsci9060106

Palermo, M. T. (2022) 'Scientism, ethics and evil: from mens rea to cerebrum reus'. *International Journal of Offender Therapy and Comparative Criminology*, 66(9): 1036–48. https://doi.org/10.1177/0306624X221104959

Paul, E. S., Sher, S., Tamietto, M., Winkielman, P. and Mendl, M. T. (2020) 'Towards a comparative science of emotion: affect and consciousness in humans and animals'. *Neuroscience and Biobehavioral Reviews*, 108: 749–70. DOI:10.1016/j.neubiorev.2019.11.014

Peppoloni, S. and Di Capua, G. (2021) *Geoetica*. Rome: Donzelli Editore.

Pippin, J. J. (2012) 'Animal research in medical sciences: seeking a convergence of science, medicine, and animal law'. *Texas Law Review*, 54: 469.

Pohja-Mykrä, M. (2016) 'Illegal hunting as rural defiance'. In J. F. Donnermeyer (ed) *The Routledge International Handbook of Rural Criminology*, London and New York: Routledge, pp 329–37.

Proulx, G., Cattet, M., Serfass, T. L. and Baker, S. E. (2020) 'Updating the AIHTS Trapping Standards to improve animal welfare and capture efficiency and selectivity'. *Animals*, 10(8): 1262.

Raible, F., Takekata, H. and Tessmar-Raible, K. (2017) 'An overview of monthly rhythms and clocks'. *Frontiers in Neurology*, 8. https://doi.org/10.3389/fneur.2017.00189

Regan, T. (2004) *The Case for Animal Rights*. Oakland, CA: University of California Press.

Ricci, C., Marinelli, N. and Puliti, L. (2016) 'The consumer as citizen: the role of ethics for a sustainable consumption'. *Agriculture and Agricultural Science Procedia* 8: 395–401. DOI:10.1016/j.aaspro.2016.02.035

Rousseau, J. J. (1987) *The Basic Political Writings*. Indianapolis: Hackett Publishing Company.

Rowlands, M. (1998) *Animal Rights: A Philosophical Defence*. London: Macmillan Press.

Salehi, B., Sestito, S., Rapposelli, S., Peron, G., Calina, D., Sharifi-Rad, M. et al (2018) 'Epibatidine: a promising natural alkaloid in health'. *Biomolecules*, 9(1): 6. DOI:10.3390/biom9010006

Sand, P. H. (2014) 'The concept of public trusteeship in the transboundary governance of biodiversity'. In L. J. Kotzé and T. Marauhn (eds) *Transboundary Governance of Biodiversity*, Leiden/Boston: Brill/Nijhoff, pp 34–64.

Sato, W., Kochiyama, T., Uono, S., Sawada, R., Kubota, Y., Yoshimura, S. and Toichi, M. (2019) 'Resting-state neural activity and connectivity associated with subjective happiness'. *Scientific Reports*, 9(1): 12098. https://doi.org/10.1038/s41598-019-48510-9

Sayer, A. (2002) 'Market, embeddedness and trust: problems of polysemy and idealism'. In S. Metcalfe and A. Warde (eds) *Market Relations and the Competitive Process*, Manchester: Manchester University Press, pp 41–57.

Siano, A., Vollero, A., Conte, F. and Amabile, S. (2017) 'More than words: expanding the taxonomy of greenwashing after the Volkswagen scandal'. *Journal of Business Research*, 71: 27–37. https://doi: 10.1016/j.jbusres.2016.11.002

Singer, I. B. (2021) *Zlateh la capra e alter storie (Zlateh the goat and other stories)*. Milan: Adelphi.

Sollund, R. A. (2015) 'Introduction: critical green criminology – an agenda for change'. in R. Sollund (ed) *Green Harms and Crimes: Critical Criminology in a Changing World*, London: Palgrave Macmillan, pp 1–26.

Sollund, R. (2016) 'The animal other: legal and illegal theriocide'. In M. Hall, J. Maher, A. Nurse, G. Potter, N. South and T. Wyatt (eds) *Greening Criminology in the 21st Century: Contemporary Debates and Future Directions in the Study of Environmental Harm*, London: Routledge, pp 93–113.

Sollund R. (2022) 'Wildlife trade and law enforcement: a proposal for a remodeling of CITES incorporating species justice, ecojustice, and environmental justice'. *International Journal of Offender Therapy and Comparative Criminology*, 66(9): 1017–35. https://doi.org/10.1177/0306624X221099492

Sollund, R. and Goyes, D. R. (2021) 'State-organized crime and the killing of wolves in Norway'. *Trends in Organized Crime*, 24: 467–84.

Stauder, J., Favilli, F., Stawinoga, A. E., Omizzolo, A. and Steifeneder, T. P. (2020) 'The attitude of society to the return of the wolf in South Tyrol (Italy)'. *European Journal of Wildlife Research*, 66(40). https://doi.org/10.1007/s10344-020-1372-5

Sternisko, A., Cichocka, A. and van Bavel, J. J. (2020) 'The dark side of social movements: social identity, non-conformity, and the lure of conspiracy theories'. *Current Opinion in Psychology*, 35: 1–6.

Stevens, J. R. (2010) 'The challenges of understanding animal minds'. *Frontiers in Psychology*, 1: 203. https://doi.org/10.3389/fpsyg.2010.00203

Stucki, S. (2020) 'Towards a theory of legal animal rights: simple and fundamental rights'. *Oxford Journal of Legal Studies*, 40(3): 533–60. https://doi.org/10.1093/ojls/gqaa007

Svancara, L. K., Brannon, R., Scott, J. M., Groves, C.R., Noss, R.F. and Pressey, R. L. (2005) 'Policy-driven versus evidence-based conservation: a review of political targets and biological needs'. *BioScience*, 55: 989–95. DOI:10.1641/0006-3568(2005)055[0989:PVECAR]2.0.CO;2

Sykes, B. C., Mullis, R. A., Hagenmuller, C., Melton, T. W. and Sartori, M. (2014) 'Genetic analysis of hair samples attributed to yeti, bigfoot and other anomalous primates'. *Proceedings: Biological Sciences*, 281(1789): 20140161. https://doi.org/10.1098/rspb.2014.0161

Tart, C. T. (2009) *The End of Materialism*. Oakland, CA: New Harbinger Publications.

Testa, A. (2017) ' "Fertility" and the carnival 2: popular Frazerism and the reconfiguration of tradition in Europe today'. *Folklore*, 128(2): 111–32. https://doi.org/10.1080/0015587X.2017.1281967

The DNA Tests (n.d.) 'How much DNA do humans share with other animals and plants?' Retrieved 23 November 2022 from thednatests.com/how-much-dna-do-humans-share-with-other-animals/

Turgut, A. C., Hall, W. A. and Turgut, M. (2021) 'Three mythic giants for common fetal malformation called "cyclopia": Polyphemus, Tepegöz, and Grendel'. *Child's Nervous System*, 37(3): 725–6.

Wada, N., Kazuki, Y., Kazuki, K., Inoue, T., Fukui, K. and Oshimura, M. (2017) 'Maintenance and function of a plant chromosome in human cells'. *ACS Synthetic Biology*, 6(2): 301–10. https://doi.org/10.1021/acssynbio.6b00180

Webster's Encyclopedic Unabridged Dictionary of the English Language (1989) New York/Avenel, NJ: Gramercy Books.

Weindling, P., von Villiez, A., Loewenau, A. and Farron, N. (2016) 'The victims of unethical human experiments and coerced research under National Socialism'. *Endeavour*, 40(1): 1–6. https://doi.org/10.1016/j.endeavour.2015.10.005

Wendler, D. (2020) 'When and how to include vulnerable subjects in clinical trials'. *Clinical Trials*, 17(6): 696–702. https://doi.org/10.1177/1740774520945601

Willerslev, R. (2015a) 'Hunting animism: human-animal transformations among the Siberian Yukaghirs'. In G. Harvey (ed) *The Handbook of Contemporary Animism*, Abingdon and New York: Routledge, pp 148–58.

Willerslev, R. (2015b) 'The One-All: the animist high god'. In G. Harvey (ed) *The Handbook of Contemporary Animism*, Abingdon and New York: Routledge, pp 275–83.

Winkelman, M. (2010) *Shamanism: A Biopsychosocial Paradigm of Consciousness and Healing* (2nd edn). Santa Barbara, CA: Praeger.

Xu, X. M. and Møller, S. G. (2011) 'The value of Arabidopsis research in understanding human disease states'. *Current Opinion in Biotechnology*, 22(2): 300–7. https://doi.org/10.1016/j.copbio.2010.11.007

12

Conclusion

Ragnhild A. Sollund and Martine S.B. Lie

An important aspect of the CRIMEANTHROP (Criminal Justice, Wildlife Conservation and Animal Rights in the Anthropocene) project was to assess to which degree freeborn animals have rights that are reflected in the implementation of two important conventions, or as consequence of the two conventions. Both were established to protect wildlife species from extinction: CITES, The Convention of Trade in Endangered Species of Wild Fauna and Flora (1973) and the Council of Europe's Convention on the Conservation of European Wildlife and Natural Habitats (1979), known as the Bern Convention. It is important to emphasize that the goal with these conventions is not to offer individual freeborn animals protection from harm and abuse, not even to individuals pertaining to species that are protected because they are endangered. Generally, although they may be included in animal welfare legislation, wildlife is not protected from harm, on the contrary they are hunted for entertainment in countries that are parties/members of these conventions.

In the countries that are included in the case studies of this book, there are thus hunting traditions, for example, the infamous fox hunting of the upper class in the UK from horseback with the use of dogs; the rabbit hunting in Spain with the use of greyhounds (galgo), who are very often mistreated and killed when the hunt is over; the wild boar hunting in Germany and Poland, and the widespread practice of catching and killing songbirds in Italy and around the Mediterranean sea for food or decorations, which is criminalized due to the devastating effects this practice has had on the bird populations (see Chapter 5 by Lorenzo Natali, Ciro Troiano, Sara Zoja and Anita Lavorgna, this volume; Brochet et al 2016). The threat to Europe's birds due to loss of habitat and legal and illegal hunting led to the establishment of the EU Birds Directive in 1979,[1] which together with the Habitats Directive implements the Bern Convention in the EU.

In Norway, like in many other countries,[2] most species that are not threatened with extinction are 'huntable species', for example in the hunting season 2022–23, according to Statistics Norway,[3] 49,301 deer and 27,487 elks were legally killed, while 21,030 red foxes lost their lives to a hunter's rifle in the 2021–22 season, many after first being trapped. Even animals of vulnerable and endangered species are 'huntable species' in Norway, such as hares, grouse and the lynx, of which 36 were shot in the 2022–23 season on so-called 'quota hunts' – a term that disguises that this is recreational hunting. Regarding the large predators, exceptions are often made from rules governing how and when freeborn animals may be hunted, which leaves them with fewer rights than freeborn animals for whom hunting rules are respected. Wolves are even hunted by means of helicopters and machine guns, despite the fact that hunting from aircraft is forbidden according to the Bern Convention's Appendix IV[4] (Lie, this volume).

As shown in Tanya Wyatt's work for the CRIMEANTHROP project, also in the UK controversial hunting takes place which is regarded as a breach of the Bern Convention, when tens of thousands of badgers are killed to control bovine tuberculosis (see Chapter 10 in this volume; Wyatt 2021). From this we argue that, while conventions exist that aim to protect species from extinction, most freeborn animals may still easily fall victim to a hunter's bullets, whether endangered, vulnerable or plentiful. The hunting that wildlife species are subject to for human entertainment is harmful and deadly. So, why then should animals who are listed on the appendices of CITES and the Bern Convention be entitled to rights, when hunting culture and traditions clearly underline that they have none (Sollund and Goyes 2021)?

Although there are provisions in regards to animal welfare in CITES, and although wildlife is accorded intrinsic value in the Bern Convention's preamble, the basis of these conventions is in both cases anthropocentric (Goyes and Sollund 2016; Sollund 2021; Goyes 2021). While animal rights are important in the CRIMEANTHROP project, the cross disciplinarity of the present book means that other issues concerning the implementation and enforcement of the two conventions have received more attention in some contributions, and that the issue of animal rights and animal welfare

---

[1] The Birds Directive (europa.eu)
[2] There are exceptions. For example, in several countries in Latin America, such as Costa Rica, Colombia and Brazil, so called sports hunting is forbidden.
[3] Jakt (ssb.no)
[4] CETS 104 – Annex IV – Convention on the Conservation of European Wildlife and Natural Habitats (coe.int)

is not overall the main focus. The chapters of this volume that pay attention to animal rights find that animal rights are largely absent, as expected. The research that has been carried out in the different countries – Norway, the UK, Spain, Germany, Italy, the Netherlands and Poland – all contribute to shed important light on the ways in which CITES and the Bern Convention succeed or fail to succeed to protect endangered species, as well as weaknesses in their implementation.

The contributions to this book also illustrate that the ways in which the conventions are implemented and enforced vary between countries. In the following we sum up some of the main findings from the chapters of this book.

The first case study in Chapter 2 looked into the mentioned large predator hunts in Norway. Martine S.B. Lie compared legal and illegal wolf and bear hunts and demonstrated that Norway's implementation and enforcement of the Bern Convention is paradoxical. Both legal and illegal hunts cause species injustice and significant harm to the animals, and both threaten their chances of survival. Moreover, those carrying out illegal hunts also participate in legal hunts, even as trusted members of the hunting communities. Additionally, the modus operandi of the crimes is strikingly similar to how legal hunts are conducted, with a considerable risk of wounding the victims in both cases. Lie concludes that the legal hunts uphold anthropocentric interests in keeping the predator populations *low*, and to fulfil only the minimum requirements of the Bern Convention.

Similarly, it is suggested by Sollund's Chapter 3, that animal trafficking victims are not saved for their intrinsic value. It appears that, while there has been some improvement in regards to the protection of trafficking victims of Appendix I species in Norway, at least formally, there is still a risk that the authorities continue to paradoxically enforce CITES through killing the animals who are seized as an enforcement measure (Sollund 2019). This means that the intrinsic value is not respected by the authorities and that the animals are not protected, rather the enforcement of CITES itself may be what entails their death. Enforcement of CITES became more complicated when reptile trade was partly legalized in Norway, not least due to the possibilities that exist for laundering of illegal animals into the legal trade, and the problems related to free trade within the EU's inner market.

This is supported by Chapter 4, by Isabella Dominguez, Marjan Hindriks, Jordi Janssen and Daan van Uhm, who are particularly concerned with reptile trafficking in the Netherlands. They find, as Sollund, that the laundering of illegal wildlife is a salient problem. Both these chapters on reptile trade reveal the role of the internet in the commercialization of reptiles and the problems this online trade entails in terms of control. The fact that reptiles are regarded as any other illegal contraband by traffickers also has consequences for animal welfare and animal rights, and it is important to note that the fact that wildlife trade is generally legal provides opportunities for trade that is actually forbidden. That wildlife trade is allowed and regulated, rather than banned and therefore a crime, adds to a normative climate that encompasses a perception of animals as goods and 'items' from which people and countries can profit. This is in direct contrast with animal rights and the recognition of the intrinsic value of sentient animals.

In Chapter 5, Lorenzo Natali, Ciro Troiano, Sara Zoja and Anita Lavorgna uncover another challenge in the enforcement of CITES and the Bern Convention, with regards to the mentioned illegal abductions and killing of birds in Italy, namely that organized crime groups take part in such crimes. This also points to the diversity of the actors involved, and the monetary interests in the trafficking of wildlife. Moreover, the criminals exhibit considerable creativity in the tools they design for abducting and killing the birds, which cause them significant harm. The Bern Convention and the legislation under which the convention is implemented, as well as other legislation related to CITES, set the rules for bird abductions and related harms in Italy. Although such crimes are considered to be the main threat to the birds' survival, they have received only limited interest in the country. In Italy, 25 per cent of the surveyed bird species are at risk of extinction. 'Poaching' – or abductions – whether or not the birds are killed, is one reason for this, which is further exacerbated by climate change and habitat loss. The authors of this chapter conclude that it is urgent to know the links between the different actors involved at different levels, and their modus operandi; to comprehend the dynamics of supply and demand causing the circulation of these 'products'; but also to grasp the underlying cultural aspects enabling and fostering these behaviours. Not least, in view of lenient sentencing, this chapter concludes that the current penalties for such crimes are insufficiently deterrent. Importantly, the authors also conclude with a call for the need of human beings to live in constant integration and harmony with the natural world, conserving its other animal species. This, they suggest, could be given further incentive through dedicated projects of sensitization and awareness-raising in the educational context and in the society as a whole.

In Chapter 6 Piotr J. Chmielewski and Agnieszka Serlikowska similarly found lenient penalties to be one of several weaknesses of the implementation and enforcement of the Bern Convention in Poland. In many judgments regarding illegal wolf killings penalties were not even imposed. As demonstrated in other chapters, enforcement agents and the criminal justice system lack training in investigating and prosecuting wildlife crimes. As Lie noted about Norway, the majority of the general public in Poland want to preserve the wolves in the country. Nevertheless, Chmielewski and Serlikowska conclude that the legislation meant to protect the Polish wolves is anthropocentric, fragmented and inefficient in attributing them with genuine protection, and favours financial interests. In the rare instances where illegal wolf killings are prosecuted, it is the financial value gained by the offence, rather than the victim wolf's intrinsic value that is taken into account in the courts' judgments.

Teresa Fajardo's analysis of the implementation and enforcement of CITES in Spain in Chapter 7 paints a more promising picture regarding the enforcement of the convention. She demonstrates the complexities of CITES from a legal perspective. CITES and European Union regulations on CITES reflect an anthropocentric approach to wildlife, in which the interests of animals are not yet taken into account. Nonetheless, Fajardo's research suggests that Spain has a rather successful enforcement of CITES compared to that found in others of the case studies. This comes from the cooperation between all enforcement authorities – CITES authorities, SEPRONA (Spanish police unit for the protection of nature) and the Public Prosecutor's Office – and the specialization of personnel that investigate and prosecute CITES crimes. However, the success in regards to enforcement is relative, since when it comes to the compliance with CITES, the legislative measures adopted by Spain create a too fragmented legal framework, similarly to the situation in Poland. The result is that many offenders are not prosecuted or are exonerated. When it comes to the rights of animal victims of trafficking, Spain has focused more on the rehabilitation and rehoming of animals who are stopped in traffic than, for example, Norway. While Spain is more successful there are also weaknesses, as there is a lack of training for enforcement agents also in this country, in addition to the legal fragmentation.

Fragmentation is also a challenge in Germany, as demonstrated by Christoph H. Stefes in Chapter 8, but for other reasons. The fragmentation of the implementation and enforcement of CITES and the Bern Convention to Germany's 16 federal states, entails a lack of training of enforcement officers involved and lenient penalties, and consequently the implementation and enforcement of these two conventions in Germany have too little effect. Stefes, therefore, strongly recommends the establishment of both a centralized authority and specialized offices, as they have in Spain. This can support street-level bureaucrats in building strong cases against offenders. Even if the enforcement of the conventions is wanting, some German states excel compared to others in terms of the number of cases they process. Stefes attributes this to personal engagement and ingenuity among some of the bureaucrats placed with the responsibility of enforcing the conventions, as found in other studies (for example, Sollund and Maher 2015).

In Chapter 9, David R. Goyes also recognizes that the success of CITES and the Bern Convention in protecting freeborn animals depends on the people involved in implementing and enforcing the conventions in the member states. He investigated the conventions' chain of effectiveness from the international to the local level in Norway, suggesting an explanation for poor compliance with the treaties in Norway and beyond. Goyes found in his analysis that although the conventions have many signatories, their obligations are ambiguous. Norway has strictly implemented CITES mandates in the CITES regulation, while taking many liberties when legislating the obligations derived from the Bern Convention, as demonstrated in Lie's chapter. Goyes explains that trade conventions will be better enforced than conservation conventions, due to the economic interests involved in trade rather than in conservation. As is evident in many of the case studies, economic interests broadly defined are more powerful than the intrinsic value of nature and its inhabitants, which is logical in capitalist/materialist societies. Last, based on interviews with parliamentarians, bureaucrats, police and NGOs, Goyes contended that CITES and the Bern Convention fail to affect the stakeholders' behaviour since the conventions were not prominent in their stories about wildlife management.

While the previous chapters painted a disheartening picture of the status of wildlife protection in Europe, Tanya Wyatt's Chapter 10 offered some optimism. She focused on the pertinent issue of rewilding, which has been witnessed in Europe over the past decades with the support of the EU Habitats Directive and the Bern Convention. Studying the public debate in regards to a possible rewilding of the lynx in the UK, Wyatt notes that when governments permit rewilding of predators, speciesism can be challenged and possibly reduced. Her analysis shows, however, that anthropocentrism is central in the debate. The arguments focus more on what harm a rewilding would encompass, than what good it would do in restoring an ecosystem that was disrupted more than a millennium ago when the lynx was hunted to extinction in Britain. A rewilding, even if successful, would be contested and the root cause for species extinction, anthropocentrism, will still present a threat to lynx. Wyatt concludes that a rewilding of the lynx will benefit both humans and nature, correct a historic wrong, and also be in line with UN recommendations to restore nature and revive ecosystems. However, this rewilding must compete with both anthropocentric and economic interests.

Chapter 11, by Mark T. Palermo, reflected further on the role of anthropocentrism in the current deficient regulation of nature and animal protection, highlighting the philosophical approaches of the CRIMEANTHROP project and this book. Similarly to Natali, Troiano, Zoja and Lavorgna, his chapter suggested that policy alone, including international agreements such as CITES and the Bern Convention, will not improve our relationship to nature and the beings within, until it is grounded in an empathic understanding for the environment. This approach resonates with care ethics (Donovan and Adams 2007; Gruen 2015), which has previously been employed as an approach in green criminology in relation to animal abuse (Beirne 1999; Sollund 2008). Of course, empathy for animals is not triggered among all people and particularly not towards animals who are cast as enemies, such as large predators in some instances. Empathy is also an emotion that needs practising, the capacity to feel empathy varies among individuals of the same species and is (sub)culturally dependent. The lack of empathic understanding of freeborn animals may contribute to the shortcomings of international wildlife conventions such as CITES and the Bern Convention, because they fail to move us. As a consequence, they allow for irresponsibility and carelessness on the part of citizens and policy makers alike.

To sum up the findings: This book shows that the implementation and enforcement of the two conventions, CITES and Bern, have shortcomings and therefore fail in conserving the species that they are meant to protect. Moreover, the conventions do not protect individual animals from harm and death. It is suggested that more effort is made to enforce CITES, which is a convention protecting wildlife trade, more than wildlife itself, because it is guided by economic interests. The Bern Convention, on the other hand, fails to be sufficiently respected, because it threatens economic and anthropocentric interests, whether related to hunting or husbandry. Additionally, the Bern Convention's diplomatic character means that it is rarely enforced by the Standing Committee, leaving its fulfilment to the member states' discretion in practice. In this regard, the Habitats Directive is better positioned to put weight behind its demands.

An important finding is that fragmentation is a concern in several countries when it comes to legislation, implementation and enforcement. This relates to another finding, which is that enforcement agents lack proper training and skills that are required to enforce the conventions. In addition, while there may be significant financial resources involved in wildlife trade, punishments for such crimes have little deterrent effect because they are generally very lenient or, indeed, absent. Therefore, such crimes should be prioritized rather than the opposite, which is generally the current situation. The CITES Convention, particularly, facilitates parallel legal and illegal markets, which suggests that a total ban on trading wildlife may be easier to enforce than the appendix system of CITES (See also Sollund 2019).

The underlying foundation for CITES is that it shall maintain, sustain and secure anthropocentric interests generally and economic interests especially, which is problematic in relation to the nature crisis. Another attitude and approach to the protection of endangered species is required than that which involves what wildlife represents *for humans*, whether aesthetic or monetary value. Freeborn animals should be protected for their intrinsic value and in respect for their interests in life, as well as for their value as part of ecosystems. This is important also in regards to the Bern Convention. As long as anthropocentrism is left to govern, both protection of endangered species specifically and nature generally fail, and rewilding encounters problems that may appear unsurmountable. From a species justice point of view, animals' intrinsic value and right not to suffer from human-inflicted abuse should be included in the conventions, not for our sake, but for theirs, and not contingent on the state of their species' vulnerability. This would mean that, particularly in regards to CITES, the convention would need a total makeover (Sollund 2022). An important way of increasing the protection of wildlife is to create awareness among people generally, as well as among politicians, about the deplorable situation and in this way create incentives for offering freeborn animals genuine protection, more than allowing the conventions to become bureaucratic paper tigers. This would entail a focus on nature and wildlife conservation in schools and universities as well as among the general public. However, this approach could be added to by accepting that the economy is crucial in human wildlife conservation, and encourage ways in which wildlife can receive stronger protection to secure both their intrinsic value, and the economy, which does not need to disrespect animals' intrinsic rights to life. For example, if the forest owners could open for wildlife safaris to offer people the possibility to track and perhaps even see the majestic species that are currently under constant threat, this could contribute to offer them greater protection, provided this was done in a responsible manner, for example by requiring authorization from the environmental authorities. Also, the efforts to include the value of nature and animals in calculations of policy effects may highlight the importance of species and nature conservation, although these calculations are, admittedly, highly anthropocentric.

Together, the contributions to this book provide a broad picture of the effects, or lack of effects, of international nature conservation conventions in protecting wildlife from harms and premature deaths caused by human action. Sadly, CITES and the Bern Convention, including their implementation and enforcement, are inadequate to protect wildlife, due to the nature of the conventions themselves. Like most other international law, agreement rather than disagreement is a goal. The conventions are formulated broadly and with possibilities for exemptions and reservations from the rules, to ensure many signatories and accommodate the member states' different interests. Moreover, conflicts that could have arisen as result of critique by the Standing Committees, are avoided,[5] through which the conventions remain silent and powerless. Therefore, the liberty states have in determining how to interpret, implement and enforce the conventions can give paradoxical results, as when endangered animals who are victims of trade are killed in

---

[5] This does not mean that social conflicts that arise from the wildlife 'management' in the countries that are parties to the conventions are avoided. On the contrary, for example, the annual culling in Norway leads to significant protest.

the hands of the authorities that should protect them, and when the states themselves organize hunts of endangered species.

Many of the case studies undoubtedly demonstrate how we are far from securing conservation and protection of freeborn animals, both as species and individuals. It is still our hope that we, with this book, have added inspiration to ways in which endangered wildlife may achieve better protection and thrive in the future, and thereby may continue to add to the natural beauty of this world, for present and future generations of all species.

References

Beirne, P. (1999). For a nonspeciesist criminology: Animal abuse as an object of study. *Criminology, 37*(1), 117–48.

Brochet, A. L., van den Bossche, W., Jbour, S., Ndang'ang'a, P. K., Jones, V. R., Abdou, W. A. L. I., et al (2016). Preliminary assessment of the scope and scale of illegal killing and taking of birds in the Mediterranean. *Bird Conservation International, 26*(1), 1–28.

Donovan, J., and Adams, C. J. (eds). (2007). *The Feminist Care Tradition in Animal Ethics: A reader.* Columbia University Press.

Goralnik, L., Millenbah, K. F., Nelson, M. P., and Thorp, L. (2012). An environmental pedagogy of care: Emotion, relationships, and experience in higher education ethics learning. *Journal of Experiential Education, 35*(3), 412–28. https://doi.org/10.1177/105382591203500303

Goyes, D. R. (2021). Contending philosophical foundations in international wildlife law: A discourse analysis of CITES and the Bern Convention. *Revista Catalana de Dret Ambiental, 12*(1), 1–35.

Goyes, D. R., and Sollund, R. (2016). Contesting and contextualising CITES: Wildlife trafficking in Colombia and Brazil. *International Journal for Crime, Justice and Social Democracy, 5*(4), 87–102.

Gruen, L. (2015). *Entangled Empathy: An alternative ethic for our relationships with animals.* Lantern books.

Sollund, R. (2008). Causes for speciesism: Difference, distance and denial. In R. Sollund (ed) *Global Harms: Ecological crime and speciesism.* Nova Science Publishers.

Sollund, R. (2019). *The Crimes of Wildlife Trafficking: Issues of justice, legality and morality.* Routledge.

Sollund, R. (2021). The development of the enforcement of CITES in Norway: Discretionary omissions and theriocides. *Revista Catalana de Dret Ambiental, 12*(1).

Sollund, R. (2022). Wildlife trade and law enforcement: A proposal for a remodeling of CITES incorporating species justice, ecojustice, and environmental justice. *International Journal of Offender Therapy and Comparative Criminology, 66*(9), 1017–35.

Sollund, R., and Goyes, D. R. (2021). State-organized crime and the killing of wolves in Norway. *Trends in Organized Crime*, *24*(4), 467–84.

Sollund, R., and Maher, J. (2015). The illegal wildlife trade: A case study report on the illegal wildlife trade in the United Kingdom, Norway, Colombia and Brazil. *A study compiled as part of the EFFACE Project*. University of Oslo and University of South Wales.

Wyatt, T. (2021). CITES and the Bern Convention in the UK: An exploration of norms and ambiguities. *Revista Catalana de Dret Ambiental*, *12*(1), 1–34.

Index

Page numbers in *italic* type refer to figures and graphs; those in **bold** refer to tables.

A

Action Plan on Wildlife Trafficking (WAP) 108, 109, 110, 111, 113, 115, 120, 121
African grey parrots 7, 41, 44
African spurred tortoises 55, 58–9
Agreement on International Humane Trapping Standards (AIHTS) 189
animal–human relations 186, 195–6
  see also anthropocentric relationship between humans, other animals and nature
animal–human transformations 188–9
Animal Protection Act 1997 (Poland) 92, 94
animal rights 186, 196–7, 206–7
  lack of an international convention for 3, 105
  NGOs, CITES and discussion of 153–4
animal welfare 49, 153–4, 206–7
  CITES' addressing of 105, 107, 206
  experimentation on animals 187–8
  hunts and suffering of animals 4, 24, 26, 29–30
  and lifting of reptile ban in Norway 44–6, 49
  references in WAP 108, 120
  rescue centres for trafficked animals 114–15, 119–20
  suffering of poached birds 73–4
Animal Welfare Act 1977 (Norway) 21, 41, 157
animals, intrinsic value of 1–2, 4, 6, 210, 211
  Bern Convention on 8, 206
  CITES on 44
Anthropocene 5, 168, 192
anthropocentric relationship between humans, other animals and nature 13–14, 185–204, 210–11
  CITES and commodification of life 190–3
  conclusions and future directions 193–7
  experimenting on animals 187–8
  philosophical framework 186
  relationships through history 188–90

anthropocentrism 3, 195
  of Bern Convention 8, 206, 211–12
  of CITES 37, 108, 206, 211–12
  of Habitats Directive 132
  regarding welfare of wolves 94, 101
anthropology beyond the human 186
Anubis 188
anxiety and guilt, apocalyptic 192, 193
Arabidopsis thaliana 194
Attenborough, D. 168
awareness, raising
  to act as a crime deterrent 64, 96–7
  of animal trafficking 43, 49
    information campaigns 114–15
  of wildlife protection 137, 212

B

Baden-Württemberg 134
badgers 172, 180, 206
Balkan lynx 172
barbary macaques 119
BArtSchV (Federal Ordinance on the Conservation of Species) 131, 139
bears, brown 17, 21
  illegal theriocides 23
  in defence 24, 25–6
  management through lethal control 21–2, 30
  protection of reproductively 'valuable' females 28
  wounding and suffering of hunted 24, 29
  see also hunting of wolves and bears in Norway
beavers 179
behavioural change, wildlife treaties and 159–62, 163
Behnke, N. 126, 128
Bennett, C. 168
Bern Convention 4–5, 8–10, 154
  anthropocentric perspective 8, 206, 211–12
  appendices 8, 21, 22, 91, 154, 172
  commitments and prohibitions 8–9

215

complaints re compliance with 9
decision-making monopoly 155
as econocentric 155
EU directives to implement 4, 9–10, 132
in Germany 131–2, 133
goals of 131–2, 154, 205
  latent as opposed to stated goals 155
in Italy 78
lynx, support for rewilding of 179–80
members 3
in Norway 5, 21, 158, 159
in Poland 91
prohibited methods of killing 172, **173**
shortcomings 4, 197, 211, 212
similarities and differences with CITES and implications for effectiveness 154–6
BfN (Federal Agency for Nature Protection) 125, 126, 131, 133, 134, 136, 141
biodiversity
  conservation 3, 143
    CITES prioritizing of 105, 106–8, 111
    Global Biodiversity Framework 107
  in Italy 70
  threats to, and loss of 18, 55, 70, 76, 168
  in UK 168, 174
biophilia 11–12, 81
bird poaching in Italy 70–86, 208
  bird species at risk of extinction 71
  CITES-related/adjunct legislation 78–9
  criminal charges 73
  economic benefits 76
  goldfinches and other *Fringillidae* 74–7
  legal framework 77–9, 80–1
    Law 150/1992 78–9
    Law 157/1992 78
    Law 503/1981 78
    Legislative Decree 121/2011 77–8
  links to organized crime 72, 75, 77
  poaching typology 71–2
  purposes of 72–3
  recommendations for future policy 80–1
  suffering of birds 73–4
birds
  African grey parrots 7, 41, 44
  Peruvian toucans 117–18, 120–1
  of prey 119, 180
  welfare of trafficked 119–20
Birds Directive, European Union 9, 132, 206
BKA (Federal Criminal Police Office) 126, 133, 136, 141, 142
BNatSchG (Federal Nature Conservation Act) 131, 132, 136, 138, 139, 141, *142*, 143
bobcats 172
bow traps 73–4
Brisman, A. 5, 6, 18, 91, 155, 167, 169–70, 180, 186
bushmeat 119

C

Canadian lynx 172
care ethics 210–11
categorical imperative 190
CBD (Convention of Biological Diversity) 91, 107
chain of effectiveness of wildlife treaties, Norwegian 13, 151–67, 209–10
  link 1, conventions 153–6, 163
  link 2, domestic legislation 156–9, 163
    Nature Diversity Act 156, 158–9
    Regulation 1276 of 15 November 2002 157–8
  link 3, behavioural change 159–62, 163
circuses, animals in 38, 154
CITES (Convention on International Trade in Endangered Species of Wild Fauna and Flora) 4–5, 7–8, 37–8, 153–4, 171–2
  annual trade reports 7–8, 37
  anthropocentric perspective 37, 108, 206, 211–12
  appendices 7, 37, 38, 154, 172
    amendment of Appendix I 41–2, 44
  biodiversity conservation 105, 106–8, 111
  commodification of life and 190–3
  Conferences of the Parties (COPs) 7, 106, 107
  decision-making monopoly 155
  as econocentric 155
  export and import permits 41, 42, 43, 112, 116, 117, 120, 172
    electronic 117
  in Germany 130–1, 132–4
  goals of 153–4, 205
    latent as opposed to stated goals 155
  in Italy 78–9
  lynx, support for rewilding of 179
  in Poland 93–5
  recommendations for a revision 212
  seized live animals and revised recommendations 44, 114–15, 119–20
  shortcomings 4, 37, 197, 211, 212
  similarities and differences with Bern Convention and implications for effectiveness 154–6
  Strategic Vision Statement 2021–30 105, 106, 107, 111, 120
  tagging requirements 47–8, **48**
CITES in Norway 11, 36–51, 207
  awareness of crimes and potential punishments 43, 49
  changes in implementation and wildlife trade regulation 41–2, 44
  incorporation into domestic law 157–8, 159
  lack of transparency in enforcement 42–3
  lifting of reptile ban 38, 41, 43–6, 49
  methodology 39
  owner certificates 42, 46–7, 48, 49

INDEX

risks of wildlife laundering 46–8, 49
statistics on crimes and ensuing
  penalties 42–3, 49
tagging requirements 47–8, **48**
transnational reptile trade 39–41
CITES in Spain 12, 105–24, 209
  control of legal trade 112
  legislation 109–10, 111–13, 115
    CITES authorities 109, 111–12, 120
    grounds for acquittal on charges of illegal
      trading 115–16
    law enforcement agencies 109, 112–13
    public prosecutor's office 113
  methodology 109–11
  Operation Quercus 112
  permit systems 112, 116, 117, 120
  practices for seized live animals 114–15,
    119–20
  SEPRONA 109, 110, 111, 112–13, 114,
    118–19, 120
  TIFIES Plan 113–19, 120
    implement and enforce existing rules
      more effectively 115–17, 120
    prevent illegal trafficking and international
      poaching of wildlife 114–15
    strengthen global partnerships on wildlife
      trafficking and poaching 117–19
  trafficking of native species 118–19
  welfare of trafficked animals 114–15, 119–20
clinical trials 187–8
commodification of life 2–3, 14, 96, 190–3
Convention of Biological Diversity
  (CBD) 91, 107
Convention on International Trade in
  Endangered Species of Wild Fauna
  and Flora *see* CITES (Convention on
  International Trade in Endangered Species
  of Wild Fauna and Flora); CITES in
  Norway; CITES in Spain
Convention on the Conservation of
  European Wildlife and Natural Habitats
  see BERN Convention
cooperation, international
  for return of trafficked animals 119
  TIFIES Plan seeking to strengthen 117–19,
    120–1
CRIMEANTHROP project 2–5, 106,
  168–9, 205
criminal gangs
  in eel trafficking 118–19
  in illegal reptile trade 56, 57, 58–9, 60,
    61–2, 63
  in poaching in Italy 72, 75, 77
cultural poaching 72
cyclopia 188

D

Dasgupta Review 173
de-extinction 169–70, 180

decision-making monopolies 155
deer 174, 176–7
dualistic principle 156

E

ecological harms 5–6
ecological justice 6, 171
ecosystems 6
  benefits of adding lynx back into 173,
    174–5, 180, 181
  de-extinction and disruption to 170
eel trafficking 118–19
empathy 6, 210–11
  -based approaches for animal-related
    crimes 80
environmental justice 6, 171
environmental victimization 170
epibatidine 187
Eurasian lynx 172, 173
Eurogroup for Animals survey 98–100, **99**
European Union (EU)
  Action Plan on Wildlife Trafficking 108,
    109, 110, 111, 113, 115, 120, 121
  Birds Directive 9, 132, 206
  Habitats Directive 4, 9, 10, 94, 132, 143,
    179, 211
  influential member of Bern Convention 10
  reptile trade 39–40, 40–1, 52–3
    facilitating illegal 63–4
  Wildlife Trade Regulations 53, 63–4,
    130–1
experiments with live animals 187–8
export and import permits 41, 42, 43, 112,
  116, 117, 120, 172
  electronic 117
extinction
  birds in Italy at risk of 71
  de-extinction 169–70, 180
  of lynx in UK 173
  numbers of species at risk of 41, 55, 168
  of species from 1970 to 2016 151
extradition orders 117–18

F

Facebook 45, 54, 60–1, 63
Fajardo, T. 109, 110, 113, 114, 116, 117, 119
Federal Agency for Nature Protection
  (*Bundesamt für Naturschutz*, BfN) 125,
  126, 131, 133, 134, 136, 141
Federal Criminal Police Office
  (*Bundeskriminalamt*, BKA) 126, 133, 136,
  141, 142
Federal Nature Conservation Act
  (*Bundesnaturschutzgesetz*, BNatSchG) 131,
  132, 136, 138, 139, 141, *142*, 143
Federal Ordinance on the Conservation
  of Species (*Bundesartenschutzverordnung*,
  BArtSchV) 131, 139
Feehan, K. 176, 177, 178, 179, 180, 181

217

Food Safety Authority (FSA) 43, 44, 46, 49
Foucault, M. 195
fowling 72, 73–4
freedoms, five 3
frogs, 'harvesting of' 187
Fuentes, J. 109, 110, 113, 116, 117

G

genotypes 194
Germany *see* wildlife protection in Germany
Global Biodiversity Framework (GBF) 107
goldfinches and other *Fringillidae*
  artistic representations 74, 75
  poaching 74–7, 76
Gosling, E. 100
Goyes, D. 8, 19, 21, 37, 89, 152, 153, 154, 155, 156, 160, 162, 187, 189, 190, 191, 192, 206
grass snakes 56
green criminology 5–7, 79, 169–71, 185, 186
green economy 193
Green Party, Germany 137, 142–3
Gruen, L. 6, 19, 210
Grundgesetz (German Constitution) 128, 131
guilt and anxiety, apocalyptic 192, 193

H

Habitats Directive, European Union 4, 9, 10, 94, 132, 143, 179, 211
Handke, P. 194
hard incorporation 157
hierarchical speciesism 44, 171
Higher Nature Protection Agencies (*Obere Naturschutzbehörde*, ONB) 134
human–animal relations 186, 195–6
  see also anthropocentric relationship between humans, other animals and nature
human–animal transformations 188–9
hunting 2–3, 205–6
  in Italy 78
  suffering of animals 4, 24, 26, 29–30
  traditional approaches to 189
  in US 190
  use of helicopters 22, 30
hunting and killing of wolves in Poland, illegal 12, 87–104, 208–9
  anthropocentrism regarding welfare 94, 101
  crime detection 101, 102
  criminal convictions for crimes against animals 88
  data collection 87
  environmental NGOs involvement in court cases 97
  financial value of a wolf 96
  implementation of CITES and Bern Convention 93–5
  jurisprudence in court cases 95–8, 101, 102
  lack of awareness of consequences for 96–7, 101
  legal status of wolves 89–93, 101, 102
    Animal Protection Act 1997 92, 94
    Hunting Law 1995 89, 92
    Polish Penal Code 89, 92–3, 95, 96–7
  methodology 88–9
  permits for killing 94–5
  property aspect 93, 94
  social factors influencing toleration of 98–101, **99**, 101–2
  theriocides 2002–20 88
  tools of poaching 88, 89, 92, 99
  training in legal protection of wild animals 97–8
hunting of wolves and bears in Norway 10–11, 17–35, 206
  comparison of legal and illegal theriocides 26–30
    actors and means 26–7
    protection of reproductively 'valuable individuals' 27–9
    suffering of animals 29–30
  'huntable species' 206
  hunting quotas 21
  illegal theriocides 23–6, 30
    alleged accidental 26
    organized hunts 23–4
    poisoning 24, 29
    suffering of animals 24, 26, 29–30
    theriocides in defence 24–6
    traps 24
  large predator management 5, 18, 21–2, 30–1
  methodology 20–1
  prosecutions and convictions 20–1, 23–4, 26, 27
  skadefelling applications 25, 28
  'species justifiability' of legal hunts 30–1
  theoretical perspective 18–19, 30–1
hybridization 56
hypothetical imperative 190

I

import and export permits 41, 42, 43, 112, 116, 117, 120, 172
  electronic 117
information campaigns on wildlife trafficking 114–15
international cooperation
  for return of trafficked animals 119
  TIFIES Plan seeking to strengthen 117–19, 120–1
international environmental law 3, 153–6
  see also Bern Convention; CITES (Convention on International Trade in Endangered Species of Wild Fauna and Flora)
Italy *see* bird poaching in Italy
ivory 117, 138

INDEX

J
Janssen, J. 8, 53, 55, 56, 64
Jung, C. 194

K
Kant, I. 190
Kohn, E. 186
Kropp, S. 126, 128
Kuszlewicz, K. 93

L
Lavorgna, A. 43, 57, 60, 70, 71, 72, 75, 77, 78, 79
law enforcement 211
  bird poaching in Italy 75–6, 77–9, 80
  CITES authorities and law enforcement agencies in Spain 111–13
  CITES implementation through TIFIES Plan in Spain 113–19, 120–1
  confrontations between farmers and 190
  consequences of lifting reptile ban in Norway 43–6, 49
  illegal killing of wolves in Poland 95–8, 101, 102
  lack of transparency in Norway 42–3
  reptile trade in Netherlands 58–9, 59–61, 63–4
  wolf and bear theriocides in Norway 26–30
  see also wildlife protection in Germany
Leupen, B. T. C. 8, 53, 56, 64
Lie, M. S. B. 19, 29, 30
LIFE EuroLargeCarnivores project 100, 101
Liljeblad, J. 151, 152
lions 2–3, 119
Lipsky, M. 129
lobby groups in Germany 138, 140
Lovdata 20, 156
Lower Nature Protection Agencies (*Untere Naturschutzbehörde*, UNB) 134, 139, 140, 141
Lower Saxony 140
lynx 169
  in Norway 176, 178
  species of 172
lynx, rewilding in United Kingdom 13, 171–84, 210
  benefits 180–1
  drivers of extinction of Eurasian lynx 173
  farmers' compensation scheme 178
  green criminology 169–71
  harms 170, 180
  legal framework 171–3, **173**
  legal practicalities 179–80
  methods 175
  opposition to 176–7
  rejection of first application 177
  rewilding and lynx 173–5
  species justice 174–5, 181
  support for 177–9

Lynx UK Trust 173, 174, 177, 178, 179, 180, 181

M
Maher, J. 45, 52, 110, 114, 119, 139, 209
markets, illegal wildlife 59, 74–5, 76
Marshall, B. M. 40, 53, 138
Ministry of Foreign Affairs, Norway 156, 158
myths 188–9, 192

N
narrative analysis 160
  of behavioural change 160–2
narrative turn 159
Natali, L. 80, 186
National Farmers Union Scotland (NFUS) 176
Nature Conservation Act 2016 (Poland) 91, 94
Nature Diversity Act (NDA) 2009 (Norway) 19, 20, 27, 38, 49, 156, 158–9
nature management 4, 5–6
  of large predators in Norway 5, 18, 21–2, 30–1
  of wolves in Poland 94–5
nature symbolism 188–9
Netherlands *see* reptile trade in Netherlands
network analysis 54, 61–2, *62*, 63
Nietzsche, F. 186
Norway
  dualistic principle 156
  'huntable species' 206
  lifting of reptile ban and positive list 38, 41, 43–6, 49
  lynx 176, 178
  nature management of large predators 5, 18, 21–2, 30–1
  parrot trade 41
  see also chain of effectiveness of wildlife treaties, Norwegian; CITES in Norway; hunting of wolves and bears in Norway
Norwegian Environment Agency (NEA) 38, 41, 42, 48

O
Olszańska, A. 100
ONB (Higher Nature Protection Agencies) 134
online reptile trade 40, 53–4, 59–61, 64
Operation Quercus 112
orthologs 194
Orwell, G. 185
otherness 195–6
owner certificates 42, 46–7, 48

P
Palermo, M. T. 190, 192, 193
Paquel, K. 87, 97, 102

parrots 7, 47
  African grey 7, 41, 44
  owner certificates 42
  trade in 41, 42, 47
Penal Code (Norway) 20, 24
Penal Code (Poland) 89, 92–3, 95, 96–7
pet trade 4, 40, 41, 45, 60
  TIFIES Plan to prevent illegal exotic 114
pharmacotherapy 187
plants, genes 194
poaching
  regulations in Poland on tools of 88, 89, 92, 99
  three types of 71–2
  TIFIES Plan
    to prevent international poaching 114–15
    to strengthen global partnerships on poaching 117–19
  see also bird poaching in Italy
poisoning 24, 29
Poland *see* hunting and killing of wolves in Poland, illegal
pre-religious and shamanistic cultures 185, 188
professional poaching 71–2
public trust doctrine (PTD) 191
public trust thinking (PTT) 191

R

Redford, K. 160
regime effectiveness studies 151
  see also chain of effectiveness of wildlife treaties, Norwegian
rehoming of wildlife victims of trafficking 42, 114–15, 119–20
reproductively 'valuable' animals, protection of 27–9
reptile trade
  harms of illegal 55–6
  largest importers and exporters 39–40, 40–1, 52–3
  lifting of ban in Norway 38, 41, 43–6, 49
  newly discovered species 40, 55
  online 40, 53–4, 59–61, 64
  risk of laundering 46, 49
  transnational 39–41
reptile trade in Netherlands 11, 52–69, 207–8
  actors 56–8
    criminal groups 56, 57, 58–9, 60, 61–2, 63
    private traders 57
    professional traders 56
  bottlenecks for regulation 63–4
  illegal trade 55–6
  methodology 54–5
  modi operandi 58–9
  network analysis 61–2, *62*, 63
  online 53–4, 59–61
    distinguishing between legal and illegal 64
  reptile fairs 59
  smuggling 58
  social media 60–1, 63

reptiles
  hybridization 56
  lack of expertise in identifying species 59
  species at risk of extinction 41, 55
  welfare concerns 44–6
rescue centres 45, 114–15, 119–20
research, using animals for 187–8
restorative justice 80
rewilding of lynx in United Kingdom 13, 171–84, 210
  benefits 180–1
  drivers of extinction of Eurasian lynx 173
  farmers' compensation scheme 178
  green criminology 169–71
  harms 170, 180
  legal framework 171–3, **173**
  legal practicalities 179–80
  methods 175
  opposition to 176–7
  rejection of first application 177
  rewilding and lynx 173–5
  species justice 174–5, 181
  support for 177–9

S

safaris, forest wildlife 212
Scanlon, J. 105, 106
seized live animals and revised CITES recommendations on 44, 114–15, 119–20
SEPRONA (Spanish police unit for protection of nature) 109, 110, 111, 112–13, 120
  fight against eel trafficking 118–19
  Operation Quercus 112
  SEPRONA in Action 114
shamanistic and pre-religious cultures 185, 188
sharks 7
sheep 174, 176, 178
Singer, P. 19, 171, 194
skadefelling applications 25, 28
smuggling 58, 140
Smuggling Act 1995 (Spain) 111, 115, 116, 117, 118
Social Ecological Thought (SET) marketing 193
social media 45, 54, 60–1, 63, 64
soft incorporation 157–8
Sollund, R. 1, 5, 6, 8, 17, 19, 20, 21, 22, 23, 26, 28, 30, 31, 37, 38, 39, 42, 43, 44, 45, 46, 47, 52, 55, 57, 59, 64, 71, 81, 89, 106, 108, 110, 114, 118, 119, 126, 132, 139, 142, 152, 154, 155, 169, 170, 171, 186, 187, 190, 191, 192, 195, 206, 207, 210, 211, 212
South, N. 5, 6, 18, 155, 169–70, 180, 192
Spain *see* CITES in Spain
species justice 6, 19, 171, 196–7, 212
  perspective on inquiry into legal and illegal hunts 18–19, 30–1
  rewilding 174–5, 181

speciesism 170, 171, 181, 195
  hierarchical 44, 171
Stockholm Declaration 153
Strategic Vision Statement 2021–30, CITES 105, 106, 107, 111, 120
street-level bureaucrats 126, 129, 134, 140, 141, 142, 143, 144
survey on illegal killing of wolves in Europe 98–100, **99**
sustainable consumer behaviours 192–3
Sweden 4, 9, 129

T

tagging requirements 47–8, **48**
therianthropes 188
theriocide of wolves and bears in Norway 10–11, 17–35, 206
  comparison of legal and illegal theriocides 26–30
    actors and means 26–7
    protection of reproductively 'valuable individuals' 27–9
    suffering of animals 29–30
  'huntable species' 206
  hunting quotas 21
  illegal theriocides 23–6, 30
    alleged accidental 26
    organized hunts 23–4
    poisoning 24, 29
    suffering of animals 24, 26, 29–30
    theriocides in defence 24–6
    traps 24
  large predator management 5, 18, 21–2, 30–1
  methodology 20–1
  prosecutions and convictions 20–1, 23–4, 26, 27
  skadefelling applications 25, 28
  'species justifiability' of legal hunts 30–1
  theoretical perspective 18–19, 30–1
theriocide of wolves in Poland, illegal 12, 87–104, 208–9
  anthropocentrism regarding welfare 94, 101
  crime detection 101, 102
  criminal convictions for crimes against animals 88
  data collection 87
  environmental NGOs involvement in court cases 97
  financial value of a wolf 96
  implementation of CITES and Bern Convention 93–5
  jurisprudence in court cases 95–8, 101, 102
  lack of awareness of consequences for 96–7, 101
  legal status of wolves 89–93, 101, 102
    Animal Protection Act 1997 92, 94
    Hunting Law 1995 89, 92
    Polish Penal Code 89, 92–3, 95, 96–7
  methodology 88–9

permits for killing 94–5
property aspect 93, 94
social factors influencing toleration of 98–101, **99**, 101–2
theriocides 2002–20 88
tools of poaching 88, 89, 92, 99
training in legal protection of wild animals 97–8
TIFIES Plan 113–19, 120
  implement and enforce existing rules more effectively 115–17, 120
  prevent illegal trafficking and international poaching of wildlife 114–15
  strengthen global partnerships on wildlife trafficking and poaching 117–19
timber trade 112
tortoises 53, 55, 56, 58–9
toucans, Peruvian 117–18, 120–1
tourism, wildlife 174, 178, 180
trade reports, annual 7–8, 37
training in wildlife protection 97–8, 110, 118
  in Germany 137, 138, 140
traps 24, 73–4, 189
Troiano, C. 70, 71, 73, 74, 78
trust, lack of 191–2
turtles 53, 54, 55

U

Uhm, D. P. van 39, 52, 53, 56, 57, 58, 63, 70, 114, 119, 151
UNB (Lower Nature Protection Agencies) 134, 139, 140, 141
United Kingdom *see* rewilding of lynx in United Kingdom
United Nations Convention on Animal Health and Protection draft 3
United States 41, 129, 190
urbanization 190

V

veterinarians, caring for reptiles 44
victimization, environmental 170

W

WAP (Action Plan on Wildlife Trafficking) 108, 109, 110, 111, 113, 115, 120, 121
welfare, animal *see* animal welfare
whales 172
White, R. 6, 19, 70, 79, 168, 170, 171, 180
wild boar 179
wildlife farms 193
wildlife laundering 46–8, 49, 55, 56, 59
  verification process to prevent 112
wildlife protection in Germany 12–13, 125–50, 209
  attitudes to wildlife crime 138–9
  criminal investigations 133, 134–5, 138–9
  Customs 133, 137

deterrent effect of legislation 137
federal system and problems of law
  enforcement 139–41, 141–2, 143
  in centralized states 140, 141
  in cooperative, mixed-centralized
    states 140–1, 142, 144
  in decentralized states 139–40, 140–1,
    142, 144
federal system, pros and cons 127–8
formidable opponents 138, 140
Green Party impact 137, 142–3
legal enforcement agencies, hierarchy
  of 135, *135*
legal enforcement, CITES and Bern
  Convention 132–5
  in centralized states 134
  in cooperative, mixed-centralized states 134
  in decentralized states 134
legal enforcement, general problems 125–6,
  137–9, 143
  general problems of **139**, 143
  insufficient allocation of
    resources 126, 137
  lack of training and expertise 137,
    138, 140
  lack of will to pursue 138–9
  lenient sentencing 138–9, 143
  low detection rates for crimes 137–8
legal framework 128–32, *130*
  Bern Convention 131–2
  CITES 130–1
methodology 126–7, 135–6
  list of interviewees 147–8
quantitative analysis of states' capacity to
  prosecute violations 141–3, *142*
  panel regression models 142, 149–50
recommendations 144
societal awareness of wildlife exploitation 137
special units (*Stabsstelle Umweltkriminalität*)
  141, 144
street-level bureaucrats 126, 129, 134, 140,
  141, 142, 143, 144

wildlife trade
  concept 192
  information campaigns 114–15
  in poached birds 74–5, 76
  regulation *see* CITES (Convention on
    International Trade in Endangered Species
    of Wild Fauna and Flora)
  TIFIES plan to prevent 113–19, 120
  unknowing participation in 47
  see also reptile trade; reptile trade
    in Netherlands
Wildlife Trade Regulations, European
  Union 53, 63–4, 130–1
wildlife treaties, Norwegian chain of
  effectiveness 13, 151–67, 209–10
  link 1, conventions 153–6, 163
  link 2, domestic legislation 156–9, 163
    Nature Diversity Act 156, 158–9
    Regulation 1276 of 15 November
      2002 157–8
  link 3, behavioural change 159–62, 163
Wilson, E. 81
wolves 3, 4, 5, 9–10, 17
  alleged accidental illegal theriocides 26
  Eurogroup for Animals survey 98–100, **99**
  inbreeding 28
  legal hunts 5, 18, 21–2, 30–1
  organized illegal hunts 23–4, 28
  protection of 'genetically valuable' 27, 28
  rewilding in US 180
  in symbolic iconography 188
  theriocides in defence 24, 25
  wounding and suffering of hunted 26, 29
  see also hunting and killing of wolves in
    Poland, illegal; hunting of wolves and
    bears in Norway
World Wildlife Fund (WWF)
  Poland 97, 98
World Wildlife Fund (WWF)
  Spain 110, 114
Wyatt, T. 8, 37, 43, 57, 70, 80, 81, 108, 114,
  118, 139, 154, 170, 171, 172, 206

www.ingramcontent.com/pod-product-compliance
Lightning Source LLC
Chambersburg PA
CBHW051539020426
42333CB00016B/2013